Barnes & Noble
BOOK OF
QUOTATIONS
REVISED AND ENLARGED

Barnes & Noble
BOOK OF
QUOTATIONS
REVISED AND ENLARGED
Edited by
Robert I. Fitzhenry

BARNES & NOBLE BOOKS

A DIVISION OF HARPER & ROW, PUBLISHERS

New York, Cambridge, Philadelphia, San Francisco, Washington
London, Mexico City, São Paulo, Singapore, Sydney

This book is published in Canada by Fitzhenry & Whiteside Limited under the title *The Fitzhenry & Whiteside Book of Quotations (Revised and Enlarged)*.

BARNES & NOBLE BOOK OF QUOTATIONS *(Revised and Enlarged)*. Copyright © 1987 by Fitzhenry & Whiteside Limited. All rights reserved. Printed in the United States of America. No part of this book may be used or reproduced in any manner whatsoever without written permission except in the case of brief quotations embodied in critical articles and reviews. For information address Harper & Row, Publishers, Inc., 10 East 53rd Street, New York, N.Y. 10022. Published simultaneously in Canada by Fitzhenry & Whiteside Limited, Toronto.

First BARNES & NOBLE edition published 1987.

Library of Congress Cataloging-in-Publication Data
Barnes & Noble book of quotations.

  (Everyday handbook ; 720)
  Reprint. Originally published: The Fitzhenry &
Whiteside book of quotations. Rev. and enl. Toronto:
Fitzhenry & Whiteside, © 1986.
  Includes index.
  1. Quotations, English.   I. Fitzhenry, Robert I.
II. Title.   III. Title: Barnes and Noble book of
quotations.
PN6081.F53   1987   082   86-45096
ISBN 0-06-463720-4 (pbk.)

---

   88 89 90 91 MPC 10 9 8 7 6 5 4 3 ·

Acknowledgements

One would think that a scissors and pastepot collection like this would require little help. Not true. A tribe of hunters and gatherers is required: there is so much to be seen for so little selected. My wife, Hilda, and my three daughters, Sharon, Bridget and Holly, gave generous assistance. Sharon, further, made the initial division into subject categories.

Peg McKelvey reviewed and corrected the manuscripts of both the first and second editions.

R.I.F.

Contents

Preface

Dan Bial and the Harper & Row editorial board have asked me to enlarge and extend my original collection of quotations. I am, of course, happy to do so, but enlarged or not it remains an idiosyncratic chrestomathy. It is published with the conceit that I have reasonable discrimination and that whatever instructs, enlightens, reinforces, amuses, titillates or solaces me has some value to the general book readership. We shall see.

Sometimes quotations are here because they propose a new thought to me. Thus Jiddu Krishnamurti's "Discipline does not mean suppression and control, nor is it adjustment to a pattern or ideology. It means a mind that sees 'what is' and learns from 'what is.' " Some quotations are here because they are thoughts I've had myself, but these are better put and return to me "with a certain alienated majesty" as Emerson would say. Thus Rollo May's "Hate is not the opposite of love; apathy is." Or André Maurois' "Business is a combination of war and sport." Some quotations are here that I do not agree with at all: for example, Clarence Darrow's "There is no such thing as justice — in or out of court." Doubtless this seemed true enough to a defence attorney striving for acquittal of the guilty as well as the innocent.

I have collected these quotations from nearly forty years of reading books and manuscripts and book reviews and advertisements and epitaphs and signs in store windows. I have collected them from other quotation books and from obituary pages and from listening to friends and strangers and associates. I have collected them from the Bible and Shakespeare and from Ralph Waldo Emerson. These three are basic and Mr. Emerson holds his own with the other two. Some years ago, I lost an election for councillor and received a telegram the following morning which I deduced was from Robert Sachs, Vice-President of Harper & Row. It said: "Shall we judge a country by the majority or by the minority? By the minority, surely." It was signed R.W. Emerson.

I remember Bushrod H. Campbell, doughty bookman that he was, saying with spirit, "If I've learned anything in my seventy years, it's that nothing's as good or as bad as it appears." It wasn't meant to be a quotation. It just came out as an eloquent conclusion to a point he was making.

No claim is made here for scholarship, or for the earliest use of a quote or even, in some cases, the precise wording. Some entries are from oral sources and perhaps these words have been honed a bit by listeners, readers, speechwriters, translators, *et al*. In my opinion, they are in this form graceful, compact and cogent.

As George Seldes says, "There are many famous, sometimes brilliant and often very great quotations attributed to notable persons, which though false or incorrect, are usually improvements by anonymous requoters." Further, there is no doubt that famous persons often get credit for quotations which they have borrowed. "In science," says Sir William Osler, "the credit goes to the man who convinces the world, not to the man to whom the idea first occurs." So it is in the humanities.

Churchill's immortal words of May 13, 1940, "I have nothing to offer but blood, toil, tears and sweat," are said to be adapted from the Garibaldi sentence, "I offer hunger, thirst, forced marches, battles and death." But they could also have come from Byron who used the phrase "blood, sweat, and tear-wrung millions" in 1823. As Voltaire said, "Originality is nothing but judicious imitation. The most original writers borrowed one from another. The instruction we find in books is like fire. We fetch it from our neighbours, kindle it at home, communicate it to others, and it becomes the property of all."

If, indeed, there is nothing new under the sun, the reservoir of thought must be finite and it is not surprising that the same perception will be struck independently. Robertson Davies said, "The eye sees only what the mind is prepared to comprehend." Louis Pasteur said, "In the field of observation, chance favours the prepared mind." Mark Twain's remark, "It is better to deserve honours and not to have them than to have them and not deserve them," echoes Cato the Elder's "I would rather have men ask why I have no monument than why I have one." Theodor Reik said, "Work and love — these are the basics. Without them there is neurosis." And the Parisian couturier, Coco Chanel, said, "There is time for work. And time for love. That leaves no other time."

Sometimes quotations appear contradictory. But I find that two seemingly conflicting thoughts which have made it to proverb or aphorism status can be, and usually are, in the ambivalence of life, both true. When Edna St. Vincent Millay says that "It is not true that life is one damn thing after another — it's one damn thing over and over," she is making a distinction that does not exist. Life is *both* one damn thing after another and one damn thing over and over.

On architecture, Mario Pei says "Good architecture lets nature in." And Leonard Baskin says, "Architecture should be dedicated to keeping the outside out and the inside in." Rudyard Kipling sums it up: "There are nine and sixty ways of constructing tribal lays, and every single one of them is right."

In addition to a similarity of thought there is a similarity of technique. The anomalous, for instance. The unexpected twist. The non-sequitor. When Babe Ruth was asked in 1930 how he felt about making more money than the president of the United States, he said, "I had a better year than he did."

When Stalin was asked in 1948 what the Pope would say to a proposed strategy, he responded, "How many divisions has the Pope?" Oscar Wilde plays the same game when he says, "If England treats her criminals the way she has treated me, she doesn't deserve to have any." So does W.C. Fields when he says, "I always keep a supply of stimulant handy in case I see a snake — which I also keep handy."

I think there is wisdom in these pages but I know there is nonsense too. I can't resist the flippant phrase. Who can hold out against Joseph Heller's "Frankly I'd like to see the government get out of war altogether and leave the whole field to private industry."

Translations, of course, are necessarily inexact. When Heinrich Heine was told on his death bed by a priest that God would forgive him, he is reported to have said, "Bien sûr qu'il me pardonnera; c'est son métier." This has been honed to "God will forgive me. It's his business." Striving for purity of expression rather than accuracy may offend some. It doesn't me. I prefer the best words in the best order and sources are secondary. I agree with Edmund Wilson who, citing *The Rubaiyat*, said that the best translations "are those that depart most widely from the originals — that is, if the translator is himself a good poet."

Another good quality is compression. Michelangelo said, "Beauty is the purgation of superfluities." Emerson took longer to say, "We ascribe beauty to that which is simple; which has no superfluous parts; which exactly answers its ends." Robert Browning said, "Less is more." Jean-Paul Sartre capsulized Freud in two words. "Childhood decides."

One tries to include new and fresh names but one cannot exclude the old ones — no matter how ubiquitous. Samuel Johnson is sometimes verbose, but always acute in articulating the English code: "Questioning is not the mode of conversation among gentlemen." And Shaw and Wilde; not only ubiquitous but often outrageous. Shaw said, "My method is to take the utmost trouble to find the right thing to say, and then to say it with the utmost levity." Shaw's levity includes inversions designed to shock. "The universal regard for money is the one hopeful fact in our civilization." Wilde likes inversions, too: "Work is the curse of the drinking classes." The arrogant, impertinent Wilde shows much more often than the sombre and tragic one.

This book does not have rich indices of key words or first lines or any of those detailed and valuable aids. I leave these to the great scholarly collections. ("To me, the charm of an encyclopedia is that it knows and I needn't." — Francis Yeats-Brown). The best of these, it seems to me, are Burton Stevenson's *Home Book of Quotations*, Bartlett's *Familiar Quotations*, George Seldes' *The Great Quotations*, Laurence J. Peter's *Peter's Quotations*, James B. Simpson's *Contemporary Quotations*, Edward F. Murphy's *The Crown Treasury of Relevant Quotations, The Oxford Dictionary of Quotations*, and *The International Thesaurus of Quotations*.

And now as an apéritif, here are some quotations I like particularly:

A man can stand almost anything except a succession of ordinary days.
Goethe

Wars are not fought for territory, but for words. Man's deadliest weapon is language. He is as susceptible to being hypnotized by slogans as he is to infectious diseases. And where there is an epidemic, the group-mind takes over.
Arthur Koestler

Shy and unready men are great betrayers of secrets; for there are few wants more urgent for the moment than the want of something to say.
Henry Taylor

Whenever you see a successful business, someone once made a courageous decision.
Peter Drucker

We have met the enemy, and he is us.
Walt Kelly

It is no use saying "we are doing our best." You have got to succeed in doing what is necessary.
Winston Churchill

Happiness to a dog is what lies on the other side of a door.
Charleton Ogburn, Jr.

In nature there are neither rewards nor punishments — there are consequences.
Robert G. Ingersoll

There is no passion like that of a functionary for his function.
Georges Clemenceau

You've got to keep fighting — you've got to risk your life every six months to stay alive.
Elia Kazan

There are three faithful friends: an old wife, an old dog, and ready money.
Benjamin Franklin

Fortunately, analysis is not the only way to resolve inner conflicts. Life itself remains a very effective therapist.
Karen Horney

Sloppy, raggedy-assed old life. I love it. I never want to die.
Dennis Trudell

You have to pay the price — but if you do you can only win.
Frank Leahy

R.I. Fitzhenry,
November, 1986

Barnes & Noble
BOOK OF
QUOTATIONS
REVISED AND ENLARGED

Ability and Achievement

It's pretty hard to be efficient without being obnoxious.   *Kin Hubbard*

What the world needs is some 'do-give-a-damn' pills. *William Menninger*

I am surprised nothing has been made of the fact that astronaut Neil Armstrong carried no sidearms when he landed on the moon.
Justice Arthur Goldberg

'What would you call the highest happiness?' Wratislaw was asked. 'The sense of competence,' was the answer, given without hesitation.
John Buchan

The winds and waves are always on the side of the ablest navigators.
Edward Gibbon

How many 'coming men' has one known? Where on earth do they all go to?   *Arthur Wing Pinero*

He is the best sailor who can steer within fewest points of the wind, and exact a motive power out of the greatest obstacles. *Henry David Thoreau*

They are able who think they are able.   *Virgil*

The biggest things are always the easiest to do because there is no competition.
William Van Horne

What we do upon some great occasion will probably depend on what we already are: and what we are will be the result of previous years of self-discipline.   *H.P. Liddon*

1

Nothing great is created suddenly, any more than a bunch of grapes or a fig. If you tell me that you desire a fig, I answer you that there must be time. Let it first blossom, then bear fruit, then ripen. *Epictetus*

Out of the strain of the Doing,
Into the peace of the Done. *Julia Louise Woodruff*

It's them that takes advantage that gets advantage i' this world.
  George Eliot

Anything you're good at contributes to happiness. *Bertrand Russell*

I think knowing what you cannot do is more important than knowing what you can do. *Lucille Ball*

There is endless merit in a man's knowing when to have done. *Thomas Carlyle*

Ad Inexplorate (Toward the Unknown)
  Motto at Edwards U.S. Air Force Test Base

It's the whole, not the detail, that matters. *German proverb*

Long is the road from conception to completion. *Molière*

One day Alice came to a fork in the road and saw a Cheshire cat in a tree.
'Which road do I take?' she asked.
His response was a question: 'Where do you want to go?'
'I don't know,' Alice answered.
'Then,' said the cat, 'it doesn't matter.' *Lewis Carroll*

Only those who dare to fail greatly can ever achieve greatly.
  Robert F. Kennedy

Back of every achievement is a proud wife and a surprised mother-in-law.
  Brooks Hays

Noise proves nothing. Often a hen who has merely laid an egg cackles as if she had laid an asteroid. *Mark Twain*

We judge ourselves by what we feel capable of doing, while others judge us by what we have already done. *Henry Wadsworth Longfellow*

Do what you can, with what you have, where you are.
  Theodore Roosevelt

About all some men accomplish in life is to send a son to Harvard.
Edgar Watson Howe

He has half the deed done who has made a beginning.   *Horace*

Give me where to stand, and I will move the earth.   *Archimedes*

The only way round is through.   *Robert Frost*

If a man does not keep pace with his companions, perhaps it is because he hears a different drummer. Let him step to the music which he hears, however measured or far away.   *Henry David Thoreau*

Is there anything in life so disenchanting as attainment?
Robert Louis Stevenson

I'm a slow walker, but I never walk back.   *Abraham Lincoln*

One small step for man, one giant leap for mankind.   *Neil Armstrong*

You cannot fly like an eagle with the wings of a wren.
William Henry Hudson

In esse I am nothing; in posse I am everything.   *John Adams*

Out of the best and most productive years of each man's life, he should carve a segment in which he puts his private career aside to serve his community and his country, and thereby serve his children, his neighbours, his fellow men, and the cause of freedom.   *David Lilienthal*

Good is not good, where better is expected.   *Thomas Fuller*

Never look down to test the ground before taking your next step; only he who keeps his eye fixed on the far horizon will find his right road.
Dag Hammarskjöld

We promise according to our hopes, and perform according to our fears.
La Rochefoucauld

Practice yourself, for heaven's sake, in little things; and thence proceed to greater.   *Epictetus*

For a man to achieve all that is demanded of him he must regard himself as greater than he is.   *Goethe*

He that leaveth nothing to Chance will do few things ill, but he will do very few things.   *George, Lord Halifax*

When spider webs unite, they can tie up a lion.   *Ethiopian proverb*

Everyone must row with the oars he has.   *English proverb*

Every calling is great when greatly pursued. *Oliver Wendell Holmes, Jr.*

Any jackass can kick down a barn, but it takes a good carpenter to build one.   *Sam Rayburn*

God gives the nuts, but he does not crack them.   *German proverb*

Let me tell you the secret that has led me to my goal. My strength lies solely in my tenacity.   *Louis Pasteur*

What one has to do usually can be done.   *Eleanor Roosevelt*

The world is all gates, all opportunities, strings of tension waiting to be struck.
Ralph Waldo Emerson

I confess that altruistic and cynically selfish talk seem to me about equally unreal. With all humility, I think 'whatsoever thy hand findeth to do, do it with thy might,' infinitely more important than the vain attempt to love one's neighbour as one's self. If you want to hit a bird on the wing you must have all your will in focus, you must not be thinking about yourself, and equally, you must not be thinking about your neighbour; you must be living with your eye on that bird. Every achievement is a bird on the wing.
Oliver Wendell Holmes, Jr.

Sometimes it is more important to discover what one cannot do, than what one can do.   *Lin Yutang*

To achieve great things, we must live as though we were never going to die.
Vauvenargues

I am easily satisfied with the very best.   *Winston Churchill*

The more we realize our minuteness and our impotence in the face of cosmic forces, the more astonishing becomes what human beings have achieved.
Bertrand Russell

Don't be afraid to take a big step if one is indicated. You can't cross a chasm in two small jumps.   *David Lloyd George*

There is nothing so useless as doing efficiently that which should not be done at all.   *Peter F. Drucker*

Each morning sees some task begun,
Each evening sees it close.
Something attempted, something done,
Has earned a night's repose.   *Henry Wadsworth Longfellow*

The reward of a thing well done, is to have done it.
                                                                    Ralph Waldo Emerson

God will not look you over for medals, degrees or diplomas, but for scars.
                                                                    Elbert Hubbard

There are two kinds of people: those who are always well and those who are always sick. Most of the evils of the world come from the first sort and most of the achievements from the second.   *Louis Dudek*

Absence

Greater things are believed of those who are absent.   *Tacitus*

Absences are a good influence in love and keep it bright and delicate.
                                                                    Robert Louis Stevenson

The longest absence is less perilous to love than the terrible trials of incessant proximity.   *Ouida*

Failing to be there when a man wants her is a woman's greatest sin, except to be there when he doesn't want her.   *Helen Rowland*

Absence diminishes little passions and increases great ones just as the wind blows out a candle and fans a fire.   *La Rochefoucauld*

It takes time for the absent to assume their true shape in our thoughts. After death they take on a firmer outline and then cease to change.   *Colette*

Sometimes, when one person is missing, the whole world seems depopulated.
                                                                    Alphonse de Lamartine

The absent are always wrong.   *English proverb*

Acting and the Theatre

Acting is not being emotional, but being able to express emotion.
Kate Reid

A good actor must never be in love with anyone but himself.
Jean Anouilh

Every actor in his heart believes everything bad that's printed about him.
Orson Welles

Actors are the only honest hypocrites.   *William Hazlitt*

Drama is life with the dull bits cut out.   *Alfred Hitchcock*

Film-making has become a kind of hysterical pregnancy. *Richard Lester*

Not to go to the theatre is like making one's toilet without a mirror.
Arthur Schopenhauer

You can't automate in the arts. Since the sixteenth century there has been
no change in the number of people necessary to produce *Hamlet*.
William T. Wylie

When actors begin to think, it is time for a change. They are not fitted for
it.   *Stephen Leacock*

Opening night is the night before the play is ready to open.
George Jean Nathan

An actor is a sculptor who carves in snow.   *Edwin Booth*

An actor's a guy who, if you ain't talking about him, ain't listening.
Marlon Brando

The unencumbered stage encourages the truth operative in everyone. The
less seen, the more heard. The eye is the enemy of the ear in real drama.
Thornton Wilder

The live entertainment Canadians like most is the intimate review, a collection of songs and sketches, preferably with a satirical bias.
Nathan Cohen

Acting is happy agony.   *Alec Guinness*

With the collapse of vaudeville new talent has no place to stink.
George Burns

When the audience knows you know better, it's satire, but when they think you can't do any better, it's corn. *Spike Jones*

The person who wants to make it has to sweat. There are no short cuts. And you've got to have the guts to be hated. *Bette Davis*

True tragedy may be defined as a dramatic work in which the outward failure of the principal personage is compensated for by the dignity and greatness of his character. *Joseph Wood Krutch*

A fan club is a group of people who tell an actor he is not alone in the way he feels about himself. *Jack Carson*

The real actor — like any real artist — has a direct line to the collective heart.
Bette Davis

The best actors do not let the wheels show. *Henry Fonda*

A talent for drama is not a talent for writing, but is an ability to articulate human relationships. *Gore Vidal*

Many plays, certainly mine, are like blank cheques. The actors and directors put their own signatures on them. *Thornton Wilder*

You need three things in the theatre — the play, the actors and the audience, and each must give something. *Kenneth Haigh*

From the point of view of the playwright, then, the essence of a tragedy, or even of a serious play, is the spiritual awakening, or regeneration, of his hero.
Maxwell Anderson

Acting consists of the ability to keep an audience from coughing.
Jean-Louis Barrault

Hamlet is the tragedy of tackling a family problem too soon after college.
Tom Masson

A film is never really good unless the camera is an eye in the head of a poet.
Orson Welles

The whole motivation for any performer is 'Look at me, Ma.'
Lenny Bruce

If you give audiences a chance they'll do half your acting for you.
Katharine Hepburn

Show business is like sex. When it's wonderful, it's wonderful. But when it isn't very good, it's still all right.
Max Wall

Actresses will happen in the best regulated families.   *Oliver Herford*

All the movies used to be 'colossal.' Now they're all 'frank.' I think I liked 'colossal' better.
Beryl Pfizer

Satire is what closes Saturday night.   *George S. Kaufman*

A play should give you something to think about. When I see a play and understand it the first time, then I know it can't be much good.
T.S. Eliot

By increasing the size of the keyhole, today's playwrights are in danger of doing away with the door.   *Peter Ustinov*

We do not go (to the theatre) like our ancestors, to escape from the pressure of reality, so much as to confirm our experience of it.   *Charles Lamb*

A play visibly represents pure existing.   *Thornton Wilder*

I sweat. If anything comes easy to me, I mistrust it.   *Lilli Palmer*

I sometimes wish they would swagger more now, buy bigger overcoats and wilder hats, and retain those traces of make-up that put them outside respectability and keep them rogues and vagabonds, which is what, at heart — bless 'em — they are.
J.B. Priestley

Actor-manager — one to whom the part is greater than the whole.
Ronald Jeans

I want him ('Hamlet') to be so male that when I come out on the stage, they can hear my balls clank.   *John Barrymore*

I know it was wonderful, but I don't know how I did it.
Laurence Olivier (after a brilliant performance as 'Othello')

Very few people go to the doctor when they have a cold, they go to the theatre instead.   *W. Boyd Gatewood*

The unique thing about Margaret Rutherford is that she can act with her chin alone. Among its many moods I especially cherish the chin command-ing, the chin in doubt, and the chin at bay.   *Kenneth Tynan*

There are five stages to an actor's career: who is Herschel Bernardi? get me Herschel Bernardi; get me a Herschel Bernardi type; get me a young Herschel Bernardi; and who is Herschel Bernardi?   *Herschel Bernardi*

On stage I make love to twenty-five thousand people; then I go home alone.
                                                                    Janis Joplin

In Hollywood, if you don't have happiness, you send out for it.
                                                                    Rex Reed

Long experience has taught me that in England nobody goes to the theatre unless he or she has bronchitis.   *James Agate*

Playing Shakespeare is very tiring. You never get to sit down, unless you're a king.   *Josephine Hull*

Theatre is simply what cannot be expressed by any other means; a complexity of words, movements, gestures that convey a vision of the world inexpres-sible in any other way.   *Eugene Ionesco*

Action

He who desires, but acts not, breeds pestilence.   *William Blake*

The frontiers are not east or west, north or south, but wherever a man fronts a fact.   *Henry David Thoreau*

If you want a thing done, go — if not, send.   *Benjamin Franklin*

All glory comes from daring to begin.   *Anon.*

Action is eloquence.   *Shakespeare, 'Coriolanus'*

From the moment of birth we are immersed in action, and can only fitfully guide it by taking thought.   *Alfred North Whitehead*

The great end of life is not knowledge, but action.   *Thomas Fuller*

The men who act stand nearer to the mass of man than the men who write; and it is in their hands that new thought gets its translation into the crude language of deeds.   *Woodrow Wilson*

We accept the verdict of the past until the need for change cries out loudly enough to force upon us a choice between the comforts of further inertia and the irksomeness of action.
                    Learned Hand

It is much easier to do and die than it is to reason why.
                    G.A. Studdert-Kennedy

There are two reasons for doing things — a very good reason and the real reason.   *Anon.*

'Mean to' don't pick no cotton.   *Anon.*

Everything comes to him who hustles while he waits. *Thomas A. Edison*

The bell never rings of itself; unless someone handles or moves it, it is dumb.
                    Plautus

It is only in marriage with the world that our ideals can bear fruit; divorced from it, they remain barren.   *Bertrand Russell*

The great end of life is not knowledge, but action.   *Thomas Huxley*

There are risks and costs to a program of action. But they are far less than the long-range risks and costs of comfortable inaction.
                    John F. Kennedy

Take time to deliberate; but when the time for action arrives, stop thinking and go in.   *Andrew Jackson*

You may be disappointed if you fail, but you are doomed if you don't try.
                    Beverly Sills

When you appeal to force, there's one thing you must never do — lose.
                    Dwight D. Eisenhower

In action, be primitive; in foresight, a strategist.   *René Char*

I am not built for academic writings. Action is my domain.   *Gandhi*

Trust only movement. Life happens at the level of events not of words. Trust movement.   *Alfred Adler*

Let us act on what we have, since we have not what we wish.
        Cardinal Newman

Nothing is often a good thing to do and always a good thing to say.
        Will Durant

A = r + p (or Adventure equals risk plus purpose.)   *Robert McClure*

For purposes of action nothing is more useful than narrowness of thought combined with energy of will.   *Henri Frédéric Amiel*

I shall tell you a great secret, my friend. Do not wait for the last judgement, it takes place every day.   *Albert Camus*

Blessed is he who carries within himself a god and an ideal and who obeys it — an ideal of art, of science, or gospel virtues. Therein lie the springs of great thoughts and great actions.   *Louis Pasteur*

I learn by going where I have to go.   *Theodore Roethke*

He who is outside his door already has a hard part of his journey behind him.   *Dutch proverb*

The shortest answer is doing.   *English proverb*

Action is consolatory. It is the enemy of thought and the friend of flattering illusions.   *Joseph Conrad*

We will either find a way, or make one.   *Hannibal*

If you have anything to tell me of importance, for God's sake begin at the end.   *Sara Jeannette Duncan*

There are only two forces that unite men — fear and interest.
        Napoleon Bonaparte

Adversity

Night brings our troubles to the light rather than banishes them.   *Seneca*

Too much happens . . . Man performs, engenders so much more than he can or should have to bear. That's how he finds that he can bear anything.
William Faulkner

A great man does not lose his self-possession when he is afflicted; the ocean is not made muddy by the falling in of its banks.   *Panchatantra*

I've had an unhappy life, thank God.   *Russell Baker*

Do not show your wounded finger, for everything will knock up against it.
Baltasar Gracián

They sicken of the calm that know the storm.   *Dorothy Parker*

Trouble is only opportunity in work clothes.   *Henry J. Kaiser*

The man who is swimming against the stream knows the strength of it.
Woodrow Wilson

The ultimate measure of a man is not where he stands in moments of comfort and convenience, but where he stands at times of challenge and controversy.   *Martin Luther King, Jr.*

Great occasions do not make heroes or cowards; they simply unveil them to the eyes of men. Silently and imperceptibly, as we wake or sleep, we grow strong or weak; and at last some crisis shows what we have become.
Brooke Foss Westcott

What does not destroy me, makes me strong.   *Friedrich Nietzsche*

I long ago came to the conclusion that all life is six to five against.
Damon Runyan

(Adversity is) the state in which a man most easily becomes acquainted with himself, being especially free from admirers then.   *Samuel Johnson*

Adversity has the same effect on a man that severe training has on the pugilist — it reduces him to his fighting weight.   *Josh Billings*

From a fallen tree, all make kindling.   *Spanish proverb*

The virtue of prosperity is temperance; the virtue of adversity is fortitude, which in morals is the heroical virtue.   *Francis Bacon*

The keenest sorrow is to recognize ourselves as the sole cause of all our adversities.   *Sophocles*

No untroubled day has ever dawned for me.   *Seneca*

You can't have more bugs than a blanketful.   *Spanish proverb*

Even in the deepest sinking there is the hidden purpose of an ultimate rising. Thus it is for all men; from none is the source of light withheld unless he himself withdraws from it. Therefore the most important thing is not to despair.   *Hasidic saying*

Trouble will rain on those who are already wet.   *Anon.*

They say a reasonable amount o' fleas is good for a dog — it keeps him from broodin' over bein' a dog mebbe.   *Edward Noyes Westcott*

There is nothing the body suffers which the soul may not profit by.
                                               George Meredith

The burden is equal to the horse's strength.   *The Talmud*

Nothing befalls a man except what is in his nature to endure.
                                               Marcus Aurelius

I am escaped by the skin of my teeth.   *Job 19:20*

Prosperity tries the fortunate; adversity the great.   *Pliny the Younger*

Be willing to have it so; acceptance of what has happened is the first step to overcoming the consequences of any misfortune.   *William James*

Ad astra per aspera. (To the stars through hardship.)
                                      Motto of the State of Kansas

If all our misfortunes were laid in one common heap, whence every one must take an equal portion, most people would be content to take their own and depart.   *Solon*

I never knew any man in my life who could not bear another's misfortunes perfectly like a Christian.   *Alexander Pope*

When the world has once begun to use us ill, it afterwards continues the same treatment with less scruple or ceremony, as men do to a whore.

Jonathan Swift

Is there no balm in Gilead?
Is there no physician there?   *Jeremiah 8:22*

Every difficulty slurred over will be a ghost to disturb your repose later on.

Frédéric Chopin

Fire tries gold, misfortune men.   *Anon.*

The fiery trials through which we pass will light us down in honour or dishonour to the latest generation.   *Abraham Lincoln*

Thou hast shown thy people hard things: thou hast made us to drink the wine of astonishment.   *Psalms 60:3*

Advertising

Advertising may be described as the science of arresting the human intelligence long enough to get money from it.   *Stephen Leacock*

Advertising is the most fun you can have with your clothes on.

Jerry Della Femina

The best ad is a good product.   *Alan H. Meyer*

The philosophy behind much advertising is based on the old observation that every man is really two men — the man he is and the man he wants to be.

William Feather

The number of agency people required to shoot a commercial on location is in direct proportion to the mean temperature of the location.

Shelby Page

Buy me and you will overcome the anxieties I have just reminded you of.

Michael Schudson

First Law of Wing Walking: Never leave go of what you've got hold of until you've got hold of something else.

I know that you believe you understand what you think I said, but I am not sure you realize that what you heard is not what I meant.

Berry & Homer Inc.

If I were starting life over again, I am inclined to think that I would go into the advertising business in preference to almost any other. The general raising of standards of modern civilization among all groups of people during the past half-century would have been impossible without that spreading of the knowledge of higher standards by means of advertising.

Franklin D. Roosevelt

Promise, large promise, is the soul of an advertisement. *Samuel Johnson*

The deeper problems connected with advertising come less from the unscrupulousness of our 'deceivers' than from our pleasure in being deceived; less from the desire to seduce than from the desire to be seduced.

Daniel J. Boorstin

Ads are the cave art of the twentieth century.   *Marshall McLuhan*

The advertisement is one of the most interesting and difficult of modern literary forms.   *Aldous Huxley*

What kills a skunk is the publicity it gives itself.   *Abraham Lincoln*

Few people at the beginning of the nineteenth century needed an adman to tell them what they wanted.   *J.K. Galbraith*

The art of publicity is a black art.   *Learned Hand*

Advertising is legalized lying.   *H.G. Wells*

Advertising is what you do when you can't go to see somebody. That's all it is.   *Fairfax Cone*

The consumer is not a moron. She's your wife.

David Ogilvy (advice to advertising copywriters)

Advice

I remember my father telling me the story of the preacher delivering an exhortation to his flock, and as he reached the climax of his exhortation, a man in the front row got up and said, 'O Lord, use me. Use me, O Lord — in an advisory capacity!'   *Adlai Stevenson*

Be frank and explicit. That is the right line to take when you wish to conceal your own mind and to confuse the minds of others.   *Benjamin Disraeli*

To make pleasure pleasant, shorten.   *Charles Buston*

Put all thine eggs in one basket and — watch that basket.   *Mark Twain*

It has seemed to be more necessary to have regard to the weight of words rather than to their number.   *Cicero*

Don't offer me advice, give me money.   *Spanish proverb*

If you aren't rich, you should always look useful.
                                                    Louis-Ferdinand Celine

He who can lick can bite.   *French proverb*

When a man comes to me for advice, I find out the kind of advice he wants, and I give it to him.   *Josh Billings*

We only make a dupe of the friend whose advice we ask, for we never tell him all; and it is usually what we have left unsaid that decides our conduct.
                                                    Diane de Poitiers

I give myself, sometimes, admirable advice, but I am incapable of taking it.   *Mary Wortley Montagu*

Advice is like snow; the softer it falls, the longer it dwells upon, and the deeper it sinks into, the mind.   *Samuel Taylor Coleridge*

The true secret of giving advice is, after you have honestly given it, to be perfectly indifferent whether it is taken or not and never persist in trying to set people right.   *Hannah Whitall Smith*

'Be yourself!' is about the worst advice you can give to some people.
                                                    Tom Masson

A bull does not enjoy fame in two herds.   *Rhodesian proverb*

The advice of the elders to young men is very apt to be as unreal as a list of the hundred best books.   *Oliver Wendell Holmes, Jr.*

Fewer things are harder to put up with than the annoyance of a good example.
Mark Twain

The only thing to do with good advice is to pass it on. It is never any use to oneself.   *Oscar Wilde*

A good scare is worth more to a man than good advice.
Edgar Watson Howe

There is little serenity comparable to the serenity of the inexperienced giving advice to the experienced.   *Anon.*

Advice is seldom welcome; and those who want it the most always like it the least.   *Lord Chesterfield*

It is well enough, when one is talking to a friend, to lodge in an odd word by way of counsel now and then; but there is something mighty irksome in its staring upon one in a letter, where one ought to see only kind words and friendly remembrances.   *Mary Lamb*

Men of much depth of mind can bear a great deal of counsel; for it does not easily deface their own character, nor render their purposes indistinct.
Arthur Helps

Have more than thou showest,
Speak less than thou knowest.   *Shakespeare, 'King Lear'*

What you don't see with your eyes, don't invent with your tongue.
Jewish proverb

If you keep your mind sufficiently open, people will throw a lot of rubbish into it.   *William A. Orton*

Don't fight forces; use them.   *Buckminster Fuller*

Drink nothing without seeing it; sign nothing without reading it.
Spanish proverb

What is important is to keep learning, to enjoy challenge, and to tolerate ambiguity. In the end there are no certain answers.   *Marina Horner*

Aging and Old Age

To be seventy years young is sometimes far more cheerful and hopeful than to be forty years old.   *Oliver Wendell Holmes, Jr.*

One of the delights known to age, and beyond the grasp of youth, is that of 'not going.'   *J.B. Priestley*

A man of sixty has spent twenty years in bed and over three years in eating.
Arnold Bennett

The role of a retired person is no longer to possess one.
Simone de Beauvoir

Middle age: when you're sitting at home on Saturday night and the telephone rings and you hope it isn't for you.   *Odgen Nash*

No Spring, nor Summer beauty hath such grace,
As I have seen in one Autumnal face.   *John Donne*

If you live long enough the venerability factor creeps in; you get accused of things you never did and praised for virtues you never had.
I.F. Stone

The worst thing, I fear, about being no longer young, is that one is no longer young.   *Harold Nicolson*

I advise you to go on living solely to enrage those who are paying your annuities. It is the only pleasure I have left.   *Voltaire*

Growing old is no more than a bad habit which a busy man has no time to form.   *André Maurois*

Old age is an island surrounded by death.   *Juan Montalvo*

It is time to be old,
To take in sail.   *Ralph Waldo Emerson*

I feel age like an icicle down my back.   *Dyson Carter*

Old age is a time of humiliations, the most disagreeable of which, for me, is that I cannot work long at sustained high pressure with no leaks in concentration.   *Igor Stravinsky*

Dignity, high station, or great riches are in some sort necessary to old men, in order to keep the younger at a distance, who are otherwise too apt to insult them upon the score of their age.   *Jonathan Swift*

The young feel tired at the end of an action;
The old at the beginning.   *T.S. Eliot*

Old foxes want no tutors.   *Thomas Fuller*

Old birds are hard to pluck.   *German proverb*

A man of fifty looks as old as Santa Claus to a girl of twenty.
                                                                            William Feather

How old would you be if you didn't know how old you are?
                                                                             Satchell Paige

The tragedy of old age is not that one is old, but that one is young.
                                                                                Oscar Wilde

The young always have the same problem — how to rebel and conform at the same time. They have now solved this by defying their parents and copying one another.   *Quentin Crisp*

Before you contradict an old man, my fair friend, you should endeavour to understand him.   *George Santayana*

Zsa Zsa Gabor, when asked which of the Gabor women was the oldest, said 'She'll never admit it, but I believe it is Mama.'

When men grow virtuous in their old age, they only make a sacrifice to God of the devil's leavings.   *Jonathan Swift*

When you are forty, half of you belongs to the past . . . And when you are seventy, nearly all of you.   *Jean Anouilh*

To an old man any place that's warm is homeland.   *Maxim Gorky*

By the time a man gets well into his seventies his continued existence is a mere miracle.   *Robert Louis Stevenson*

One trouble with growing older is that it gets progressively tougher to find a famous historical figure who didn't amount to much when he was your age.   *Bill Vaughan*

Forty is the old age of youth; fifty is the youth of old age. *Victor Hugo*

Middle age is youth without its levity,
And age without decay.   *Daniel Defoe*

And he (King David) died in a good old age, full of days, riches and honour.
                                                                          1 Chronicles 29:28

I never dared be radical when young
For fear it would make me conservative when old.   *Robert Frost*

Old age is by nature rather talkative.   *Cicero*

Old age, especially an honoured old age, has so great authority, that this
is of more value than all the pleasures of youth.   *Cicero*

Age has a good mind and sorry shanks.   *Pietro Aretino*

To me, old age is always fifteen years older than I am. *Bernard Baruch*

Few people know how to be old.   *La Rochefoucauld*

First you forget names, then you forget faces, then you forget to pull your
zipper up, then you forget to pull your zipper down.   *Leo Rosenberg*

I really believe that more harm is done by old men who cling to their influence
than by young men who anticipate it.   *Owen D. Young*

He had come to that time in his life (it varies for every man) when a human
being gives himself over to his demon or to his genius, according to a
mysterious law which orders him either to destroy or to surpass himself.
                                                              Marguerite Yourcenar

The individual succumbs, but he does not die if he has left something to
mankind.   *Will Durant*

It is always in season for old men to learn.   *Aeschylus*

So, lively brisk old fellow, don't let age get you down. White hairs or not,
you can still be a lover.   *Goethe*

He that has seen both sides of fifty has lived to little purpose if he has no
other views of the world than he had when he was much younger.
                                                              William Cowper

Let us respect gray hairs, especially our own. *J.P. Senn*

The spiritual eyesight improves as the physical eyesight declines. *Plato*

A man over ninety is a great comfort to all his elderly neighbours: he is a picket-guard at the extreme outpost: and the young folks of sixty and seventy feel that the enemy must get by him before he can come near their camp.
Oliver Wendell Holmes, Jr.

An old codger, rampant, and still learning. *Aldous Huxley*

A person is always startled when he hears himself seriously called an old man for the first time. *Oliver Wendell Holmes, Jr.*

Many a man that couldn't direct ye to th' drug store on th' corner when he was thirty will get a respectful hearin' when age has further impaired his mind. *Finley Peter Dunne*

The denunciation of the young is a necessary part of the hygiene of older people, and greatly assists the circulation of their blood.
Logan Pearsall Smith

Never have I enjoyed youth so thoroughly as I have in my old age. In writing *Dialogues in Limbo, The Last Puritan*, and now all these descriptions of the friends of my youth and the young friends of my middle age, I have drunk the pleasure of life more pure, more joyful than it ever was when mingled with all the hidden anxieties and little annoyances of actual living. Nothing is inherently and invincibly young except spirit. And spirit can enter a human being perhaps better in the quiet of old age and dwell there more undisturbed than in the turmoil of adventure. *George Santayana*

The arctic loneliness of age. *S. Weir Mitchell*

When pain ends, gain ends too. *Robert Browning*

No gains without pains. *Adlai Stevenson*

The trombone age (moving the page back and forth).
Oliver Wendell Holmes, Jr.

Longevity is having a chronic disease and taking care of it.
Oliver Wendell Holmes, Jr.

Age is a high price to pay for maturity. *Tom Stoppard*

I'm very pleased with each advancing year. It stems back to when I was forty. I was a bit upset about reaching that milestone, but an older friend consoled me. 'Don't complain about growing old — many people don't have that privilege.'   *Earl Warren*

Life has got to be lived — that's all there is to it. At seventy, I would say the advantage is that you take life more calmly. You know that 'this, too, shall pass!'   *Eleanor Roosevelt*

It is the fear of being as dependent as a young child, while not being loved as a child is loved, but merely being kept alive against one's will.
                                                                    Malcolm Cowley

Happy the man who gains sagacity in youth, but thrice happy he who retains the fervour of youth in age.   *Dagobert Runes*

Your old men shall dream dreams, your young men shall see visions.
                                                                        Joel 2:28

I am long on ideas, but short on time. I expect to live only about a hundred years.   *Thomas A. Edison*

How beautifully the leaves grow old. How full of light and colour are their last days.   *John Burroughs*

In the last few years everything I'd done up to sixty or so has seemed very childish.   *T.S. Eliot*

What makes old age so sad is not that our joys but our hopes cease.
                                                                    Jean Paul Richter

The young man knows the rules but the old man knows the exceptions.
                                                                Oliver Wendell Holmes

To know how to grow old is the master-work of wisdom, and one of the most difficult chapters in the great art of living.   *Henri Frédéric Amiel*

When you reach your sixties, you have to decide whether you're going to be a sot or an ascetic. In other words if you want to go on working after you're sixty, some degree of asceticism is inevitable.
                                                                Malcolm Muggeridge

Old age is not so bad when you consider the alternatives.
                                                                Maurice Chevalier

Yes, I'm 68, but when I was a boy I was too poor to smoke, so knock off ten years. That makes me 58. And since I never developed the drinking habit, you can knock off ten more years. So I'm 48 — in the prime of my life. Retire? Retire to what?   *W.A.C. Bennett*

When I was very young, I was disgracefully intolerant but when I passed the thirty mark I prided myself on having learned the beautiful lesson that all things were good, and equally good. That, however, was really laziness. Now, thank goodness, I've sorted out what matters and what doesn't. And I'm beginning to be intolerant again.   *G.B. Stern*

Senescence begins
And middle age ends,
The day your descendants
Outnumber your friends.   *Ogden Nash*

Time must needs call the tune and man must follow it.   *Alain*

On the day of his death, in his eightieth year, Elliot, 'the Apostle of the Indians,' was found teaching an Indian child at his bedside. 'Why not to rest from your labours now?' asked a friend. 'Because,' replied the venerable man, 'I have prayed God to render me useful in my sphere, and he has heard my prayers; for now that I can no longer preach, he leaves me strength enough to teach this poor child the alphabet.'   *S. Chaplin*

As the world is wearie of me so am I of it.   *John Knox*

Middle age is when you have a choice of two temptations and choose the one that will get you home earlier.   *Anon.*

No wise man ever wished to be younger.   *Jonathan Swift*

The end comes when we no longer talk with ourselves. It is the end of genuine thinking and the beginning of the final loneliness.   *Eric Hoffer*

Every man who has lived his life to the full should, by the time his senior years are reached, have established a reserve inventory of unfinished thinking.   *Clarence Randall*

For the unlearned, old age is winter; for the learned, it is the season of the harvest.   *Hasidic saying*

My opportunities were still there; nay, they multiplied tenfold; but the strength and youth to cope with them began to fail, and to need eking out with the shifty cunning of experience.   *George Bernard Shaw*

I must be getting absent-minded. Whenever I complain that things aren't what they used to be, I always forget to include myself.   *George Burns*

We grow neither better nor worse as we get old, but more like ourselves
                                                    May Lamberton Becker

It's never too late to have a fling
For autumn is just as nice as spring
And it's never too late to fall in love.   *Sandy Wilson*

Growing old — it's not nice, but it's interesting.   *August Strindberg*

Golden lads and girls all must,
As chimney-sweepers, come to dust.   *Shakespeare, 'Cymbeline'*

If you think that I am going to bother myself again before I die about social improvement, or read any of those stinking upward and onwarders — you err — I mean to have some good out of being old.
                                                    Oliver Wendell Holmes, Jr.

They tell you that you'll lose your mind when you grow older. What they don't tell you is that you won't miss it very much.   *Malcolm Cowley*

I have learned little from the years that fly; but I have wrung the colour from the years.   *Frances Pollock*

America and Americans

America is a willingness of the heart.   *F. Scott Fitzgerald*

(A country where) the young are always ready to give to those who are older than themselves the full benefits of their inexperience.   *Oscar Wilde*

We are now at the point where we must decide whether we are to honour the concept of a plural society which gains strength through diversity, or whether we are to have bitter fragmentation that will result in perpetual tension and strife.   *Earl Warren*

Part of the American dream is to live long and die young.
                                                    Edgar Z. Friedenberg

Why, if you're not in New York you are camping out.
Thomas W. Dewing

Nothing ever gets settled in this town (Washington). It's not like running a company or even a university. It's a seething debating society, in which the debate never stops; in which people never give up, including me, and that's the atmosphere in which you administer.
Secretary of State, George P. Shultz

The skyline of New York is a monument of a splendour that no pyramids or palaces will ever equal or approach. *Ayn Rand*

Whoever wants to know the hearts and minds of America had better learn baseball. *Jacques Barzun*

Americans are like a rich father who wishes he knew how to give his son the hardships that made him rich. *Robert Frost*

America . . . an economic system prouder of the distribution of its products than of the products themselves. *Murray Kempton*

The United States was born in the country and moved to the city in the nineteenth century. *Anon.*

Delaware: a state that has three counties when the tide is out, and two when it is in. *J.J. Ingalls*

Washington is an endless series of mock palaces clearly built for clerks.
Ada Louise Huxtable

The Americans believe they answered all first questions in 1776: since then they've just been hammering out the practical details. *Ray Smith*

The trouble with the American public is that it thinks something is better than nothing. *Alfred Stieglitz*

Our national flower is the concrete cloverleaf. *Lewis Mumford*

Americans have a special horror of letting things happen their own way, without interference. They would like to jump down their stomachs, digest the food, and shovel the shit out. *William Burroughs*

When asked by an anthropologist what the Indians called America before the white man came, an Indian said simply 'Ours.' *Vine Deloria, Jr.*

In the United States 'First' and 'Second' class can't be painted on railroad cars, for all passengers, being Americans, are equal and it would be 'unAmerican.' But paint 'Pullman' on a car and everyone is satisfied.
Owen Wister

The true America is the Middle West, and Columbus discovered nothing at all except another Europe.
W.L. George

America once had the clarity of a pioneer axe.
Robert Osborn

By the laws of probability, North America ought to speak French, not English, today.
Alan Gowans

In the United States there is more space where nobody is than where anybody is. This is what makes America what it is.
Gertrude Stein

You say to your soldier, 'Do this' and he does it. But I am obliged to say to the American, 'This is why you ought to do this' and then he does it.
Baron von Steuben

The greatest American superstition is belief in facts.
Hermann Keyserling

America should care more for its poor and reform itself in other ways; but even if it won't do those things, it remains the least constrained society on earth.
Robert M. Adams

Florida: God's waiting room.
Glenn le Grice

If I were to go over my life again, I would be a shoemaker rather than an American statesman.
John Adams

The Englishman is under no constitutional obligation to believe that all men are created equal. The American agony is therefore scarcely intelligible, like a saint's self-flagellation viewed by an atheist.
John Updike

There is nothing the matter with Americans except their ideals. The real American is all right; it is the ideal American who is all wrong.
G.K. Chesterton

Nobody ever went broke underestimating the taste of the American public.
H.L. Mencken

Good Americans, when they die, go to Paris.
Thomas Gold Appleton

The sorrows and disasters of Europe always brought fortune to America.
Stephen Leacock

The American's conversation is much like his courtship . . . He gives an inkling and watches for a reaction; if the weather looks fair, he inkles a little more. Wishing neither to intrude nor be intruded upon, he advances by stages of acceptance, by levels of agreement, by steps of concurrence.
Donald Lloyd

The central fact of North American history is that there were fifteen British Colonies before 1776. Thirteen rebelled and two did not. *June Callwood*

The word for New York is activity.   *V.S. Pritchett*

A natural New Yorker is a native of the present tense.   *V.S. Pritchett*

New York is notoriously inhospitable to the past, disowning it whenever it can.   *John D. Rosenberg*

That enfabled rock, that ship of life, that swarming, million-footed, tower-masted, sky-soaring citadel that bears the magic name of the Island of Manhattan.   *Thomas Wolfe*

I don't like the life here in New York. There is no greenery. It would make a stone sick.   *Nikita S. Khrushchev*

New York, the nation's thyroid gland.   *Christopher Morley*

You will find the Americans much as the Greeks found the Romans: great, big, vulgar, bustling people more vigorous than we are and also more idle, with more unspoiled virtues but also more corrupt.   *Harold Macmillan*

As for what you're calling hard luck — well, we made New England out of it. That and codfish.   *Stephen Vincent Benét*

The lusts of the flesh can be gratified anywhere; it is not this sort of licence that distinguishes New York. It is, rather, a lust of the total ego for recognition, even for eminence. More than elsewhere, everybody here wants to be Somebody.   *Sydney J. Harris*

After twenty annual visits, I am still surprised each time I return to see this giant asparagus bed of alabaster and rose and green skyscrapers.
Cecil Beaton

He speaks English with the flawless imperfection of a New Yorker.

Gilbert Millstein

A town that has no ceiling price,
A town of double-talk;
A town so big men name her twice,
Like so: 'N'Yawk, N'Yawk.'

Christopher Morley

And this is good old Boston
The home of the bean and the cod —
Where the Lowells talk to the Cabots,
And the Cabots talk only to God.

J.C. Bossidy

A Bostonian — an American, broadly speaking.

G.E. Woodberry

The swaggering underemphasis of New England.

Heywood Broun

New England is a finished place. Its destiny is that of Florence or Venice, not Milan, while the American empire careens onward toward its predicted end . . . it is the first American section to be finished, to achieve stability in the conditions of its life. It is the first old civilization, the first permanent civilization in America.

Bernard de Voto

A well-established village in New England or the northern Middle-West could afford a town drunkard, a town atheist, and a few Democrats.

D.W. Brogan

I shall enter on no encomium upon Massachussets; she needs none. There she is. Behold her, and judge for yourselves.

Daniel Webster

The most serious charge which can be brought against New England is not Puritanism but February.

Joseph Wood Krutch

Boston is a moral and intellectual nursery always busy applying first principles to trifles.

George Santayana

America — the best poor man's country in the world.

William Allen

Chicago — a facade of skyscrapers facing a lake and behind the facade every type of dubiousness.

E.M. Forster

I'm from Indiana, the home of more first-rate second-class men than any other state in the union.

Thomas R. Marshall

Pennsylvania, the state that has produced two great men: Benjamin Franklin of Massachusetts, and Albert Gallatin of Switzerland. *J.J. Ingalls*

Stormy, husky, brawling,
City of the Big Shoulders. *Carl Sandburg, 'Chicago'*

I come from a state that raises corn and cotton and cockleburs and Democrats, and frothy eloquence neither convinces nor satisfies me. I am from Missouri. You have got to show me. *Willard D. Vandiver*

Washington is a place where men praise courage and act on elaborate personal cost-benefit calculations. *J.K. Galbraith*

Anger

Never go to bed mad. Stay up and fight. *Phyllis Diller*

Never forget what a man says to you when he is angry.
Henry Ward Beecher

Who can refute a sneer? *William Paley*

I never work better than when I am inspired by anger; for when I am angry, I can write, pray, and preach well, for then my whole temperament is quickened, my understanding sharpened, and all mundane vexations and temptations depart. *Martin Luther*

There is no passion so much transports the sincerity of judgement as doth anger. *Montaigne*

Don't get mad, get even. *Robert F. Kennedy*

Anger raiseth invention, but it overheateth the oven.
George, Lord Halifax

Beware the fury of a patient man. *John Dryden*

I was angry with my friend:
I told my wrath, my wrath did end.
I was angry with my foe:
I told it not, my wrath did grow. *William Blake*

When angry, count four; when very angry, swear.   *Mark Twain*

A good indignation brings out all one's powers.   *Ralph Waldo Emerson*

Anger makes dull men witty, but it keeps them poor.
Attributed to Queen Elizabeth I

Heaven has no rage like love to hatred turned,
Nor hell a fury like a woman scorned.   *William Congreve*

Anger as soon as fed is dead —
'Tis starving makes it fat.   *Emily Dickinson*

Many people lose their tempers merely from seeing you keep yours.
Frank Moore Colby

Animals

The quizzical expression of the monkey at the zoo comes from his wondering whether he is his brother's keeper, or his keeper's brother.
Evan Esar

You have now learned to see
That cats are much like you and me
And other people whom we find
Possessed of various types of mind.   *T.S. Eliot*

No animal admires another animal.   *Blaise Pascal*

The great pleasure of a dog is that you may make a fool of yourself with him and not only will he not scold you, but he will make a fool of himself too.   *Samuel Butler*

Newfoundland dogs are good to save children from drowning, but you must have a pond of water handy and a child, or else there will be no profit in boarding a Newfoundland.   *H.W. Shaw*

All animals are equal, but some animals are more equal than others.
George Orwell

To his dog, every man is Napoleon; hence the constant popularity of dogs.
Aldous Huxley

Cats — a standing rebuke to behavioural scientists . . . least human of all creatures.
Lewis Thomas

I'd rather have an inch of dog than miles of pedigree.
Dana Burnet

There are no limits to God's compassion with Paradises over their one, universally felt want; he immediately created other animals besides. God's first blunder: Man didn't find the animals amusing — he dominated them, and didn't even want to be an 'animal.'
Friedrich Nietzsche

Cats seem to go on the principle that it never does any harm to ask for what you want.
Joseph Wood Krutch

Animals are such agreeable friends — they ask no questions, they pass no criticisms.
George Eliot

It is the way of a dog that if he is hit by a stone, he bites a fellow dog.
The Zohar

I never saw a wild thing sorry for itself.
D.H. Lawrence

A robin redbreast in a cage
Sets all heaven in a rage.
William Blake

I think one reason we admire cats, those of us who do, is their proficiency in one-upmanship. They always seem to come out on top, no matter what they are doing — or pretend they do. Rarely do you see a cat discomfited. They have no conscience, and they never regret. Maybe we secretly envy them.
Barbara Webster

I think I could turn and live with animals
    they are so placid and self-contain'd,
I stand and look at them long and long,
They do not sweat and whine about their condition,
They do not lie awake in the dark and weep for their sins,
They do not make me sick discussing their duty to God,
Not one is dissatisfied, not one is demented with the
    mania of owning things,
Not one kneels to another, nor to his kind that liveth thousands
    of years ago,
Not one is respectable or unhappy over the whole earth. *Walt Whitman*

Cats are living adornments.
Edwin Lent

The dog is the god of frolic.
Henry Ward Beecher

Anxiety and Worry

If I had a formula for bypassing trouble, I wouldn't pass it around. Wouldn't be doing anybody a favour. Trouble creates a capacity to handle it. I don't say embrace trouble. That's as bad as treating it as an enemy. But I do say, meet it as a friend, for you'll see a lot of it and had better be on speaking terms with it.   *Oliver Wendell Holmes Jr.*

Trouble is the common denominator of living. It is the great equalizer.
Ann Landers

Trouble is a part of your life, and if you don't share it, you don't give the person who loves you a chance to love you enough.   *Dinah Shore*

Anxiety is essential to the human condition. The confrontation with anxiety can relieve us from boredom, sharpen the sensitivity and assure the presence of tension that is necessary to preserve human existence.   *Rollo May*

We poison our lives with fear of burglary and shipwreck, and, ask anyone, the house is never burgled, and the ship never goes down. *Jean Anouilh*

Anxiety is the experience of Being affirming itself against non-Being.
Rollo May

Neurosis is the way of avoiding non-being by avoiding being.
Paul Tillich

Anxiety is the dizziness of freedom.   *Søren Kierkegaard*

Anxiety is fear of one's self.   *Wilhelm Stekel*

Fear ringed by doubt is my eternal moon.   *Malcolm Lowry*

Worries go down better with soup than without.   *Jewish proverb*

Neurotic means he is not as sensible as I am, and psychotic means he's even worse than my brother-in-law.   *Karl Menninger*

Anxiety is the interest paid on trouble before it is due.   *William R. Inge*

Anxiety is a thin stream of fear trickling through the mind. If encouraged, it cuts a channel into which all other thoughts are drained.
Arthur Somers Roche

There is a difference between a psychopath and a neurotic. A psychopath thinks two and two are five. A neurotic knows that two and two are four, but he worries about it.   *Anon.*

Worrying helps you some. It seems as if you are doing something when you're worrying.   *Lucy Maud Montgomery*

Everything great in the world comes from neurotics. They alone have founded our religions, and composed our masterpieces. Never will the world know all it owes to them, nor all they have suffered to enrich us.
                                                      Marcel Proust

Architects and Architecture

In architecture the pride of man, his triumph over gravitation, his will to power, assume a visible form. Architecture is a sort of oratory of power by means of forms.   *Friedrich Nietzsche*

The materials of city planning are sky, space, trees, steel and cement in that order and in that hierarchy.   *Le Corbusier*

Buildings should be good neighbours.   *Paul Thiry*

Pictures deface walls oftener than they decorate them.
                                                  Frank Lloyd Wright

Life is rich, always changing, always challenging, and we architects have the task of transmitting into wood, concrete, glass and steel, of transforming human aspirations into habitable and meaningful space. *Arthur Erickson*

A building is a string of events belonging together.   *Chris Fawcett*

Good architecture is like a piece of beautifully composed music crystallized in space that elevates our spirits beyond the limitation of time.   *Tao Ho*

Architecture (is) a theatre stage setting where the leading actors are the people, and to dramatically direct the dialogue between these people and space is the technique of designing.   *Kisho Kurokawa*

I saw the bathroom fixtures as a kind of American Trinity.
                                                  Claes Oldenberg

Architecture is the will of an epoch translated into space.

Mies van der Rohe

When you look on one of your contemporary 'good copies' of historical remains, ask yourself the question: Not what style, but in what civilization is this building? And the absurdity, vulgarity, anachronism and solecism of the modern structure will be revealed to you in a most startling fashion.

Louis H. Sullivan

Light, God's eldest daughter, is a principal beauty in a building.

Thomas Fuller

No architecture can be truly noble which is not imperfect.   *John Ruskin*

Architecture is inhabited sculpture.   *Constantin Brancusi*

The flowering of geometry.   *Ralph Waldo Emerson*

Society needs a good image of itself. That is the job of the architect.

Walter Gropius

Architecture begins when you place two bricks *carefully* together.

Mies van der Rohe

An arch never sleeps.   *Hindu proverb*

Develop an infallible technique and then place yourself at the mercy of inspiration.   *Ralph Rapson*

The reality of the building does not consist in the roof and walls, but in the space within to be lived in.   *Lao-Tzu*

Good architecture lets nature in.   *Mario Pei*

Architecture should be dedicated to keeping the outside out and the inside in.   *Leonard Baskin*

Early in life I had to choose between arrogance and hypocritical humility. I chose honest arrogance and have seen no occasion to change.

Frank Lloyd Wright

No house should ever be on a hill, or on anything. It should be of the hill. Hill and house should live together, each the happier for the other.

Frank Lloyd Wright

How can we expect our students to become bold and fearless in thought and action if we encase them in sentimental shrines feigning a culture which has long since disappeared?   *Walter Gropius*

The house does not frame the view: it projects the beholder into it.
                                        Harwell Hamilton Harris

Architecture is space structured to serve man and to move him.
                                        Étienne Gaboury

Take nothing for granted as beautiful or ugly, but take every building to pieces, and challenge every feature. Learn to distinguish the curious from the beautiful. Get the habit of analysis — analysis will in time enable synthesis to become your habit of mind. 'Think simples' as my old master used to say — meaning to reduce the whole of its parts into the simplest terms, getting back to first principles.   *Frank Lloyd Wright*

Always design a thing by considering it in its next larger context — a chair in a room, a room in a house, a house in an environment, an environment in a city plan.   *Eero Saarinen*

In speculative buildings, which is most of our business, there are really only three chances to make architecture: the lobby or entrance sequence, the top and the elevator cab.   *Chao-Ming Wu*

A house is a machine for living.   *Buckminster Fuller*

A doctor can bury his mistakes, but an architect can only advise his clients to plant vines.   *Frank Lloyd Wright*

The White House was designed by Hoban, a noted Irish-American architect, and I have no doubt that he believed by incorporating several features of the Dublin style he would make it more homelike for any President of Irish descent. It was a long wait, but I appreciate his efforts.
                                        John F. Kennedy

Genius is personal, decided by fate, but it expresses itself by means of system. There is no work of art without system.   *Le Corbusier*

We shape our buildings; thereafter they shape us.   *Winston Churchill*

I call architecture 'petrified music.'   *Goethe*

Form ever follows function.   *Louis H. Sullivan*

Arguments and Quarrels

Arguments are to be avoided — they are always vulgar and often convincing.
Oscar Wilde

We're eyeball to eyeball, and the other fellow just blinked.   *Dean Rusk*

Weakness on both sides is, as we know, the motto of all quarrels.
Voltaire

There is no good arguing with the inevitable. The only argument available with an east wind is to put on your overcoat.   *James Russell Lowell*

It is not necessary to understand things in order to argue about them.
Beaumarchais

I learned long ago never to wrestle with a pig. You get dirty, and besides, the pig likes it.   *Cyrus Ching*

The test of a man or woman's breeding is how they behave in a quarrel.
George Bernard Shaw

I have never in my life learned anything from any man who agreed with me.
Dudley Field Malone

Better be quarrelling than lonesome.   *Irish proverb*

Quarrels would not last long if the fault was only on one side.
La Rochefoucauld

When we quarrel, how we wish we had been blameless.
Ralph Waldo Emerson

The most savage controversies are those about matters as to which there is no good evidence either way.   *Bertrand Russell*

Every story has three sides to it — yours, mine and the facts.
Foster Meharny Russell

Art and the Artist

Art is I, science is we. *Claude Bernard*

The artist, like the God of the creation, remains within or behind or beyond or above his handiwork, invisible, refined, out of existence, indifferent, paring his fingernails. *James Joyce*

Designers and free lance artists and editors can set their hourly rates by dividing their annual income needs by 1000. *Mike Rider*

Children, like animals, use all their senses to discover the world. Then artists come along and discover it the same way all over again.
Eudora Welty

When power leads man toward arrogance, poetry reminds him of his limitations. When power narrows the areas of men's concern, poetry reminds him of the richness and diversity of his experience. When power corrupts, poetry cleanses. For art establishes the basic human truths which must serve as the touchstones of our judgement. The artist . . . faithful to his personal vision of reality, becomes the last champion of the individual mind and sensibility against an intrusive society and an offensive state. *John F. Kennedy*

Art disease is caused by a hardening of the categories. *Adina Reinhardt*

Art is the expression of an enormous preference. *Wyndham Lewis*

Conception, my boy, fundamental brainwork, is what makes the difference in all art. *Dante Gabriel Rossetti*

An artist may visit a museum but only a pedant can live there.
George Santayana

All profoundly original art looks ugly at first. *Clement Greenberg*

Pioneers did not produce original works of art, because they were creating original human environments; they did not imagine utopias because they were shaping them. *George Woodcock*

Art is a human activity, consisting in this, that one man consciously, by means of external signs, hands on to others feelings he has worked through, and other people are infected by these feelings and also experience them.
Leo Tolstoy

A picture lives by companionship. It dies by the same token. It is therefore risky to send it out into the world. How often it must be impaired by the eyes of the unfeeling.   *Mark Roth Ko*

Abstract art is uniquely modern. It is a fundamentally romantic response to modern life — rebellious, individualistic, unconventional, sensitive, irritable.   *Robert Motherwell*

Culture is something you cannot buy, something you cannot import, something you cannot learn or produce at will. A writer, an artist or musician cannot sit down and say 'Now I will produce culture.' Culture is something that evolves out of the simple, enduring elements of everyday life; elements most truthfully expressed in the folk arts and crafts of a nation.
                                                    Thor Hansen

Dance is the only art of which we ourselves are the stuff of which it is made.
                                                    Ted Shawn

Art is not an end in itself, but a means of addressing humanity.
                                                    Modest Petrovich Mussorgsky

It is from the artist that society gains its loftier images of itself.
                                                    Joseph Wood Krutch

All art is a revolt against man's fate.   *André Malraux*

Art is a delayed echo.   *George Santayana*

Art is a kind of illness.   *Giacomo Puccini*

A work of art is a corner of creation seen through a temperament.
                                                    Emile Zola

Art washes away from the soul the dust of everyday life.   *Pablo Picasso*

Art gropes, it stalks like a hunter lost in the woods, listening to itself and to everything around it, unsure of itself, waiting to pounce.
                                                    John W. Gardner

Man in Canadian art is rarely in command of his environment or ever at home in it.   *Elizabeth Kilbourn*

What's an artist, but the dregs of his work — the human shambles that follows it around?   *William Gaddis*

Art has no other object than to set aside the symbols of practical utility, the generalities that are conventionally and socially accepted, everything in fact which masks reality from us, in order to set us face to face with reality itself.
Henri Bergson

Every artist preserves deep within him a single source from which, throughout his lifetime, he draws what he is and what he says and when the source dries up the work withers and crumbles.   *Albert Camus*

As an artist grows older, he has to fight disillusionment and learn to establish the same relation to nature as an adult as he had when a child.
Charles Burchfield

Perpetual modernness is the measure of merit in every work of art.
Ralph Waldo Emerson

Nothing can come out of an artist that is not in the man. *H.L. Mencken*

It is not in life but in art that self-fulfillment is to be found.
George Woodcock

An artist never really finishes his work, he merely abandons it.
Paul Valéry

Interviews with artists are portentous and prejudicial things. Even when they fail in their objective — as they so often do — they can be dangerously affecting.

I approach them with profound misgivings and am always sorry afterwards that I approached them at all. They tend to reveal parts of the artist's character that have nothing to do with the public effect of his work, but that linger on under your skin, colouring your opinion of that work.

I am convinced it is a mistake to find an artist human outside his work. If you cannot find him human in and through his work, you are better not to know it when you come to formulate an opinion of his public value.
Kenneth Winters

One must work, nothing but work, and one must have patience.
Auguste Rodin

Art does not reproduce the visible; rather it makes it visible.   *Paul Klee*

The more horrifying this world becomes, the more art becomes abstract.
Paul Klee

One of the recognizable features of the authentic masterpiece is its capacity to renew itself, to endure the loss of some kinds of immediate relevance while still answering the most important questions men can ask, including new ones they are just learning how to frame.   *Arnold Stein*

Every child is an artist. The problem is how to remain an artist once he grows up.   *Pablo Picasso*

Art is man's nature; nature is God's art.   *P.J. Bailey*

With the pride of the artist, you must blow against the walls of every power that exists, the small trumpet of your defiance.   *Norman Mailer*

All art is a kind of confession, more or less oblique. All artists, if they are to survive, are forced, at last, to tell the whole story; to vomit the anguish up.   *James Baldwin*

History repeats itself, but the special call of an art which has passed away is never reproduced. It is utterly gone out of the world as the song of a destroyed wild bird.   *Joseph Conrad*

This is the artist, then — life's hungry man, the glutton of eternity, beauty's miser, glory's slave.   *Thomas Wolfe*

If you ask me what I came to do in this world, I, an artist, I will answer you: 'I am here to live out loud.'   *Emile Zola*

Illustrations have as much to say as the text. The trick is to say the same thing, but in a different way. It's no good being an illustrator who is saying a lot that is on his or her mind, if it has nothing to do with the text . . . the artist must override the story, but he must also override his own ego for the sake of the story.   *Maurice Sendak*

In any evolutionary process, even in the arts, the search for novelty becomes corrupting.   *Kenneth Boulding*

All art has this characteristic — it unites people.   *Leo Tolstoy*

The cheap, no matter how charming, how immediate, does not wear so well. It has a way of telling its whole story the first time through.
                                                              William Littler

Art at its most significant is a Distant Early Warning System that can always be relied on to tell the old culture what is beginning to happen to it.
                                                            Marshall McLuhan

It is well with me only when I have a chisel in my hand.   *Michelangelo*

Art is based on order. The world is full of 'sloppy Bohemians' and their work betrays them.   *Eduard Weston*

Living is a form of not being sure, not knowing what next or how. The moment you know how, you begin to die a little. The artist never entirely knows. We guess. We may be wrong, but we take leap after leap in the dark.
                                                   Agnes de Mille

Art is called art because it is not nature.   *Goethe*

The artist, like the idiot, or clown, sits on the edge of the world, and a push may send him over it.   *Osbert Sitwell*

Art-speech is the only truth. An artist is usually a damned liar but his art, if it be art, will tell you the truth of his day. And that is all that matters. Away with eternal truth. The truth lives from day to day, and the marvelous Plato of yesterday is chiefly bosh today.   *D.H. Lawrence*

Art isn't something you marry, it's something you rape.   *Edgar Dégas*

Art is a lie that makes us realize truth.   *Pablo Picasso*

It's not what you see that is art, art is the gap.   *Marcel Duchamp*

Art is either plagiarist or revolutionist.   *Paul Gauguin*

I always suspect an artist who is successful before he is dead.
                                                   John Murray Gibbon

An artist has to take life as he finds it. Life by itself is formless wherever it is. Art must give it form.   *Hugh MacLennan*

Art upsets, science reassures.   *Georges Braque*

An artist has been defined as a neurotic who continually cures himself with his art.   *Lee Simonson*

In a sense, the modern artist is the liberal who can't believe in himself, the man who, as Robert Frost has put it, can't take his own side in a quarrel, and whose search into anarchy is a confession of his only strong intolerance — an intolerance of himself and his role.   *Malcolm Bradbury*

Painting, n: the art of protecting flat surfaces from the weather and exposing them to the critic.   *Ambrose Bierce*

Art is either plagiarism or revolution.   *Paul Gauguin*

The father of every good work is discontent, and its mother is diligence.
Lajos Kassak

A work should contain its total meaning within itself and should impress it on the spectator before he even knows the subject.   *Henri Matisse*

The terror of art lies in the representation of the hidden reality with its shattering effect.   *Martin Greenburg*

I paint objects as I think them, not as I see them.   *Pablo Picasso*

Art is all that cannot be suppressed.   *Anon.*

Drawing is speaking to the eye; talking is painting to the ear.
Joseph Joubert

We should comport ourselves with the masterpieces of art as with exalted personages — stand quietly before them and wait till they speak to us.
Arthur Schopenhauer

There is no such thing as art. There are only artists.   *Ernest Gombrich*

Be regular and orderly in your life like a bourgeois, so that you may be violent and original in your work.   *Gustave Flaubert*

The painting rises from the brushstrokes as a poem rises from the words. The meaning comes later.   *Joan Miro*

Caricature is rough truth.   *George Meredith*

A work of art is an exaggeration.   *André Gide*

Art not only imitates nature, but also completes its deficiencies.
Aristotle

When one admires an artist it is important not to know him personally.
Jacinto Benaventey Martinez

Beauty

Beauty is unbearable, drives us to despair, offering us for a minute the glimpse of an eternity that we should like to stretch out over the whole of time.
Albert Camus

Beauty is truth — truth, beauty — that is all
Ye know on earth, and all ye need to know.   *John Keats*

Ask a toad what is beauty? . . . a female with two great round eyes coming out of her little head, a large flat mouth, a yellow belly and a brown back.
Voltaire

Grace is the absence of everything that indicates pain or difficulty, hesitation or incongruity.   *William Hazlitt*

Though we travel the world over to find the beautiful, we must carry it with us or we find it not.   *Ralph Waldo Emerson*

Beauty is an ecstacy; it is as simple as hunger. There is really nothing to be said about it.   *W. Somerset Maugham*

She is a peacock in everything but beauty.   *Oscar Wilde*

As a beauty I am not a star,
There are others more handsome by far,
But my face — I don't mind it
For I am behind it.
It's the people in front get the jar.   *Anthony Euwer*

Until I saw Chardin's painting, I never realized how much beauty lay around me in my parents' house, in the half-cleared table, in the corner of a tablecloth left awry, in the knife beside the empty oyster shell.   *Marcel Proust*

The beauty of the animal form is in exact proportion to the amount of moral and intellectual virtue expressed by it.   *John Ruskin*

Do you love me because I'm beautiful, or am I beautiful because you love me?   *Oscar Hammerstein, II*

Beauty is everlasting
And dust is for a time.   *Marianne Moore*

Judgement of beauty can err, what with the wine and the dark.   *Ovid*

Beauty, more than bitterness
Makes the heart break.

Sara Teasdale

The beautiful rests on the foundations of the necessary.

Ralph Waldo Emerson

Things are beautiful if you love them.

Jean Anouilh

We ascribe beauty to that which is simple; which has no superfluous parts;
which exactly answers its ends.

Ralph Waldo Emerson

Something wonderful and strange that the artist fashions out of the chaos
of the world in the torment of his soul.

W. Somerset Maugham

Beauty is the purgation of superfluities.

Michelangelo

Beauty will save the world.

Fyodor Dostoevsky

Beauty — the adjustment of all parts proportionately so that one cannot add
or subtract or change without impairing the harmony of the whole.

Leon Battista Alberti

Underneath this stone doth lie
As much beauty as could die.

Ben Jonson

The only beautiful things are the things that do not concern us.

Oscar Wilde

There is no excellent beauty that hath not some strangeness in the proportion.

Francis Bacon

A very beautiful woman hardly ever leaves a clear-cut impression of features
and shape in the memory: usually there remains only an aura of living colour.

William Bolitho

Female beauty is an important minor sacrament . . . I am not at all sure that
neglect of it does not constitute a sin of some kind.   *Robertson Davies*

The excellence of every art is its intensity, capable of making all disagreeables
evaporate, from their being in close relationship with beauty and truth.

John Keats

It is amazing how complete is the delusion that beauty is goodness.

Leo Tolstoy

Exuberance is beauty.   *William Blake*

The Bible

That kind of so-called housekeeping where they have six Bibles and no cork-
screw.   *Mark Twain*

The total absence of humour in the Bible is one of the most singular things
in all literature.   *Alfred North Whitehead*

The Old and New Testaments are the Great Code of Art. *William Blake*

The fathers have eaten a sour grape, and the children's teeth are set on edge.
                                                    Jeremiah 31:29

I have fought a good fight, I have finished my course, I have kept the faith.
                                                    2 Timothy 4:7

I am fearfully and wonderfully made.   *Psalms 139:14*

The whole head is sick, and the whole heart faint.   *Isaiah 1:5*

It is better to dwell in a corner of the housetop, than with a brawling woman
in a wide house.   *Proverbs 21:9*

Hast thou given the horse strength? Hast thou clothed his neck with thunder?
                                                    Job 39:19

Oh my Father, if it be possible, let this cup pass from me: nevertheless, not
as I will, but as thou wilt.   *Matthew 26:39*

A prophet is not without honour, save in his own country.
                                                    Matthew 13:57

Be not curious in unnecessary matters: for more things are shewed unto thee
than men understand.   *Ecclesiasticus 3:24-25*

Seek not out the things that are too hard for thee, neither search the things
that are above thy strength.   *Ecclesiasticus 3:22*

How beautiful upon the mountains are the feet of him that bringeth good
tidings, that publisheth peace.   *Isaiah 52:7*

His countenance was like lightning, and his raiment white as snow.
Matthew 28:3

Ye have not chosen me, but I have chosen you.   *John 15:16*

Be not deceived; God is not mocked: for whatsoever a man soweth, that shall he also reap.   *Galations 6:7*

Watchman, what of the night?   *Isaiah 21:11*

Man goeth to his long home, and the mourners go about the streets.
Ecclesiastes 12:5

The letter killeth, but the spirit giveth life.   *2 Corinthians 3:6*

For if the trumpet give an uncertain sound, who shall prepare himself to the battle?   *1 Corinthians 14:8*

Borne the burden and heat of the day.   *Matthew 20:12*

The wilderness and the solitary place shall be glad for them and the desert shall rejoice, and blossom as the rose.   *Isaiah 35:1*

Whither thou goest, I will go; and where thou lodgest, I will lodge; thy people shall be my people and thy God my God: where thou diest will I die, and there will I be buried; the Lord do so to me, and more also, if ought but death part thee and me.   *Ruth 1:16-17*

We have piped unto you, and ye have not danced; we have mourned to you, and ye have not wept.   *Luke 7:32*

I know thy works, that thou art neither cold nor hot: I would thou wert cold or hot.   *Revelation 3:15*

They are as stubble before the wind, and as chaff that the storm carrieth away.   *Job 21:18*

Neither do men light a candle and put it under a bushel, but on a candlestick; and it giveth light unto all that are in the house.   *Matthew 5:15*

Bone of my bones, and flesh of my flesh: she shall be called woman.
Genesis 2:23

When caught reading the Bible, W.C. Fields said 'I'm looking for loop-holes.'

The Bible is nothing but a succession of civil rights struggles by the Jewish people against their oppressors.   *Jesse Jackson*

Now Barabbas was a robber.   *John 18:40*

Out of the mouths of babes and sucklings hast thou ordained strength.
Psalms 8:2

Unto everyone that hath shall be given, and he shall have abundance: but from him that hath not shall be taken away even that which he hath.
Matthew 25:29

He that is not with me is against me.   *Matthew 12:30*

Man is born unto trouble, as the sparks fly upward.   *Job 5:7*

For what is your life? It is even a vapour, that appeareth for a little time, and then vanisheth away.   *James 4:14*

My days are swifter than a weaver's shuttle.   *Job 7:6*

I know thy pride, and the naughtiness of thine heart.   *1 Samuel 17:28*

The bible should be taught so early and so thoroughly that it sinks straight to the bottom of the mind where everything that comes along can settle on it.   *Northrop Frye*

Birth

Being pregnant is a very boring six months. I am not particularly maternal. It's an occupational hazard of being a wife.   *Princess Anne*

The government is concerned about the population explosion, and the population is concerned about the government explosion.   *Ruth Rankin*

We have been God-like in our planned breeding of our domestic plants and animals, but rabbit-like in our unplanned breeding of ourselves.
Arnold Toynbee

Some are born to sweet delight,
Some are born to endless night.   *William Blake*

In my beginning is my end. *T.S. Eliot*

When I was born I did lament and cry
And now each day doth shew the reason why. *Richard Watkyns*

Where, unwilling, dies the rose,
Buds the new, another year. *Dorothy Parker*

And when I was born, I drew in the common air, and fell upon the earth, which is of like nature, and the first voice which I uttered was crying, as all others do . . . For all men have one entrance into life.
The Apocrypha

Monday's child is fair of face,
Tuesday's child is full of grace,
Wednesday's child is full of woe,
Thursday's child has far to go,
Friday's child is loving and giving,
Saturday's child works hard for a living,
But the child born on the Sabbath day
Is happy and wise and good and gay. *Anon.*

As the births of living creatures at first are ill-shapen, so are all innovations, which are the births of time. *Francis Bacon*

Husbands don't really count . . . in the miracle of birth. *Doug Spettigue*

Books and Reading

'Sartor Resartus' is simply unreadable, and for me that always sort of spoils a book. *Harry S. Truman*

You should read it, though there is much that is skip-worthy.
Herbert Asquith

The greatest masterpiece in literature is only a dictionary out of order.
Jean Cocteau

When you read a classic you do not see in the book more than you did before. You see more in *you* than there was before. *Clifton Fadiman*

Properly we should read for power. Man reading should be man intensely alive. The book should be a ball of light in one's hand. *Ezra Pound*

Best-sellerism is the star system of the book world. A (best-seller) is a celebrity among books. It is a book known primarily (sometimes exclusively) for its well-knowness. *Daniel J. Boorstin*

The central theme of the novel is that they were glad to see each other. *Gertrude Stein*

Reading after a certain (time) diverts the mind too much from its creative pursuits. Any man who reads too much and uses his own brain too little falls into lazy habits of thinking. *Albert Einstein*

The most technologically efficient machine that man has ever invented is the book. *Northrop Frye*

Literature is news that *stays* news. *Ezra Pound*

Just the knowledge that a good book is awaiting one at the end of a long day makes that day happier. *Kathleen Norris*

Laws die, books never. *Edward Bulwer-Lytton*

Master books, but do not let them master you. Read to live, not live to read. *Edward Bulwer-Lytton*

A good book is the precious life-blood of a master spirit, embalmed and treasured up on purpose to a life beyond life. *John Milton*

Any book which is at all important should be re-read immediately. *Arthur Schopenhauer*

Do give books — religious or otherwise — for Christmas. They're never fattening, seldom sinful, and permanently personal. *Lenore Hershey*

A boy has to peddle his book. *Truman Capote*

Truth may be stranger than fiction, but fiction is truer. *Frederic Raphael*

Never lend books — nobody ever returns them; the only books I have in my library are those which people have lent me. *Anatole France*

Discretion is not the better part of biography. *Lytton Strachey*

A dictionary should be descriptive, not prescriptive. *Phillip B. Grove*

Book lovers never go to bed alone.   *Anon.*

It circulated for five years, through the halls of fifteen publishers, and finally ended up with Vanguard Press, which as you can see is rather deep into the alphabet.
       Patrick Dennis (Edward Everett Tanner) of his novel Auntie Mame

The first book of the nation is the dictionary of its language.
                              Contanitin, Comte de Volney

A novel is a mirror carried along a main road.   *Stendhal*

I read part of it all the way through.   *Sam Goldwyn*

A successful book cannot afford to be more than ten percent new.
                                   Marshall McLuhan

First publication is a pure, carnal leap into that dark which one dreams is life.   *Hortense Calisher*

Books give not wisdom where none was before.
But where some is, there reading makes it more.   *John Harington*

A good book has no ending.   *R. D. Cumming*

Oh that my words were now written! Oh that they were printed in a book!
                                        Job 19:23

What a sense of security in an old book which time has criticized for us!
                                   James Russell Lowell

I hate books; they teach us only to talk about what we do not know.
                                   Jean-Jacques Rousseau

'Tis the good reader that makes the good book.   *Ralph Waldo Emerson*

The telephone book is full of facts but it doesn't contain a single idea.
                                   Mortimer J. Adler

In the case of good books, the point is not to see how many of them you can get through, but rather how many can get through to you.
                                   Mortimer J. Adler

Books think for me.   *Charles Lamb*

Dictionaries are like watches. The worst is better than none at all and even the best cannot be expected to run quite true.   *Samuel Johnson*

No furniture is so charming as books.   *Sydney Smith*

Does it afflict you to find your books wearing out? I mean literally . . . the mortality of all inanimate things is terrible to me, but that of books most of all.   *William Dean Howells*

The true university of these days is a collection of books.
   Thomas Carlyle

I keep my books at the British Museum and at Mudies.   *Samuel Butler*

One man is as good as another until he has written a book.
   Benjamin Jowett

If a book is worth reading, it is worth buying.   *John Ruskin*

Reading is sometimes an ingenious device for avoiding thought.
   Arthur Helps

The oldest books are still only just out to those who have not read them.
   Samuel Butler

A book is a mirror: if an ass peers into it, you can't expect an apostle to look out.   *G. C. Lichtenberg*

The man who does not read good books has no advantage over the man who can't read them.   *Mark Twain*

Where is human nature so weak as in the bookstore?
   Henry Ward Beecher

Ordinary people know little of the time and effort it takes to learn to read. I have been eighty years at it, and have not reached my goal.   *Goethe*

I am a part of all I have read.   *John Kieran*

Reading is the work of the alert mind, is demanding, and under ideal conditions produces finally a sort of ecstasy. This gives the experience of reading a sublimity and power unequalled by any other form of communication.
   E. B. White

I do not know any reading more easy, more fascinating, more delightful than a catalogue.   *Anatole France*

To me the charm of an encyclopedia is that it knows — and I needn't.
                                                      Francis Yeats-Brown

A best-seller was a book which somehow sold well simply because it was sell-ing well.   *Daniel J. Boorstin*

A good title is the title of a successful book.   *Raymond Chandler*

Books should be tried by a judge and jury as though they were crimes.
                                                          Samuel Butler

Reading, like prayer, remains one of our few private acts.
                                                      William Jovanovich

My education was the liberty I had to read indiscriminately and all the time, with my eyes hanging out.   *Dylan Thomas*

A publisher is somebody looking for someone who has something to say.
                                                          Lorne Pierce

There are perhaps no days of our childhood we lived so fully as those we believe we left without having lived them: those we spent with a favourite book.   *Marcel Proust*

Some books are to be tasted, others to be swallowed, and some few to be chewed and digested.   *Francis Bacon*

If you would understand your own age, read the works of fiction produced in it. People in disguise speak freely.   *Arthur Helps*

Camerado, this is no book.
Who touches this, touches a man.   *Walt Whitman*

A book is like a garden carried in the pocket.   *Chinese proverb*

The walls of books around him, dense with the past, formed a kind of insu-lation against the present world and its disasters.   *Ross MacDonald*

There are still a few of us booklovers around despite the awful warnings of Marshall McLuhan with his TV era and his pending farewell to Gutenberg.
                                                          Frank Davies

Bores and Boredom

Some people can stay longer in an hour than others can in a week.
William Dean Howells

A bore is a man who deprives you of solitude without providing you with
company. *Gian Vincenzo Gravina*

A bore is a man who, when you ask him how he is, tells you.
Bert Leston Taylor

The man who suspects his own tediousness has yet to be born.
Thomas Bailey Aldrich

Ennui has made more gamblers than avarice, more drunkards than thirst,
and perhaps as many suicides as despair. *Charles Caleb Colton*

The inexorable boredom that is at the core of life.
Jacques-Bénigne Bossuet

He has returned from Italy a greater bore than ever; he bores on architecture, painting, statuary and music. *Sydney Smith*

O wad some power the giftie gie us to see some people before they see us.
Ethel Watts Mumford

The most costly disease is not cancer or coronaries. The most costly disease
is boredom — costly for both individual and society. *Norman Cousins*

The devil's name is dullness. *Robert E. Lee*

The basic fact about human existence is not that it is a tragedy, but that it
is a bore. *H. L. Mencken*

His shortcoming is his long staying. *Lewis L. Lewisohn*

Uncertainty and mystery are energies of life. Don't let them scare you un-
duly, for they keep boredom at bay and spark creativity. *R.I. Fitzhenry*

Boredom is a vital problem for the moralist, since at least half the sins of
mankind are caused by the fear of it. *Bertrand Russell*

Dullness is a misdemeanour. *Ethel Wilson*

When people are bored, it is primarily with their own selves.

Eric Hoffer

A variety of nothing is superior to a monotony of something.

Jean Paul Richter

We often forgive those who bore us, but can't forgive those whom we bore.

La Rochefoucauld

A man can stand almost anything except a succession of ordinary days.

Goethe

Any idiot can face a crisis — it's this day-to-day living that wears you out.

Anton Chekhov

The secret of boring people lies in telling them everything.   *Voltaire*

Boredom turns a man to sex, a woman to shopping, and it drives newscasters berserk.   *Bruce Herschensohn*

Blessed is the man who, having nothing to say, refrains from giving wordy evidence of the fact.   *George Eliot*

Boredom is rage spread thin.   *Paul Tillich*

Almost all human affairs are tedious. Everything is too long. Visits, dinners, concerts, plays, speeches, pleadings, essays, sermons, are too long. Pleasure and business labour equally under this defect, or, as I should rather say, this fatal superabundance.   *Arthur Helps*

Business, Capitalism and Corporate Enterprise

Christmas is over, and Business is Business.   *Franklin Pierce Adams*

Another thing about capitalism — everybody knows who's in Grant's tomb.

Louis Nelson Bowman

People of privilege will always risk their complete destruction rather than surrender any material part of their advantage.   *J. K. Galbraith*

Competition means decentralized planning by many separate persons.
Friedrich Hayek

All business sagacity reduces itself in the last analysis to a judicious use of sabotage.
Thorstein Veblen

Expansion means complexity and complexity decay.
Northcote Parkinson

One man's wage rise is another man's price increase.
Harold Wilson

Meetings are indispensable when you don't want to do anything.
J. K. Galbraith

Few have heard of Fra Luca Parioli, the inventor of double entry bookkeeping, but he has probably had more influence on human life than has Dante or Michelangelo.
Herbert J. Muller

When you've got them by their wallets, their hearts and minds will follow.
Fern Naito

Chaplin is no businessman — all he knows is that he can't take anything less.
Sam Goldwyn

What kind of society isn't structured on greed? The problem of social organization is how to set up an arrangement under which greed will do the least harm; capitalism is that kind of a system.
Milton Friedman

We are dying of accuracy.
Couteli, French humorist

Barbaric accuracy — whimpering humility.
G.C. Lichtenberg

In economics, the majority is always wrong.
J.K. Galbraith

Patience is a most necessary quality for business; many a man would rather you heard his story than grant his request.
Lord Chesterfield

A holding company is the people you give your money to while you're being searched.
Will Rogers

Pounds are the sons, not of pounds, but of pence.
Charles Buxton

Whenever you see a successful business, someone once made a courageous decision.
Peter Drucker

In matters of commerce the fault of the Dutch
Is offering too little and asking too much.
The French are with equal advantage content,
So we clap on Dutch bottoms just 20%.   *George Canning*

Business? It's quite simple. It's other people's money.
                                    Alexandre Dumas the Younger

A man isn't a man until he has to meet a payroll.   *Ivan Shaffer*

As a rule, from what I've observed, the American Captain of Industry doesn't do anything out of business hours. When he has put the cat out and locked up the office for the night, he just relapses into a state of coma from which he emerges only to start being a Captain of Industry again.
                                    P.G. Wodehouse

One of the greatest pieces of economic wisdom is to know what you do not know.   *J. K. Galbraith*

I don't believe in just ordering people to do things. You have to sort of grab an oar and row with them.   *Harold Geneen*

Executive ability is deciding quickly and getting somebody else to do the work.   *J. G. Pollard*

Capitalism in the United States has undergone profound modification, not just under the New Deal but through a consensus that continued to grow after the New Deal. Government in the U.S. today is a senior partner in every business in the country.   *Norman Cousins*

Going to work for a large company is like getting on a train. Are you going sixty miles an hour or is the train going sixty miles an hour and you're just sitting still?   *Paul Getty*

The happiest time in any man's life is when he is in red-hot pursuit of a dollar with a reasonable prospect of overtaking it.   *Josh Billings*

In a hierarchy every employee tends to rise to his level of incompetence.
                                    Laurence J. Peter

What recommends commerce to me is its enterprise and bravery. It does not clasp its hands and pray to Jupiter.   *Henry David Thoreau*

Business is a combination of war and sport.   *André Maurois*

Invest in inflation. It's the only thing going up.   *Will Rogers*

Net — the biggest word in the language of business.   *Herbert Casson*

The secret of business is to know something that nobody else knows.
Aristotle Onassis

Don't gamble; take all your savings and buy some good stock and hold it
till it goes up, then sell it. If it don't go up, don't buy it.   *Will Rogers*

Good management consists of showing average people how to do the work
of superior people.   *John D. Rockefeller*

Big business is basic to the very life of this country; and yet many — perhaps
most — Americans have a deep-seated fear and an emotional repugnance
to it. Here is monumental contradiction.   *David Lilienthal*

All business proceeds on beliefs, on judgements of probabilities, and not on
certainties.   *Charles W. Eliot*

Corporations cannot commit treason, nor be outlawed, nor excommunicated,
for they have no souls.   *Edward Coke*

People of the same trade seldom meet together, even for merriment and diversion, but the conversation ends in a conspiracy against the public, or in some
contrivance to raise prices.   *Adam Smith*

Capital is past savings accumulated for future production.
Jackson Martindell

The business of America is business.   *Calvin Coolidge*

Power over a man's subsistence amounts to a power over his will.
Alexander Hamilton

In the history of enterprise, most of the protagonists of major new products
and companies began their education — not in the classroom, where the old
ways are taught, but in the factories and labs where new ways are wrought
. . . nothing has been so rare in recent years as an Ivy League graduate who
has made a significant innovation in American enterprise. *George Gilder*

If a cluttered desk is an indication of a cluttered mind, what is indicated by
an empty desk?   *Anon.*

A businessman is a hybrid of a dancer and a calculator.   *Paul Valéry*

Had there been a computer a hundred years ago, it would probably have predicted that by now there would be so many horse-drawn vehicles it would be impossible to clear up all the manure.   *K. William Kapp*

All professions are a conspiracy against the country.
George Bernard Shaw

The Middle East is a region where oil is thicker than blood.
James Holland

Labour is not a commodity, or a standard, or a means to an ulterior end, but an end in itself.   *George Brockway*

Without some dissimulation no business can be carried on at all.
Lord Chesterfield

A criminal is a person with predatory instincts who has not sufficient capital to form a corporation.   *Howard Scott*

Profitability is the sovereign criterion of the enterprise.   *Peter Drucker*

Business is more exciting than any game.   *Lord Beaverbrook*

A company is judged by the president it keeps.   *James Hulbert*

Inflation is defined as the quality that makes balloons larger and candy bars smaller.   *General Features Corporation*

I think that there is nothing, not even crime, more opposed to poetry, to philosophy, ay, to life itself than this incessant business.
Henry David Thoreau

It is not the employer who pays wages — he only handles the money. It is the product that pays wages.   *Henry Ford*

Business is really more agreeable than pleasure; it interests the whole mind . . . more deeply. But it does not look as if it did.   *Walter Bagehot*

Along this tree
From root to crown
Ideas flow up
And vetoes down.   *A senior executive, quoted by Peter Drucker*

The ability to deal with people is as purchasable a commodity as sugar or coffee. And I pay more for that ability than for any other under the sun.
John D. Rockefeller

In all modern depressions, recessions, or growth-correction, as variously they are called, we never miss the goods that are not produced. We miss only the opportunities for the labour — for the jobs — that are not provided.
J. K. Galbraith

The solid wealth of insurance companies and the success of those who organize gambling are some indication of the profits to be derived from the efficient use of chance.   *Edward de Bono*

To convert an hourly wage to an approximate yearly salary, double the wage and change the decimal to a comma.   *Don Tichnor*

After an eight-hour day, workers require three overtime hours to produce two regular hours of results.   *Illinois Institute of Technology*

Meetings are indispensable when you don't want to do anything.
J.K. Galbraith

Gross National Product is our Holy Grail.   *Steward Udall*

When two men in business always agree, one of them is unnecessary.
William Wrigley, Jr.

Few great men could pass Personnel.   *Paul Goodman*

You build on cost and you borrow on value.   *Paul Reichmann*

By pursuing his own interest (the individual) frequently promotes that of the society more effectually than when he really intends to promote it. I have never known much good done by those who affected to trade for the public good.   *Adam Smith*

Management is now where the medical profession was when it decided that working in a drug store was not sufficient training to become a doctor.
Lawrence Appley

The Bell System is like a damn big dragon. You kick it in the tail, and two years later, it feels it in its head.
Frederick Kappel (Chairman, American Telephone and Telegraph Co.)

Anybody who has any doubt about the ingenuity or the resourcefulness of a plumber never got a bill from one.   *George Meany*

Benefits should be granted little by little, so that they may be better enjoyed.
                                                            Niccolo Machievelli.

The price spoils the pleasure.   *French proverb*

Whose bread I eat, his song I sing.   *German proverb*

Buying and Selling

Everyone lives by selling something.   *Robert Louis Stevenson*

It is naught, it is naught; saith the buyer. But when he is gone his way, then he boasteth.   *Proverbs 20:14*

Piracy, n: commerce without its folly-swaddles — just as God made it.
                                                            Ambrose Bierce

A study of economics usually reveals that the best time to buy anything is last year.   *Marty Allen*

A consumer is a shopper who is sore about something.   *Harold Coffin*

Who buys has need of two eyes
But one's enough to sell the stuff.   *Anon.*

Bargain: something you can't use at a price you can't resist.
                                                            Franklin P. Jones

Don't buy the house; buy the neighborhood.   *Russian proverb*

A fair price for oil is whatever you can get plus ten to twenty per cent.
                                                                  Anon.

A decision is the action an executive must take when he has information so incomplete that the answer does not suggest itself.
                                                    Arthur William Radford

An extravagance is anything you buy that is of no earthly use to your wife.
                                                            Franklin P. Jones

What costs nothing is worth nothing.   *Anon.*

Keep thy shop and thy shop will keep thee.   *Ben Jonson*

Everything is worth what its purchaser will pay for it.   *Publilius Syrus*

There is hardly anything in the world that some man can't make a little worse and sell a little cheaper, and the people who consider price only are this man's lawful prey.   *John Ruskin*

Cheat me in the price but not in the goods.   *Thomas Fuller*

When you buy, use your eyes and your mind, not your ears.
                                          Czechoslovakian proverb

People will buy anything that's one to a customer.   *Sinclair Lewis*

Canada and Canadians

Look here
You've never seen this country
It's not the way you thought it was
Look again.   *Al Purdy*

The whole history of the Canadian north can be divided into two periods — before and after the aeroplane.   *Hugh Keenleyside*

The father of confederation is deadlock.   *Goldwin Smith*

The first time I ever felt the necessity or inevitableness of verse, was in the desire to reproduce the peculiar quality of feeling which is induced by the flat spaces and wide horizons of the virgin prairie of western Canada.
                                          T.E. Hulme

Québec is the original heart, the hardest and deepest kernel, the core of first time. All round, nine other provinces form the flesh of this still-bitter fruit called Canada.   *Anne Hébert*

The Lord said 'let there be wheat' and Saskatchewan was born.
                                          Stephen Leacock

Ottawa — a sub-arctic lumber-village converted by royal mandate into a political cockpit.   *Goldwin Smith*

Americans like to make money: Canadians like to audit it. I know no country where accountants have a higher social and moral status.

Northrop Frye

I suppose the half-breeds in Manitoba, in 1870, did not fight for two hundred forty acres of land, but it is to be understood there were two societies
who treated together. One was small, but in its smallness it had its rights.
The other was great, but in its greatness it had no greater rights than the
rights of the small, because the right is the same for everyone.

Louis Riel

Canada's national bird is the grouse.   *Stuart Keate*

Separatism is a very healthy movement within culture. It's a disastrous movement within politics and economics.   *Northrop Frye*

An arena
large as Europe
Silent
waiting the contest   *F. R. Scott*

There has never been a war of Canadian origin, nor for a Canadian cause.
William Arthur Deacon

Canada is a collection of ten provinces with strong governments loosely connected by fear.   *Dave Broadfoot*

Canada is a good country to be from. It has a gentler, slower pace — it lends
perspective.   *Paul Anka*

My generation of Canadians grew up believing that, if we were very good
or very smart, or both, we would some day graduate from Canada.

Robert Fulford

We are being swallowed up by the popular culture of the United States, but
then the Americans are being swallowed up by it too. It's just as much a
threat to American culture as it is to ours.   *Northrop Frye*

Never hear anything bad about Canada, that's one thing — in fact, I guess
it's the only thing.
Walter Stewart (quoting a student in Indiana, U.S.A.)

Canada should divert rivers to the U.S., deriving revenue from the sale of
water.   *Lord Thomson of Fleet*

Canada is a society, rather than a nation.   *Kildare Dobbs*

Living next to the United States is in some ways like sleeping with an elephant. No matter how friendly and even-tempered is the beast, one is affected by every twitch and grunt.   *Pierre Elliott Trudeau*

A sentry between the United States and Canada would be about as appropriate as a fire extinguisher on top of the Great Pyramid.   *Vincent Massey*

Canada reminds me of vichyssoise — it's cold, half-French and difficult to stir.   *Stuart Keate*

Our country has shown a lack of will to resist its own disintegration . . . Canada is practically the only country left in the world which is a pure colony; colonial in psychology as well as in mercantile economics.
            Northrop Frye

Americans assume Canada to be bestowed as a right and accept this bounty, as they do air, without thought or appreciation.   *Dean Acheson*

Americans are benevolently ignorant about Canada, while Canadians are malevolently well informed about the United States.   *J. Bartlet Brebner*

'Old Tomorrow.'   *Nickname for Sir John A. Macdonald*

'Rich by nature, poor by policy' might be written over Canada's door.
            Goldwin Smith

Canadian politics in British Columbia is an adventure, on the Prairies a cause, in Ontario a business, in Québec a religion, in the Maritimes a disease.
            Paul St. Pierre

The average American's knowledge of Canada amounts to a benevolent ignorance.   *Edward Miles*

When I stand on a street in a Canadian city and look across the street, it couldn't be anywhere but Canada, but how can I prove it?
            Margaret Mead

(Canada) — the most parochial nationette on earth . . . I have been living in this sanctimonious icebox . . . painting portraits of the opulent Methodists of Toronto. Methodism and money in this city have produced a sort of hell of dullness.   *Wyndham Lewis*

Newfoundland is a great English ship, moored near the Banks during the fishing season for the convenience of the English fishermen.

A. H. McIntosh

The Newfoundland fisheries are a nursery for seamen.   *Anon.*

The land too poor for any other crop, is best for raising men.

R. Pocock

I want history to jump on Canada's spine with sharp skates.

Leonard Cohen

Is heaven more beautiful than the country of the muskox in summer when sometimes the mist blows over the lakes, and sometimes the water is blue, and the loons cry very often?   *Saltatha Inuit*

Our sense of identity is our sense of density.   *Marshall McLuhan*

Much will have to change in Canada if the country is to stay the same.

Abraham Rotstein

The Greeks, who knew everything, understood that without the orgy there is no middle ground between bedlam and Toronto . . . we need the healing grace of the orgy in this country.   *Hugh MacLennan*

Canada is a live country — live, but not, like the States, kicking.

Rupert Brooke

There was a small boy of Quebec
Who was buried in snow to the neck:
When they said 'Are you friz?'
He replied 'Yes, I is —
But we don't call this cold in Quebec!'   *Rudyard Kipling*

The mighty voice of Canada will ever call to me.   *Arthur Conan Doyle*

Saskatchewan is much like Texas — except it's more friendly to the United States.   *Adlai Stevenson*

If the national mental illness of the United States is megalomania, that of Canada is paranoid schizophrenia.   *Margaret Atwood*

Canada is not a country for the cold of heart or the cold of feet.

Pierre Elliott Trudeau

We sing about the North, but live as far south as possible.

J. B. McGeachy

Canada has no cultural unity, no linguistic unity, no religious unity, no economic unity, no geographic unity. All it has is unity.

Kenneth Boulding

So long as the majority of Canadians have two countries, one here and one in Europe, national unity will remain a myth and a constant source of internecine quarrels. *Henri Bourassa*

We French-Canadians belong to one country, Canada: Canada is for us the whole world: but the English-Canadians have two countries, one here and one across the sea. *Wilfrid Laurier*

My father spoke French with a Bank of Montreal accent.

Hartland deMontarville Molson

If a player continues transgressing the rules, his side shall lose him.

Rugby Football rules in Toronto, circa 1880

That one never asks a question unless he knows the answer is basic to parliamentary questioning. *John G. Diefenbaker*

Love Canada or give it back. *Indian saying in Saskatchewan*

The Americans are our best friends — whether we like it or not.

Robert Thompson

Scenery here in Canada is by the mile, whereas in England it is by the foot. In England there is a great wealth of 'pretty bits.' In Canada there is a great lack of them. But there are grandeur, vastness and expansive views.

A. Brooker Klugh

Canada's climate is nine months winter and three months late in the fall.

Evan Esar

The Canadian is often a baffled man because he feels different from his British kindred and his American neighbours, sharply refused to be lumped together with either of them, yet cannot make plain his difference. *J. B. Priestley*

A Canadian is someone who knows he is going somewhere, but isn't sure where. *W. L. Morton*

He wants to be different from everyone else
and daydreams of winning the global race,
Parents unmarried and living abroad,
relatives keen to bag the estate,
schizophrenia not excluded,
will he learn to grow up before it's too late?   *Earle Birney*

To be Canadian is to live in relative calm and with great dignity.
William Davis

John Kenneth Galbraith and Marshall McLuhan are the two greatest modern
Canadians that the U.S. has produced.   *Anthony Burgess*

Canadians have been accustomed to define themselves by saying what they
are not.   *William Kilbourn*

I know that through the grace of God, I am the founder of Manitoba.
Louis Riel

Actually, when it comes to knocking the Canadian cultural scene, nobody
outdoes Canadians, myself included. We are veritable masters of self-
deprecation.   *Mordecai Richler*

Canadians are generally indistinguishable from Americans, and the surest
way of telling the two apart is to make the observation to a Canadian.
Richard Staines

A Torontonian is a man who leaves culture to his wife.   *Brendan Behan*

Toronto has no social classes — only the Masseys and the masses.
B. K. Sandwell

The Scots are the backbone of Canada. They are all right in their three vital
parts — head, heart and haggis.   *William Osler*

Listen your Lordship, I'm a respecter of institutions. Even in Paris, I remained a Canadian. I puffed hashish, but I didn't inhale.
Mordecai Richler

One man out of every five who lands on our shores is a foreigner — i.e.
non-Anglo-Saxon. He comes here with a foreign tongue, foreign ideals,
foreign religion, with centuries of ignorance and oppression behind him, often
bringing with him problems that the best statesmen of Europe have failed
to solve.   *W.D. Reid*

I think a stalwart peasant in a sheepskin coat, born on the soil, whose forefathers have been farmers for ten generations, with a stout wife and a half-dozen chickens, is good quality.   *Clifford Sifton*

If we can find out why the *idea* rather than the *nation* of Canada can win a growing loyalty rather than commanding it, then, it seems to me, we shall have come very near to trapping the elusive creature, the Canadian Identity.
George Woodcock

Beneath their work the moral core of Canadian nationhood is found in the fact that Canada is a monarchy and in the nature of monarchial allegiance. As America is united at bottom by the covenant, Canada is united at the top by allegiance. Because Canada is a nation founded on allegiance and not on compact, there is no pressure for uniformity, there is no Canadian way of life. Any one, French, Irish, Ukrainian or Eskimo, can be a subject of the Queen and a citizen of Canada without in any way changing or ceasing to be himself.   *W. L. Morton*

The Canadian spirit is cautious, observant and critical where the American is assertive.   *V. S. Pritchett*

If ever Confederation fails, it will not be because Québec — the political voice of French Canada — has separated from it. It will be because the way to keep Québec in it has not been found.   *Jean Lesage*

When the white man came, we had the land and they had the bibles. Now they have the land and we have the bibles.   *Chief Dan George*

We shall be Canadians first, foremost, and always, and our policies will be decided in Canada and not dictated by any other country.
John G. Diefenbaker

The line which marks off the frontier and the farmstead, the wilderness from the baseline, the hinterland from the metropolis, runs through every Canadian psyche.   *W. L. Morton*

The situation is one something like living with your wife. Sometimes it is difficult and even irritating to live with her, but it is always impossible to live without her.   *Lester Pearson (defining attitude toward U.S.)*

The Ottawa river flows out of Protestant Ontario into Catholic Quebec.
Hugh MacLennan

The twentieth century belongs to Canada.   *Wilfrid Laurier*

We often say that we fear no invasion from the south, but the armies of the south have already crossed the border — American enterprise, American capital is taking rapid possession of our mines and our water power, our oil areas and our timber limits.   *Sara Jeannette Duncan*

The Canadian dialect of English . . . seems roughly to be the result of applying British syntax to an American vocabulary.   *Lister Sinclair*

What a mine of inspiration there is in the history of French Canada! Fit theme indeed for poet, novelist, historian and painter!   *Thomas O'Hagan*

The *habitant* is the true Canadian, for he has no other country.
                                                          Ramsay Traquair

The immigrant who comes to Canada really sees the country much more as a whole. He doesn't know the nuances which are so important and so dearly beloved by the Torontonian or the Montrealer.   *Brian Moore*

Give us men to match our mountains,
Give us men to match our plains:
Men with empires in their purpose
And new eras in their brains.   *H. T. Miller*

Ottawa is a city where nobody lives, though some of us may die there.
                                                        Michael Macklem

Canada was settled, in the main, by people with a lower middle-class outlook, and a respect, rather than an affectionate familiarity, for the things of the mind.   *Robertson Davies*

Where else in the world could you find another case like ours — three thousand miles of forts, and not a single frontier?   *Stephen Leacock*

The trouble with this whole country is that it's divided up into little puddles with big fish in each one of them.   *Hugh MacLennan*

Historically, a Canadian is an American who rejects the Revolution.
                                                          Northrop Frye

nobody
belongs anywhere,
even the
Rocky Mountains
are still
moving.
                                                        George Bowering

The trouble with Canadians is that they spend half their time convincing the Americans that they're not British and other half convincing the British they're not Americans — which leaves them no time to be themselves.
From McGill's Red and White Review — *'My Fur Lady'*

Let us be French as the Americans are English.   *Henri Bourassa*

Confederation is only yet in the gristle, and it will require five years more before it hardens into bone.   *John A. Macdonald*

You are a big country now, but you still tend to feel small and fragile. If the United States gets a cold, you get pneumonia.   *Herman Kahn*

I was brought up in southwestern Ontario where we were taught that Canadian patriotism should not withstand anything more than a five-dollar-a-month wage differential. Anything more than that and you went to Detroit.
J. K. Galbraith

You can be a French Canadian or an English Canadian, but not a Canadian. We know how to live without an identity, and this is one of our marvellous resources.   *Marshall McLuhan*

Not necessarily conscription, but conscription if necessary.
William Lyon Mackenzie King

Whenever the Germans found the Canadian Corps coming into the line, they prepared for the worst.   *David Lloyd George*

Canadian nationalism was systematically encouraged and exploited by American capital. Canada moved from colony to nation to colony.
Harold A. Innis

Ours is a sovereign nation
Bows to no foreign will
But whenever they cough in Washington
They spit on Parliament Hill.   *Joe Wallace*

Of course, Canadians are different. There is no malice in us. We are the family doctor whom no one has called in for consultation. We are the children of the midday who see all in the clear, shallow light.   *Charles Ritchie*

I know that Nature designs that this whole continent, not merely these thirty-six states, shall be, sooner or later, within the magic circle of the American union.   *William Seward*

Censorship

To limit the press is to insult a nation; to prohibit reading of certain books is to declare the inhabitants to be either fools or slaves.

Claude Adrien Helvetius

The dirtiest book of all is the expurgated book.   *Walt Whitman*

No member of a society has a right to teach any doctrine contrary to what society holds to be true.   *Samuel Johnson*

There is no such thing as a moral or an immoral book. Books are well written or badly written.   *Oscar Wilde*

Persons who undertake to pry into, or cleanse out all the filth of a common sewer, either cannot have very nice noses, or will soon lose them.

William Hazlitt

Knowledge cannot defile, nor consequently the books, if the will and conscience be not defiled.   *John Milton*

We can never be sure that the opinion we are endeavouring to stifle is a false opinion; and if we were sure, stifling it would be an evil still.

John Stuart Mill

No government ought to be without censors; and where the press is free, no one ever will.   *Thomas Jefferson*

Censorship, like charity, should begin at home; but unlike charity, it should end there.   *Clare Boothe Luce*

Obscenity is whatever gives a judge an erection.

Anonymous American Lawyer

You censure this with difficulty because you have allowed it to become customary.   *St. Jerome*

Chance and Fortune

Unless a man has trained himself for his chance, the chance will only make him ridiculous.   *W. Matthews*

Chance is always powerful. Let your hook be always cast. In the pool where you least expect it, will be a fish. *Ovid*

Chance is the pseudonym of God when he did not want to sign. *Anatole France*

The harder you work, the luckier you get. *Gary Player*

I think we consider too much the good luck of the early bird, and not enough the bad luck of the early worm. *Franklin D. Roosevelt*

Fortune favours the bold. *Terence*

The luck of having talent is not enough; one must also have a talent for luck. *Hector Berlioz*

In the field of observation, chance favours the prepared mind. *Louis Pasteur*

Throw a lucky man into the sea, and he will come up with a fish in his mouth. *Arabic proverb*

If you were born lucky, even your rooster will lay eggs. *Russian proverb*

Depend on the rabbit's foot if you will, but remember it didn't work for the rabbit! *R.E. Shay*

Those who mistake their good luck for their merit are inevitably bound for disaster. *J. Christopher Herold*

Luck is being ready for the chance. *J. Frank Dobie*

Every man, even the most blessed, needs a little more than average luck to survive this world. *Vance Bourjaily*

With luck on your side you can do without brains. *Giordano Bruno*

If fortune turns against you, even jelly breaks your tooth. *Persian proverb*

Fortune brings in some boats that are not steered. *Shakespeare, 'Cymbeline'*

I'm a great believer in luck. I find the harder I work, the more I have of
it.   *Stephen Leacock*

Vexed sailors curse the rain
For which poor shepherds prayed in vain.
                                                          Edmund Waller

Change and Transience

Everything changes but change itself.   *John F. Kennedy*

What is actual is actual only for one time.
And only for one place.   *T.S. Eliot*

As one gets older, one discovers everything is going to be exactly the same
with different hats on.   *Noel Coward*

All changes, even the most longed for, have their melancholy, for what we
leave behind us is a part of ourselves; we must die to one life before we can
enter into another.   *Anatole France*

When you get there, there isn't any there there.   *Gertrude Stein*

Change must be measured from a known base line.   *Evan Shute*

I can generally bear the separation, but I don't like the leave-taking.
                                                           Samuel Butler

All things must change to something new, to something strange.
                                             Henry Wadsworth Longfellow

I see gr-reat changes takin' place ivry day, but no change at all ivry fifty
years.   *Finley Peter Dunne*

'Change' is scientific, 'progress' is ethical; change is indubitable, whereas
progress is a matter of controversy.   *Bertrand Russell*

Turbulence is life force. It is opportunity. Let's love turbulence and use it
for change.   *Ramsay Clark*

Would that life were like the shadow cast by a wall or a tree, but it is like
the shadow of a bird in flight.   *The Talmud*

Fame is a vapour, popularity an accident; the only earthly certainty is oblivion. *Mark Twain*

Every new adjustment is a crisis in self-esteem. *Eric Hoffer*

Character and Personality

It is native personality, and that alone, that endows a man to stand before presidents or generals, or in any distinguished collection, with aplomb — and not culture, or any intellect whatever. *Walt Whitman*

Talents are best nurtured in solitude: character is best formed in the stormy billows of the world. *Goethe*

Style, personality — deliberately adopted and therefore a mask — is the only escape from the hot-faced bargainers and money-changers. *William Butler Yeats*

Show me a good and gracious loser, and I'll show you a failure. *Knute Rockne*

Everyone is a moon and has a dark side which he never shows to anybody. *Mark Twain*

I'd rather be strongly wrong than weakly right. *Tallulah Bankhead*

Altruism declares that any action taken for the benefit of others is good, and any action taken for one's own benefit is evil. Thus the beneficiary of an action is the only criterion of moral value — and so long as that beneficiary is anybody other than oneself, anything goes. *Ayn Rand*

To enjoy the things we ought, and to hate the things we ought, has the greatest bearing on excellence of character. *Aristotle*

Character building begins in our infancy, and continues until death. *Eleanor Roosevelt*

Character is perfectly educated will. *Novalis*

Character is long-standing habit. *Plutarch*

I was born modest; not all over, but in spots. *Mark Twain*

Character, in great and little things, means carrying through what you feel able to do.   *Goethe*

Moderation is an ostentatious proof of our strength of character.
                                                                  La Rochefoucauld

If you think about what you ought to do for other people, your character will take care of itself.   *Woodrow Wilson*

You cannot dream yourself into a character; you must hammer and forge yourself one.   *James A. Froude*

A modest man is usually admired — if people ever hear of him.
                                                                  Edgar Watson Howe

The clock struck eleven with the respectful unobtrusiveness of one whose mission in life is to be ignored.   *Saki*

Some people approach every problem with an open mouth.
                                                                  Adlai Stevenson

My specialty is detached malevolence.   *Alice Roosevelt Longworth*

Every one is as God made him and oftentimes a good deal worse.
                                                                  Cervantes

Character is that which can do without success.   *Ralph Waldo Emerson*

Character is what God and the angels know of us; reputation is what men and women think of us.   *Horace Mann*

If you create an act, you create a habit. If you create a habit, you create a character. If you create a character, you create a destiny.
                                                                  André Maurois

One can acquire everything in solitude except character.   *Stendhal*

Every man has three characters — that which he exhibits, that which he has, and that which he thinks he has.   *Alphonse Kan*

If I take care of my character, my reputation will take care of itself.
                                                                  D. L. Moody

A wise and an understanding heart.   *1 Kings 3:12*

Everyone ought to bear patiently the results of his own conduct.

Phaedrus

Every man has his follies — and often they are the most interesting things he has got. *Josh Billings*

The temper of mind that sees tragedy in life has not for its opposite the temper that sees joy. The opposite pole to the tragic view of life is the sordid view. When humanity is seen as devoid of dignity and significance, trivial, mean and sunk in dreary hopelessness, then the spirit of tragedy departs.

Edith Hamilton

Indecision is like a stepchild: if he doesn't wash his hands, he is called dirty; if he does, he is wasting the water. *African proverb*

Learn to say 'No'; it will be of more use to you than to be able to read Latin.

Charles Haddon Spurgeon

To dream of the person you would like to be is to waste the person you are.

Anon.

Character is like a tree, and reputation like its shadow. The shadow is what we think of it; the tree is the real thing. *Anon.*

Every man in the world is better than some one else. And not as good as some one else. *William Saroyan*

'Tis e'er the wont of simple folk to prize the deed and overlook the motive, and of learned folk to discount the deed and lay open the soul of the doer.

John Barth

In Victorian times the purpose of life was to develop a personality once and for all and then stand on it. *Ashley Montagu*

Charm is a way of getting the answer yes without having asked any clear question. *Albert Camus*

Children and Childhood

Childhood — a period of waiting for the moment when I could send everyone and everything connected with it to hell. *Igor Stravinsky*

A child thinks twenty shillings and twenty years can scarce ever be spent.
Benjamin Franklin

If children grew up according to early indications, we should have nothing but geniuses.
Goethe

What children expect from grownups is not to be 'understood,' but only to be loved, even though this love may be expressed clumsily or in sternness. Intimacy does not exist between generations — only trust. *Carl Zucker*

Healthy children will not fear life if their elders have integrity enough not to fear death.
Erik Erikson

William Blake really is important, my cornerstone. Nobody ever told me before he did that childhood was such a damned serious business.
Maurice Sendak

Out of the mouths of babes and sucklings hast thou ordained strength.
Psalms 8:2

When I was a child, I spake as a child, I understood as a child, I thought as a child; but when I became a man I put away childish things.
1 Corinthians 13:11

Children have more need of models than of critics.   *Joseph Joubert*

Children are remarkable for their intelligence and ardour, for their curiosity, their intolerance of shams, the clarity and ruthlessness of their vision.
Aldous Huxley

The events of childhood do not pass but repeat themselves like seasons of the year.   *Eleanor Farjeon*

Children have never been very good at listening to their elders, but they have never failed to imitate them.   *James Baldwin*

Ask your child what he wants for dinner only if he is buying.
Fran Lebowitz

If a child lives with approval, he learns to live with himself.
Dorothy Law Nolte

Your children are not dead. They are just waiting until the world deserves them.   *The Pied Piper*

What's done to children, they will do to society.   *Karl Menninger*

The hardest job kids face today is learning good manners without seeing any.
Fred Astaire

Unlike grownups, children have little need to deceive themselves. *Goethe*

We've had bad luck with our kids — they've all grown up.
Christopher Morley

There are only two lasting bequests we can hope to give our children. One of these is roots, the other, wings.   *Hodding Carter*

Give me the children until they are seven and anyone may have them afterwards.   *St. Francis Xavier*

There are only two things a child will share willingly — communicable diseases and his mother's age.   *Benjamin Spock*

Do not mistake a child for his symptom.   *Erik Erikson*

Babies are such a nice way to start people.   *Don Herold*

All children wear the sign: 'I want to be important NOW.' Many of our juvenile delinquency problems arise because nobody reads the sign.
Dan Pursuit

Children need love, especially when they do not deserve it.
Harold S. Hulbert

If a child is to keep alive his inborn sense of wonder without any such gift from the fairies, he needs the companionship of at least one adult who can share it, rediscovering with him the joy, excitement and mystery of the world we live in.   *Rachel Carson*

Nothing has a stronger influence psychologically on their environment, and especially on their children, than the unlived lives of the parents.
Carl Jung

Christians and Christianity

Somewhere, and I can't find where, I read about an Eskimo hunter who asked the local missionary priest, 'If I did not know about God and sin, would I go to hell?' 'No,' said the priest, 'not if you did not know.' 'Then why,' asked the Eskimo earnestly, 'did you tell me?'   *Annie Dillard*

Christians have burned each other, quite persuaded
That all the apostles would have done as they did.   *Lord Byron*

Christian: one who believes that the New Testament is a divinely inspired book admirably suited to the spiritual needs of his neighbour.
                                                                    Ambrose Bierce

Most people believe that the Christian commandments are intentionally a little too severe — like setting a clock half an hour ahead to make sure of not being late in the morning.   *Søren Kierkegaard*

A Christian is nothing but a sinful man who has put himself to school for Christ for the honest purpose of becoming better.   *Henry Ward Beecher*

A Christian is a man who feels
Repentance on a Sunday
For what he did on Saturday
And is going to do on Monday.   *Thomas R. Ybarra*

Hatred of Judaism is at bottom hatred of Christianity.   *Sigmund Freud*

I believe in Christianity as I believe that the sun has risen. Not only because I see it, but because I see everything by it.   *C. S. Lewis*

It is not by driving away our brother that we can be alone with God.
                                                                    George Macdonald

If only God would give me some clear sign! Like making a large deposit in my name at a Swiss bank.   *Woody Allen*

God will forgive me. That's his business.   *Heinrich Heine*

Ethical man — a Christian holding four aces.   *Mark Twain*

People in general are equally horrified at hearing the Christian religion doubted, and at seeing it practised.   *Samuel Butler*

Christian life consists of faith and charity. *Martin Luther*

Many a sober Christian would rather admit that a wafer is God than that God is a cruel and capricious tyrant. *Edward Gibbon*

If you go to church, and like the singing better than the preaching, that's not orthodox. *Edgar Watson Howe*

The City and the Country

The country has charms only for those not obliged to stay there.
Edouard Manet

A great city, a great solitude. *Old proverb*

In small settlements everyone knows your affairs. In the big city, everyone does not — only those you choose to tell will know about you. This is one of the attributes of cities that is precious to most city people.
Jane Jacobs

If you would be known, and not know, vegetate in a village; if you would know and not be known, live in a city. *Charles Caleb Colton*

What is the city in which we sit here, but an aggregate of incongruous materials, which have obeyed the will of some man?
Ralph Waldo Emerson

Farmers worry only during the growing season, but town people worry all the time. *Edgar Watson Howe*

What is the city but the people? *Shakespeare, 'Coriolanus'*

As a remedy to life in society, I would suggest the big city. Nowadays it is the only desert within our reach. *Albert Camus*

All cities are mad: but the madness is gallant. All cities are beautiful: but the beauty is grim. *Christopher Morley*

The chicken is the country's, but the city eats it. *George Herbert*

Cities force growth and make men talkative and entertaining, but they make them artificial. *Ralph Waldo Emerson*

The mobs of great cities add just so much to the support of pure government as sores do to the strength of the human body.   *Thomas Jefferson*

The city is a cultural invention enforcing on the citizen knowledge of his own nature. And this we do not like. That we are aggressive beings, easily given to violence; that we get along together because we must more than because we want to, and that the brotherhood of man is about as far from reality today as it was two thousand years ago; that reason's realm is small; that we never have been and never shall be created equal; that if the human being is perfectible, he has so far exhibited few symptoms — all are considerations of man from which space tends to protect us.   *Robert Ardrey*

There is nothing good to be had in the country, or, if there be, they will not let you have it.   *William Hazlitt*

Anybody can be good in the country. There are no temptations there.
Oscar Wilde

The axis of the earth sticks out visibly through the centre of each and every town or city.   *Oliver Wendell Holmes*

We will neglect our cities to our peril, for in neglecting them we neglect the nation.   *John F. Kennedy*

To say the least, a town life makes one more tolerant and liberal in one's judgement of others.   *Henry Wadsworth Longfellow*

Commuters give the city its tidal restlessness, natives give it solidity and continuity, but the settlers give it passion.   *E. B. White*

It is only in the country that we can get to know a person or a book.
Cyril Connolly

At present, I am a sojourner in the city again, but here in the green warmth of a city backyard, I see only the countenance of spring in the country.
E. B. White

Summertime, oh, summertime, pattern of life indelible, the fade-proof lake, the woods unshatterable, the pasture with the sweetfern and the juniper forever and ever . . . the cottages with their innocent and tranquil design, their tiny docks with the flagpole and the American flag floating against the white clouds in the blue sky, the little paths over the roots of the trees leading from camp to camp. This was the American family at play, escaping the city heat.   *E. B. White*

There is no solitude in the world like that of the big city.

Kathleen Norris

Civilization

A civilized society is one that exhibits the five qualities of truth, beauty, adventure, art and peace.   *Alfred North Whitehead*

There is such a thing as too much couth.   *S. J. Perelman*

We are in the first age since the dawn of civilization in which people have dared to think it practicable to make the benefits of civilization available to the whole human race.   *Arnold Toynbee*

Let us humour if we can
The vertical man
Though we value none
But the horizontal one.   *W. H. Auden*

The human landscape of the New World shows a conquest of nature by an intelligence that does not love it.   *Northrop Frye*

Any sufficiently advanced technology is indistinguishable from magic.
Arthur C. Clarke

Technological man can't believe in anything that can't be measured, taped, or put into a computer.   *Clare Boothe Luce*

Our lifetime may be the last that will be lived out in a technological society.
Isaac Asimov

To be able to fill leisure intelligently is the last product of civilization.
Arnold Toynbee

So I should say that civilizations begin with religion and stoicism: they end with scepticism and unbelief, and the undisciplined pursuit of individual pleasure. A civilization is born stoic and dies epicurean.   *Will Durant*

We are all afraid — for our confidence, for the future, for the world. That is the nature of the human imagination. Yet every man, every civilization, has gone forward because of its engagement with what it has set itself to do. The personal commitment and the emotional commitment working together as one, has made the Ascent of Man.   *Jacob Bronowski*

Civilization is just a slow process of learning to be kind.

Charles L. Lucas

Civilization is a movement — not a condition; a voyage — not a harbour.

Arnold Toynbee

Since barbarism has its pleasures it naturally has its apologists.

George Santayana

We sit by and watch the barbarian. We tolerate him in the long stretches of peace, we are not afraid. We are tickled by his irreverence; his comic inversion of our old certitudes and our fixed creed refreshes us; we laugh. But as we laugh we are watched by large and awful faces from beyond, and on these faces there are no smiles.   *Hilaire Belloc*

Without culture, and the relative freedom it presumes, society, even when perfect, is no more than a jungle. This is why every authentic creation is a gift to the future.   *Albert Camus*

Civilizations die from philosophical calm, irony, and the sense of fair play quite as surely as they die of debauchery.   *Joseph Wood Krutch*

The three great elements of modern civilization, Gunpowder, Printing, and the Protestant Religion.   *Thomas Carlyle*

No matter how much you feed a wolf, he will always return to the forest.

Russian proverb

A savage is simply a human organism that has not received enough news from the human race.   *John Ciardi*

A race preserves its vigour so long as it harbours a real contrast between what has been and what may be, and so long as it is nerved by the vigour to adventure beyond the safeties of the past. Without adventure, civilization is in full decay.   *Alfred North Whitehead*

This is the way the world ends
Not with a bang but a whimper.   *T. S. Eliot*

A tablecloth restaurant is still one of the great rewards of civilization.

Harry Golden

The end of the human race will be that it will eventually die of civilization.

Ralph Waldo Emerson

If you would civilize a man, begin with his grandmother.   *Victor Hugo*

I know I am among civilized men because they are fighting so savagely.
Voltaire

The only way a man can get civilized is to become a contemporary of himself.
J. Frank Dobie

To be a man is to feel that one's own stone contributes to building the edifice of the world.   *Antoine de Saint Exupéry*

Committees, Clubs and Institutions

The ideal committee is one with me as chairman, and two other members in bed with flu.   *Lord Milverton*

If Moses had been a committee, the Israelites would still be in Egypt.
J. B. Hughes

A committee of one gets things done.   *Joe Ryan*

A camel is a horse designed by a committee.   *Anon.*

If Columbus had had an advisory committee he would probably still be at the dock.   *Justice Arthur Goldberg*

An institution is the lengthening shadow of one man.
Ralph Waldo Emerson

I do not care to belong to a club that accepts people like me as members.
Groucho Marx

Those mausoleums of inactive masculinity are places for men who prefer armchairs to women.   *V. S. Pritchett*

What is a committee? A group of the unwilling, picked from the unfit, to do the unnecessary.   *Richard Harkness*

No grand idea was ever born in a conference, but a lot of foolish ideas have died there.   *F. Scott Fitzgerald*

Conscience

Conscience is a mother-in-law whose visit never ends.   *H. L. Mencken*

Conscience is a cur that will let you get past it but that you cannot keep from barking.   *Anon.*

Conscience is but a word that cowards use,
Devised at first to keep the strong in awe.   *Shakespeare, 'Richard III'*

Conscience reigns but it does not govern.   *Paul Valéry*

A man's vanity tells him what is honour; a man's conscience what is justice.
                                        Walter Savage Landor

Conscience does make cowards of us all.   *Shakespeare, 'Hamlet'*

Conscience is thoroughly well-bred, and soon leaves off talking to those who do not wish to hear it.   *Samuel Butler*

Conscience is a coward, and those faults it has not strength enough to prevent, it seldom has justice enough to accuse.   *Oliver Goldsmith*

My conscience hath a thousand several tongues,
And every tongue brings in a several tale,
And every tale condemns me for a villain.   *Shakespeare, 'Richard III'*

I feel bad that I don't feel worse.   *Michael Frayn*

Shame arises from the fear of man; conscience from the fear of God.
                                        Samuel Johnson

Consistency

Inconsistency is the only thing in which men are consistent.
                                        Horace Smith

Nothing that is not a real crime makes a man appear so contemptible and little in the eyes of the world as inconsistency.   *Joseph Addison*

Like all weak men he laid an exaggerated stress on not changing one's mind.
                                        W. Somerset Maugham

A foolish consistency is the hobgoblin of little minds, adored by little statesmen and philosophers and divines. With consistency a great soul has simply nothing to do. He may as well concern himself with his shadow on the wall. Speak what you think now in hard words and tomorrow speak what tomorrow thinks in hard words again, though it contradict everything you said today.   *Ralph Waldo Emerson*

Consistency requires you to be as ignorant today as you were a year ago.
                                                                Bernard Berenson

Consistency is the last refuge of the unimaginative.   *Oscar Wilde*

Conservatism is the maintenance of conventions already in force.
                                                               Thorstein Veblen

There are those who would misteach us that to stick in a rut is consistency — and a virtue, and that to climb out of the rut is inconsistency — and a vice.   *Mark Twain*

People who honestly mean to be true, really contradict themselves much more rarely than those who try to be 'consistent.'   *Oliver Wendell Holmes*

The only man who can change his mind is the man who's got one.
                                                          Edward Noyes Westcott

.

Conversation

He was one of those men whose constitutional inability to make small talk forfeits all one's sympathy, and makes one think that social grace is sometimes a moral duty.   *James Morris*

He (Macaulay) has occasional flashes of silence that make his conversation perfectly delightful.   *Sydney Smith*

As I got warmed up, and felt perfectly at home in talk, I heard myself boasting, lying, exaggerating. Oh, not deliberately, far from it. It would be unconvivial and dull to stop and arrest the flow of talk, and speak only after carefully considering whether I was telling the truth.   *Bernard Berenson*

Men always talk about the most important things to perfect strangers.
                                                             G. K. Chesterton

Not a sentence or a word is independent of the circumstances under which it is uttered.   *Alfred North Whitehead*

Communication is and should be hell fire and sparks as well as sweetness and light.   *Aman Vivian Rakoff*

The really important things are said over cocktails and are never done.
Peter F. Drucker

You never say a word of yourself, dear Lady Grey. You have that dreadful sin of anti-egotism.   *Sydney Smith*

He talked with more claret than clarity.   *Susan Ertz*

The real art of conversation is not only to say the right thing in the right place but to leave unsaid the wrong thing at the tempting moment.
Dorothy Nevill

Listen or thy tongue will keep thee deaf.   *American Indian proverb*

People love to talk but hate to listen. Listening is not merely not talking, though even that is beyond most of our powers; it means taking a vigorous, human interest in what is being told us. You can listen like a blank wall or like a splendid auditorium where every sound comes back fuller and richer.
Alice Duer Miller

A man who listens because he has nothing to say can hardly be a source of inspiration. The only listening that counts is that of the talker who alternately absorbs and expresses ideas.   *Agnes Repplier*

When I think over what I have said, I envy dumb people.   *Seneca*

That is the happiest conversation where there is no competition, no vanity, but a calm quiet interchange of sentiments.   *Samuel Johnson*

John Wesley's conversation is good, but he is never at leisure. He is always obliged to go at a certain hour. This is very disagreeable to a man who loves to fold his legs and have his talk out as I do.   *Samuel Johnson*

She had lost the art of conversation, but not, unfortunately, the power of speech.   *George Bernard Shaw*

I often quote myself. It adds spice to my conversation.
George Bernard Shaw

Too much agreement kills a chat.   *Eldridge Cleaver*

You can never hope to become a skilled conversationalist until you learn how to put your foot tactfully through the television set. *M. Dale Baughman*

Some persons talk simply because they think sound is more manageable than silence.   *Margaret Halsey*

While the right to talk may be the beginning of freedom, the necessity of listening is what makes the right important.   *Walter Lippmann*

Listening is a magnetic and strange thing, a creative force. The friends who listen to us are the ones we move toward, and we want to sit in their radius. When we are listened to, it creates us, makes us unfold and expand.
Karl Menninger

A ceremony of self-wastage — good talkers are miserable, they know that they have betrayed themselves, that they have taken material which should have a life of its own, to disperse it in noises upon the air.
Cyril Connolly

Wit is the salt of conversation, not the food.   *William Hazlitt*

Conviction and Belief

It is a perplexing and unpleasant truth that when men already have 'something worth fighting for,' they do not feel like fighting.   *Eric Hoffer*

Martyrdom has always been a proof of the intensity, never of the correctness of a belief.   *Arthur Schnitzler*

Belief is better than anything else, and it is best when rapt — above paying its respects to anybody's doubt whatsoever.   *Robert Frost*

The peak of tolerance is most readily achieved by those who are not burdened with convictions.   *Alexander Chase*

A belief is not merely an idea the mind possesses; it is an idea that possesses the mind.   *Robert Bolton*

Every man who attacks my belief diminishes in some degree my confidence in it, and therefore makes me uneasy, and I am angry with him who makes me uneasy.   *Samuel Johnson*

Penetrating so many secrets, we cease to believe in the unknowable. But there it sits nevertheless, calmly licking its chops.   *H. L. Mencken*

Believe not your own brother — believe, instead, your own blind eye.
                                                                Russian proverb

Whether you are really right or not doesn't matter; it's the belief that counts.
                                                            Robertson Davies

I love an opposition that has convictions.   *Frederick the Great*

You are fully convinced of the purity of your ideals and the high virtue of your goals. But each man has the same conviction, with the exception of a few cynics who are convinced of the high virtue of cynicism.   *Anon.*

Every man is encompassed by a cloud of comforting convictions, which move with him like flies on a summer day.   *Bertrand Russell*

Convictions are the mainsprings of action, the driving powers of life. What a man lives are his convictions.   *Bishop Francis Kelly*

The best lack all conviction, while the worst
Are full of passionate intensity.   *William Butler Yeats*

(Conviction) is possible only in a world more primitive than ours can be perceived to be. A man can achieve a simply gnomic conviction only by ignoring the radical describers of his environment, or by hating them, as convinced men have hated, say, Darwin and Freud, as agents of some devil.
                                                                    John Ciardi

Faith is the substance of things hoped for, the evidence of things not seen.
                                                                    St. Paul

Those who serve a cause are not those who love that cause. They are those who love the life which has to be led in order to serve it — except in the case of the very purest, and they are rare.   *Simone Weil*

The great thing in this world is not so much where we stand, as in what direction we are moving.   *Oliver Wendell Holmes*

Orthodoxy is my doxy — heterodoxy is another man's doxy.
William Warburton

Every dogma has its day.   *Abraham Rotstein*

A man can believe in a considerable deal of rubbish, and yet go about his
daily work in a rational and cheerful manner.   *Norman Douglas*

Every life is a possession of faith, and exercises an inevitable and silent propaganda.   *Henri Frédéric Amiel*

Soon after a hard decision something inevitably occurs to cast doubt. Holding
steady against that doubt usually proves that decision.   *R. I. Fitzhenry*

I may have faults but being wrong ain't one of them.   *Jimmy Hoffa*

Courage and Bravery

Here I stand. I can do no other. God help me. Amen.   *Martin Luther*

Many become brave when brought to bay.   *Norwegian proverb*

O God, give us serenity to accept what cannot be changed; courage to change
what should be changed, and wisdom to distinguish the one from the other.
Reinhold Niebuhr

The first virtue in a soldier is endurance of fatigue; courage is only the second
virtue.   *Napoleon Bonaparte*

Courage is fear holding on a minute longer.   *George S. Patton*

We could be cowards, if we had courage enough.   *Thomas Fuller*

A decline in courage may be the most striking feature which an outside
observer notices in the West in our days. The Western world has lost its civic
courage, both as a whole and separately, in each country, in each government, in each political party, and, of course, in the United Nations. Such
a decline in courage is particularly noticeable among the ruling groups and
the intellectual elite, causing an impression that the loss of courage extends
to the entire society.   *Aleksandr Solzhenitsyn*

Showing up is eighty percent of life. *Woody Allen*

A high station in life is earned by the gallantry with which appalling experiences are survived with grace. *Tennessee Williams*

Courage is doing what you're afraid to do. There can be no courage unless you're scared. *Eddie Rickenbacker*

One man with courage makes a majority. *Andrew Jackson*

If one is forever cautious, can one remain a human being? *Aleksandr Solzhenitsyn*

Never let your head hang down. Never give up and sit down and grieve. Find another way. And don't pray when it rains if you don't pray when the sun shines. *Satchel Paige*

The Ancient Mariner said to Neptune during a great storm, 'O God, you will save me if you wish, but I am going to go on holding my tiller straight.' *Montaigne*

Fight on, my merry men all,
I'm a little wounded, but I am not slain;
I will lay me down for to bleed a while,
Then I'll rise and fight with you again. *John Dryden*

The paradox of courage is that a man must be a little careless of his life even in order to keep it. *G. K. Chesterton*

The last thing a woman will consent to discover in a man whom she loves, or on whom she simply depends, is want of courage. *Joseph Conrad*

Please understand there is no depression in this house and we are not interested in the possibilities of defeat. They do not exist. *Victoria, Queen of England*

To be brave one short instant is no easy matter; it is easier to die for a cause than to live for it. *Comtesse Diane (Marie de Beausacq)*

Have the courage to act instead of react. *Earlene Larson Jenks*

Courage! I have shown it for years; think you I shall lose it at the moment when my sufferings are to end? *Marie Antoinette on the way to the guillotine*

Necessity does the work of courage. *George Eliot*

Now the trumpet summons us again — not as a call to bear arms, though arms we need; not as a call to battle, though embattled we are; but a call to bear the burden of a long twilight struggle, year in and year out, 'rejoicing in hope, patient in tribulation,' a struggle against the common enemies of man: tyranny, poverty, disease and war itself. *John F. Kennedy*

The courage we desire and prize is not the courage to die decently, but to live manfully. *Thomas Carlyle*

Courage is a quality so necessary for maintaining virtue that it is always respected, even when it is associated with vice. *Samuel Johnson*

The courage of life is often a less dramatic spectacle that the courage of a final moment; but it is no less a magnificent mixture of triumph and tragedy. A man does what he must — in spite of personal consequences, in spite of obstacles and dangers and pressures — and that is the basis of all morality. *John F. Kennedy*

He was a bold man that first ate an oyster. *Jonathan Swift*

Unless one says goodbye to what one loves, and unless one travels to completely new territories, one can expect merely a long wearing away of oneself. *Jean Dubuffet*

A decent boldness ever meets with friends. *Homer*

Courage is resistance to fear, mastery of fear, not absence of fear. *Mark Twain*

One doesn't discover new lands without consenting to lose sight of the shore for a very long time. *André Gide*

The fly ought to be used as the symbol of impertinence and audacity; for whilst all other animals shun man more than anything else, and run away even before he comes near them, the fly lights upon his very nose. *Arthur Schopenhauer*

Never undertake anything for which you wouldn't have the courage to ask the blessings of heaven. *G. C. Lichtenberg*

Valour lies just halfway between rashness and cowardice. *Cervantes*

As to moral courage, I have very rarely met with the two o'clock in the morning kind. I mean unprepared courage, that which is necessary on an unexpected occasion, and which, in spite of the most unforeseen events, leaves full freedom of judgement and decision.   *Napoleon Bonaparte*

The guts carry the feet, not the feet the guts.   *Cervantes*

Clothes and courage have much to do with each other.
Sara Jeannette Duncan

A great part of courage is the courage of having done the thing before.
Ralph Waldo Emerson

Courage — fear that has said its prayers.   *Dorothy Bernard*

Courage is rightly esteemed the first of human qualities because it is the quality which guarantees all others.   *Winston Churchill*

Constant exposure to dangers will breed contempt for them.   *Seneca*

(Courage) a perfect sensibility of the measure of danger, and a mental willingness to endure it.   *William T. Sherman*

Not simply one of the virtues but the form of every virtue at the testing point, which means at the point of highest reality.   *C. S. Lewis*

Never look behind you. Something may be gaining on you.
Satchel Paige

At the bottom of a good deal of the bravery that appears in the world there lurks a miserable cowardice. Men will face powder and steel because they cannot face public opinion.   *E. H. Chapin*

Whether it be to failure or success, the first need of being is endurance — to endure with gladness if we can, with fortitude in any event.
Bliss Carman

Creation and Creativity

Human Salvation lies in the hands of the creatively maladjusted.
Martin Luther King, Jr.

In the creative state a man is taken out of himself. He lets down as it were a bucket into his subconscious, and draws up something which is normally beyond his reach. He mixes this thing with his normal experiences and out of the mixture he makes a work of art.   *E. M. Forster*

I do not seek. I find.   *Pablo Picasso*

The creation of a thousand forests is in one acorn.
      Ralph Waldo Emerson

The life of the creative man is led, directed and controlled by boredom. Avoiding boredom is one of our most important purposes.
      Saul Steinberg

An artist is a creature driven by demons. He doesn't know why they choose him and he's usually too busy to wonder why.   *William Faulkner*

No artist is ahead of his time. He is his time. It is just that others are behind the time.   *Martha Graham*

Doodling is the brooding of the hand.   *Saul Steinberg*

I am a choreographer. A choreographer is a poet. I do not create. God creates. I assemble, and I will steal from everywhere to do it.
      George Balanchine

Workaholics are energized rather than enervated by their work — their energy paradoxically expands as it is expended.   *Marilyn Machlowitz*

You lose it if you talk about it.   *Ernest Hemingway*

In creating, the only hard thing's to begin;
A grass-blade's no easier to make than an oak.   *James Russell Lowell*

The End of every maker is himself.   *St. Thomas Aquinas*

Now I really make the little idea from clay, and I hold it in my hand. I can turn it, look at it from underneath, see it from one view, hold it against the sky, imagine it any size I like, and really be in control, almost like God creating something.   *Henry Moore*

I can always be distracted by love, but eventually I get horny for my creativity.
      Gilda Radner

No matter how old you get, if you can keep the desire to be creative, you're keeping the man-child alive.   *John Cassavetes*

What is originality? Undetected plagiarism.   *William R. Inge*

Originality is nothing but judicious imitation.   *Voltaire*

A hunch is creativity trying to tell you something.   *Frank Capra*

Style is a simple way of saying complicated things.   *Jean Cocteau*

What another would have done as well as you, do not do it. What another would have said as well as you, do not say it. What another would have written as well, do not write it. Be faithful to that which exists nowhere but in yourself — and thus make yourself indispensable.   *André Gide*

It seems that the creative faculty and the critical faculty cannot exist together in their highest perfection.   *Thomas Babington Macaulay*

I must create a system or be enslaved by another man's.
I will not reason and compare;
My business is to create.   *William Blake*

Crime and Punishment

The study of crime begins with the knowledge of oneself.   *Henry Miller*

Fear succeeds crime — it is its punishment.   *Voltaire*

The number of malefactors authorizes not the crime.   *Thomas Fuller*

All punishment is mischief. All punishment in itself is evil.
                    Jeremy Bentham

Speaking generally, punishment hardens and numbs, it produces concentration, it sharpens the consciousness of alienation, it strengthens the power of resistance.   *Friedrich Nietzsche*

He only may chastise who loves.   *Rabindranath Tagore*

If England treats her criminals the way she has treated me, she doesn't deserve to have any.   *Oscar Wilde*

It is fairly obvious that those who are in favour of the death penalty have more affinity with assassins than those who are not.
Rémy de Gourmont

Prisons don't rehabilitate, they don't punish, they don't protect, so what the hell do they do?
Jerry Brown

Capital punishment is as fundamentally wrong as a cure for crime as charity is wrong as a cure for poverty.
Henry Ford

The reformative effect of punishment is a belief that dies hard, chiefly, I think, because it is so satisfying to our sadistic impulses.
Bertrand Russell

Much as he is opposed to lawbreaking, he is not bigoted about it.
Damon Runyon

Crime, like virtue, has its degrees.
Racine

Critics and Criticism

Two and two continue to make four, in spite of the whine of the amateur for three, or the cry of the critic for five.
James McNeill Whistler

Tomorrow night I appear for the first time before a Boston audience — 4000 critics.
Mark Twain

He has a right to criticize, who has a heart to help.
Abraham Lincoln

More and more people think of the critic as an indispensable middle man between writer and reader, and would no more read a book alone, if they could help it, than have a baby alone.
Randall Jarrell

It is not expected of critics that they should help us to make sense of our lives; they are bound only to attempt the lesser feat of making sense of the ways we try to make sense of our lives.
Frank Kermode

Analysis kills spontancity. The grain once ground into flour springs and germinates no more.
Henri Frédéric Amiel

His words leap across rivers and mountains, but his thoughts are still only six inches long.
E. B. White

When critics disagree, the artist is in accord with himself.   *Oscar Wilde*

The factor in human life provocative of a noble discontent is the gradual emergence of a sense of criticism, founded upon appreciation of beauty, and of intellectual distinction, and of duty.   *Alfred North Whitehead*

To many people dramatic criticism must seem like an attempt to tattoo soap bubbles.   *John Mason Brown*

Never criticize a man until you've walked a mile in his moccasins.
American Indian proverb

The test of a good critic is whether he knows when and how to believe on insufficient evidence.   *Samuel Butler*

Reprove not a scorner, lest he hate thee; rebuke a wise man and he will love thee.   *Proverbs 9:8*

In judging others, folks will work overtime for no pay.
Charles Edwin Carruthers

A critic is a man who knows the way but can't drive the car.
Kenneth Tynan

If you are willing to take the punishment, you're halfway through the battle. That the issues may be trivial, the battle ugly, is another point.
Lillian Hellman

A critic is a legless man who teaches running.   *Channing Pollock*

Vilify! Vilify! Some of it will always stick.   *Beaumarchais*

Always bring money along with your complaints.   *Plautus*

Nature fits all her children with something to do,
He who would write and can't write, can surely review.
James Russell Lowell

Nature, when she invented, manufactured and patented her authors, contrived to make critics out of the chips that were left.
Oliver Wendell Holmes

To escape criticism — do nothing, say nothing, be nothing.
Elbert Hubbard

Any fool can criticize, and many of them do.   *Archbishop C. Garbett*

Critics are like eunuchs in a harem: they know how it's done, they've seen it done every day, but they're unable to do it themselves.
Brendan Behan

I am sitting in the smallest room in my house. I have your review in front of me. Soon it will be behind me.   *Max Reger*

The good critic is he who narrates the adventures of his soul among master-pieces.   *Anatole France*

Of all the cants which are canted in this canting world, tho' the cant of hypocrites may be the worst, the cant of criticism is the most tormenting.
Laurence Sterne

The critic is the duenna in the passionate affair between playwrights, actors and audiences — a figure dreaded, and occasionally comic, but never welcome, never loved.   *Robertson Davies*

A critic at best is a waiter at the great table of literature.   *Louis Dudek*

Crowds and the Masses

Every crowd has a silver lining.   *P. T. Barnum*

Insanity in individuals is rare — but in groups, parties, nations, and epochs, it is the rule.   *Friedrich Nietzsche*

When a hundred men stand together, each of them loses his mind and gets another one.   *Friedrich Nietzsche*

Wherever there is a crowd there is untruth.   *Søren Kierkegaard*

The time when, most of all, you should withdraw into yourself is when you are forced to be in a crowd.   *Epicurus*

You cannot make a man by standing a sheep on its hind legs. But by standing a flock of sheep in that position you can make a crowd of men.
Max Beerbohm

The average man's opinions are much less foolish than they would be if he thought for himself.   *Bertrand Russell*

Custom, Habit and Tradition

Without the aid of prejudice and custom, I should not be able to find my way across the room.   *William Hazlitt*

Custom, that unwritten law,
By which the people keep even kings in awe.   *Charles Davenport*

Habit is stronger than reason.   *George Santayana*

Laws are never as effective as habits.   *Adlai Stevenson*

Habituation is a falling asleep or fatiguing of the sense of time; which explains why young years pass slowly, while later life flings itself faster and faster upon its course.   *Thomas Mann*

The one thing more difficult than following a regimen is not imposing it on others.   *Marcel Proust*

Charlotte, having seen his body borne before her on a shutter, like a well conducted person, went on cutting bread and butter.
William Makepeace Thackeray

The gnarled fidelity of an old habit.   *Rainer Maria Rilke*

One of the advantages of being disorderly is that one is constantly making exciting discoveries.   *A. A. Milne*

We do not really mean, we do not really mean, that what we are going to say is true.   *Usual beginning, Ashanti folktales*

What thou lovest well remains, the rest is dross.   *Ezra Pound*

The most unendurable thing, to be sure, the really terrible thing, would be a life without habits, a life which continually required improvisation.
Friedrich Nietzsche

Historic continuity with the past is not a duty, it is only a necessity.
Oliver Wendell Holmes, Jr.

Tradition means giving votes to the most obscure of all classes — our ancestors. It is the democracy of the dead. Tradition refuses to submit to the small and arrogant oligarchy of those who merely happen to be walking around.   *G. K. Chesterton*

What an enormous magnifier is tradition! How a thing grows in the human memory and in the human imagination, when love, worship, and all that lies in the human heart, is there to encourage it.   *Thomas Carlyle*

Tradition, thou art for suckling children
Thou are the enlivening milk for babes,
But no meat for men is in thee.   *Stephen Crane*

It seems, in fact, as though the second half of a man's life is made up of nothing but the habits he has accumulated during the first half.
Fyodor Dostoevsky

To renew ties with the past need not always be daydreaming; it may be tapping old sources of strength for new tasks.   *Simeon Strunsky*

I have not been afraid of excess: excess on occasion is exhilarating. It prevents moderation from acquiring the deadening effect of a habit.
W. Somerset Maugham

Habit is the enormous flywheel of society, its most precious conservative agent. There is no more miserable human being than one in whom nothing is habitual but indecision. Full half the time of such a man goes to the deciding, or regretting, of matters which ought to be so ingrained in him as practically not to exist for his consciousness at all.   *William James*

Chaos often breeds life, when order breeds habit.   *Henry Adams*

The main dangers in this life are the people who want to change everything — or nothing.   *Lady Astor*

The chains of habit are too weak to be felt until they are too strong to be broken.   *Samuel Johnson*

When you are accustomed to anything, you are estranged from it.
George Cabot Lodge

Cynicism

Cynicism such as one finds very frequently among the most highly educated young men and women of the West, results from the combination of comfort and powerlessness.   *Bertrand Russell*

A cynic is a man who, when he smells flowers, looks around for a coffin.
H. L. Mencken

Cynicism — the intellectual cripple's substitute for intelligence.
Russell Lynes

Cynicism is that blackguard defect of vision which compels us to see the world as it is, instead of as it should be.
Ambrose Bierce

Cynicism is intellectual dandyism, without the coxcomb's feathers.
George Meredith

There is nothing to which men, while they have food and drink, cannot reconcile themselves.
George Santayana

It's not that the Irish are cynical. It's rather that they have a wonderful lack of respect for everything and everybody.
Brendan Behan

Watch what people are cynical about, and one can often discover what they lack.
Harry Emerson Fosdick

What is a cynic? A man who knows the price of everything and the value of nothing.
Oscar Wilde

A cynic can chill and dishearten with a single word.
Ralph Waldo Emerson

We can destroy ourselves by cynicism and disillusion just as effectively as by bombs.
Kenneth Clark

Cynicism is an unpleasant way of saying the truth.   *Lillian Hellman*

Death and Dying

Do not go gentle into that good night
Old age should burn and rave at close of day;
Rage, rage against the dying of the light.   *Dylan Thomas*

The stroke of death is as a lover's pinch,
Which hurts and is desired.   *Shakespeare, 'Antony and Cleopatra'*

Nothing in his life
Became him like the leaving it.   *Shakespeare, 'Macbeth'*

Things have a terrible permanence when people die.   *Joyce Kilmer*

A solemn funeral is inconceivable to the Chinese mind.   *Lin Yutang*

At its most basic root, the death or disintegration of one's parents is a harsh
reminder of one's own mortality.   *Janet Harris*

I don't want to achieve immortality through my work. I want to achieve immortality through not dying.   *Woody Allen*

Die and endow a cat or a college.   *Alexander Pope*

Mausoleum, n: the final and funniest folly of the rich.   *Ambrose Bierce*

No, 'tis not so deep as a well, nor so wide as a church door; but 'tis enough,
'twill serve: ask for me tomorrow, and you shall find me a grave man. I am
peppered, I warrant, for this world.   *Shakespeare, 'Romeo and Juliet'*

Human life consists in mutual service. No grief, pain, misfortune, or 'broken
heart' is excuse for cutting off one's life while any power of service remains.
But when all usefulness is over, when one is assured of an unavoidable and
imminent death, it is the simplest of human rights to choose a quick and
easy death in place of a slow and horrible one.
          Suicide note, Charlotte Perkins Gilman

Poisons pain you;
Rivers are damp;
Acid stains you;
And drugs cause cramp.
Guns aren't lawful;
Nooses give;
Gas smells awful;
You might as well live.   *Dorothy Parker*

Epitaph, n: an inscription on a tomb showing that virtues acquired by death
have a retroactive effect.   *Ambrose Bierce*

Dying is a wild night and a new road.   *Emily Dickinson*

The reports of my death are greatly exaggerated.   *Mark Twain*

And I looked, and behold, a pale horse: and his name that sat on him was
Death. *Revelation 6:8*

There is no man so blessed that some who stand by his deathbed won't hail
the occasion with delight. *Marcus Aurelius*

There may be little or much beyond the grave,
But the strong are saying nothing until they see. *Robert Frost*

All human things are subject to decay,
And when fate summons, monarchs must obey. *John Dryden*

When Andrew Jackson died someone asked a friend if he thought Old
Hickory would go to heaven. 'He will if he wants to,' was the reply.

On his death bed Disraeli declined a visit from Queen Victoria. 'No, it is
better not,' he said, 'she would only ask me to take a message to Albert.'

I am a broken machine. I am ready to go.
Woodrow Wilson's last words

Let the tent be struck. *Robert E. Lee's last words*

You can lose a man like that by your own death, but not by his.
George Bernard Shaw (of William Morris)

We die only once, and for such a long time! *Molière*

Because I could not stop for Death
He kindly stopped for me —
The carriage held but just ourselves
And Immortality. *Emily Dickinson*

When a man dies, he does not just die of the disease he has: he dies of his
whole life. *Charles Péguy*

The long habit of living indisposeth us for dying. *Thomas Browne*

Most people would die sooner than think; in fact, they do.
Bertrand Russell

One should be ever booted and spurred and ready to depart. *Montaigne*

He who must die must die in the dark, even though he sells candles.
Colombian proverb

A dead man
Who never caused others to die
Seldom rates a statue.   *Anon.*

Nothing you can lose by dying is half so precious as the readiness to die,
which is man's charter of nobility.   *George Santayana*

Man dies when he wants, as he wants, of what he chooses.
                                                      Jean Anouilh

After sixty years the stern sentence of the burial service seems to have a meaning that one did not notice in former years. There begins to be something
personal about it.   *Oliver Wendell Holmes*

Death be not proud, though some have called Thee
Mighty and dreadful, for thou art not so.
                                                      John Donne

Let us eat and drink; for tomorrow we shall die.   *Isaiah 22:13*

Toward the person who has died we adopt a special attitude: something like
admiration for someone who has accomplished a very difficult task.
                                                      Sigmund Freud

You have to learn to do everything, even to die.   *Gertrude Stein*

When a man knows he is to be hanged in a fortnight, it concentrates his mind
wonderfully.   *Samuel Johnson*

I'm not afraid to die. I just don't want to be there when it happens.
                                                      Woody Allen

Oh death, you can wait; keep your distance.   *André Chenier*

Body and mind, like man and wife, do not always agree to die together.
                                                  Charles Caleb Colton

The undiscovered country from whose bourn no traveller returns.
                                                  Shakespeare, 'Hamlet'

A thousand goodbyes come after death — the first six months of bereave-
ment.   *Alan Gregg*

You don't die in the United States, you underachieve.   *Jerzy Kosinski*

Life is a great surprise. I do not see why death should not be an even greater
one. 　　　　　　　　　　　　　　　　　　　　　　*Vladimir Nabokov*

If life must not be taken too seriously — then so neither must death.
　　　　　　　　　　　　　　　　　　　　　　　　　Samuel Butler

Death is terrible to Cicero, desirable to Cato, and indifferent to Socrates.
　　　　　　　　　　　　　　　　　　　　　　　　　　　　Anon.

The crash of the whole solar and stellar systems could only kill you once.
　　　　　　　　　　　　　　　　　　　　　　　　Thomas Carlyle

In nature, there is less death and destruction than death and transmutation.
　　　　　　　　　　　　　　　　　　　　　　　Edwin Way Teale

A man's dying is more the survivors' affair than his own. *Thomas Mann*

I hate funerals, and would not attend my own if it could be avoided, but
it is well for every man to stop once in a while to think of what sort of a
collection of mourners he is training for his final event.
　　　　　　　　　　　　　　　　　　　　　　　Robert T. Morris

If this is dying, I don't think much of it. 　　　　　*Lytton Strachey*

Human life, because it is marked by a beginning and an end, becomes whole,
an entirety in itself that can be subjected to judgement only when it has ended
in death. Death not merely ends life, it also bestows upon it a silent com-
pleteness, snatched from the hazardous flux to which all things human are
subject. 　　　　　　　　　　　　　　　　　　　　　*Hannah Arendt*

Men use one another to assure their personal victory over death.
　　　　　　　　　　　　　　　　　　　　　　　　　Ernest Becker

Any man's death diminishes me, because I am involved in mankind; and
therefore never send to know for whom the bell tolls; it tolls for thee.
　　　　　　　　　　　　　　　　　　　　　　　　　　John Donne

A belief in hell and the knowledge that every ambition is doomed to frustration at the hands of a skeleton have never prevented the majority of human
beings from behaving as though death were no more than an unfounded
rumour, and survival a thing not beyond the bounds of possibility.
　　　　　　　　　　　　　　　　　　　　　　　　　Aldous Huxley

Make sure to send a lazy man for the Angel of Death. 　*Jewish proverb*

It cost me never a stab nor squirm
To tread by chance upon a worm.
'Aha, my little dear' I say,
'Your clan will pay me back one day.'   *Dorothy Parker*

I cannot forgive my friends for dying: I do not find these vanishing acts of
theirs at all amusing.   *Logan Pearsall Smith*

Around, around the sun we go:
The moon goes round the earth.
We do not die of death:
We die of vertigo.   *Archibald MacLeish*

There is no such thing as death,
In nature, nothing dies:
From each sad moment of decay
Some forms of life arise.   *Charles Mackay*

I am going to seek a great Perhaps.   *François Rabelais' dying words.*

Deception

Everything that deceives may be said to enchant.   *Plato*

We are never deceived; we deceive ourselves.   *Goethe*

All charming people have something to conceal, usually their total dependence
on the appreciation of others.   *Cyril Connolly*

You k'n hide de fier, but what you guine do wid de smoke?
          Joel Chandler Harris

Deep versed in books and shallow in himself.   *John Milton*

What we need is a rebirth of satire, of dissent, of irreverence, of an uncompromising insistance that phoniness is phony and platitudes are platitudinous.
          Arthur Schlesinger, Jr.

Half the work that is done in the world is to make things appear what they
are not.   *E. R. Beadle*

If the world will be gulled, let it be gulled.   *Robert Burton*

I give you bitter pills in sugar coating. The pills are harmless: the poison is in the sugar. *Stanislaw Lec*

I have known a vast quantity of nonsense talked about bad men not looking you in the face. Don't trust that conventional idea. Dishonesty will stare honesty out of countenance, any day in the week, if there is anything to be got by it. *Charles Dickens*

One should seek for the salutary in the unpleasant: if it is there, it is after all nectar. One should seek for the deceitful in the pleasant: if it is there it is after all poison. *Panchatantra*

Deceive not thy physician, confessor, nor lawyer. *George Herbert*

Frank and explicit — this is the right line to take when you wish to conceal your own mind and to confuse the mind of others. *Benjamin Disraeli*

Defeat

Do not be afraid of defeat. You are never so near to victory as when defeated in a good cause. *Henry Ward Beecher*

To lose
Is to learn. *Anon.*

We have fought this fight as long, and as well as we know how. We have been defeated. For us, as a Christian people, there is now but one course to pursue. We must accept the situation. *Robert E. Lee*

I let the American people down, and I have to carry that burden for the rest of my life. My political life is over. I will never again have an opportunity to serve in any official position. Maybe I can give a little advice from time to time. *Richard Nixon*

What is defeat? Nothing but education, nothing but the first step toward something better. *Wendell Phillips*

Who, apart
From ourselves, can see any difference between
Our victories and our defeats? *Christopher Fry*

They were never defeated, they were only killed.
(said of the French Foreign Legion)

The mountain remains unmoved at seeming defeat by the mist.

Rabindranath Tagore

Democracy

Democracy is based upon the conviction that there are extraordinary possibilities in ordinary people.   *Harry Emerson Fosdick*

In a democracy, the opposition is not only tolerated as constitutional, but must be maintained because it is indispensable.   *Walter Lippmann*

It has been said that Democracy is the worst form of government except all those other forms that have been tried from time to time.

Winston Churchill

Democracy is based on the conviction that man has the moral and intellectual capacity, as well as the inalienable right, to govern himself with reason and justice.   *Harry S. Truman*

If you want to understand democracy, spend less time in the library with Plato, and more time in the buses with people.   *Simeon Strunsky*

Democracy is a small hard core of common agreement, surrounded by a rich variety of individual differences.   *James Bryant Conant*

People often say that, in a democracy, decisions are made by a majority of the people. Of course, that is not true. Decisions are made by a majority of those who make themselves heard and who vote — a very different thing.

Walter H. Judd

The democracy which embodies and guarantees our freedom is not powerless, passive or blind, nor is it in retreat. It has no intention of giving way to the savage fantasies of its adversaries. It is not prepared to give advance blessing to its own destruction.   *Pierre Elliott Trudeau*

Democracy means government by the uneducated, while aristocracy means government by the badly educated.   *G. K. Chesterton*

My definition of a free society is a society where it is safe to be unpopular.

Adlai Stevenson

It is the greatest good to the greatest number which is the measure of right and wrong. *Jeremy Bentham*

The greatest blessing of our democracy is freedom. But in the last analysis, our only freedom is the freedom to discipline ourselves. *Bernard Baruch*

Democracy is the recurrent suspicion that more than half of the people are right more than half of the time. *E. B. White*

The worst form of inequality is to try to make unequal things equal. *Aristotle*

What men value in the world is not rights, but privileges. *H. L. Mencken*

As I would not be a slave, so I would not be a master. This expresses my idea of democracy. *Abraham Lincoln*

Democracy is a festival of mediocrity. *E.M. Cioran*

Drink, Drinking and Drinkers

I like liquor — its taste and its effects — and that is just the reason why I never drink it. *Thomas (Stonewall) Jackson*

The Persians are very fond of wine . . . It is also their general practice to deliberate upon affairs of weight when they are drunk; and then in the morning, when they are sober, the decision to which they came the night before is put before them by the master of the house in which it was made; and if it is then approved they act on it; if not, they set it aside. Sometimes, however, they are sober at their first deliberations, but in this case they always reconsider the matter under the influence of wine. *Herodotus*

Drunkenness is temporary suicide: the happiness that it brings is merely negative, a momentary cessation of unhappiness. *Bertrand Russell*

Bacchus has drowned more men than Nepture. *Guiseppe Garibaldi*

Temperance is the control of all the functions of our bodies. The man who refuses liquor, goes in for apple pie and develops a paunch, is no ethical leader for me. *John Erskine*

Nothing ever tasted any better than a cold beer on a beautiful afternoon with nothing to look forward to but more of the same.   *Hugh Hood*

Moderation is commonly firm, and firmness is commonly successful.
Samuel Johnson

Abstinence is as easy for me as temperance would be difficult.
Samuel Johnson

I drink to make other people interesting.   *George Jean Nathan*

One of the disadvantages of wine is that is makes a man mistake words for thoughts.   *Samuel Johnson*

The innkeeper loves the drunkard, but not for a son-in-law.
Jewish proverb

Whisky drowns some troubles and floats a lot more. *Robert C. Edwards*

Malt does more than Milton can
To justify God's ways to man.   *A. E. Housman*

A man hath no better thing under the sun, than to eat, and to drink, and to be merry.   *Ecclesiastes 8:15*

Drink not the third glass — which thou can'st not tame when once it is within thee.   *George Herbert*

An Irish queer: a fellow who prefers women to drink.   *Sean O'Faolain*

Jellinek's disease (alcoholism) is responsible for:
    50 percent of all auto fatalities
    80 percent of all home violence
    30 percent of all suicides
    60 percent of all child abuse
    65 percent of all drownings
It is estimated that when a woman contracts the disease, her husband leaves her in nine out of ten cases; when a man contracts it, his wife leaves in one out of ten cases.   *Kathleen Whalen Fitzgerald*

Eat bread at pleasure, drink wine by measure.   *Randle Cotgrave*

It's a naive domestic burgundy without any breeding, but I think you'll be amused by its presumption.   *James Thurber*

Drunkenness is nothing but voluntary madness.   *Seneca*

We frequently hear of people dying from too much drinking. That this happens is a matter of record. But the blame almost always is placed on whisky. Why this should be I never could understand. You can die from drinking too much of anything — coffee, water, milk, soft drinks and all such stuff as that. And so long as the presence of death lurks with anyone who goes through the simple act of swallowing, I will make mine whisky.

W. C. Fields

There are more old drunkards than old physicians.   *Rabelais*

He is . . . like many other geniuses, a greater friend to the bottle, than the bottle is to him.   *William Lyon Mackenzie*

Boys should abstain from all use of wine until their eighteenth year, for it is wrong to add fire to fire.   *Plato*

Woe unto them that rise up early in the morning, that they may follow strong drink; that continue until night, till wine inflame them.   *Isaiah 5:11*

I always keep a supply of stimulant handy in case I see a snake — which I also keep handy.   *W. C. Fields*

We had gone out there to pass the beautiful day of high summer like true Irishmen — locked in the dark Snug of a public house.   *Brendan Behan*

The whole world is about three drinks behind.   *Humphrey Bogart*

Education

Education should be gentle and stern, not cold and lax.   *Joseph Joubert*

The schools ain't what they used to be and never was.   *Will Rogers*

Educate a man and you educate an individual — educate a woman and you educate a family.   *Agnes Cripps*

The things taught in schools are not an education but the means of an education.   *Ralph Waldo Emerson*

The university is the last remaining platform for national dissent.

Leon Eisenberg

The freshmen bring a little knowledge in and the seniors take none out, so it accumulates through the years.   *A.L. Lowell, President of Harvard*

Surely the shortest commencement address in history — and for me one of the most memorable — was that of Dr. Harold E. Hyde, President of New Hampshire's Plymouth State College. He reduced his message to the graduating class to these three ideals: 'Know yourself — Socrates. Control yourself — Cicero; Give yourself — Christ.'   *Walter T. Tatara*

There is that indescribable freshness and unconsciousness about an illiterate person that humbles and mocks the power of the noblest expressive genius.
Walt Whitman

Intelligence appears to be the thing that enables a man to get along without education. Education appears to be the thing that enables a man to get along without the use of his intelligence.   *A.E. Wiggan*

Most men of education are more superstitious than they admit — nay, than they think.   *G.C. Lichtenberg*

A university is what a college becomes when the faculty loses interest in students.   *John Ciardi*

Education is indoctrination, if you're white — subjugation if you're black.
James Baldwin

The investigation of the meaning of words is the beginning of education.
Antisthenes

Learning to learn is to know how to navigate in a forest of facts, ideas and theories, a proliferation of constantly changing items of knowledge. Learning to learn is to know what to ignore but at the same time not rejecting innovation and research.   *Raymond Queneau*

By learning you will teach; by teaching you will learn.   *Latin proverb*

A good education should leave much to be desired.   *Alan Gregg*

'Whom are you?' he asked, for he had been to night school.
George Ade

Education with inert ideas is not only useless; it is above all things harmful.
Alfred North Whitehead

Schoolmasters and parents exist to be grown out of.   *John Wolfenden*

A child educated only at school is an uneducated child.

George Santayana

No one can become really educated without having pursued some study in which he took no interest. For it is part of education to interest ourselves in subjects for which we have no aptitude. *T.S. Eliot*

It is in fact a part of the function of education to help us to escape, not from our own time — for we are bound by that — but from the intellectual and emotional limitations of our time. *T.S. Eliot*

Nothing in education is so astonishing as the amount of ignorance it accumulates in the form of inert facts. *Henry Adams*

You can lead a man up to the university, but you can't make him think.

Finley Peter Dunne

It is a greater work to educate a child, in the true and larger sense of the word, than to rule a state. *William Ellery Channing*

There is less flogging in our great schools than formerly, but then less is learned there; so that what the boys get at one end they lose at the other.

Samuel Johnson

Education is not the filling of a pail, but the lighting of a fire.

William Butler Yeats

If you think education is expensive — try ignorance. *Derek Bok*

Perhaps the most valuable result of all education is the ability to make yourself do the thing you have to do, when it ought to be done, whether you like it or not; it is the first lesson that ought to be learned, and however early a man's training begins, it is probably the last lesson that he learns thoroughly.

Thomas Huxley

Some men are graduated from college cum laude, some are graduated summa cum laude, and some are graduated mirabile dictu.

William Howard Taft

Education is the ability to listen to almost anything without losing your temper or your self-confidence. *Robert Frost*

We must reject that most dismal and fatuous notion that education is a preparation for life. *Northrop Frye*

It is of interest to note that while some dolphins are reported to have learned English — up to fifty words used in correct context — no human being has been reported to have learned dolphinese.   *Carl Sagan*

And if the student finds that this is not to his taste, well, that is regrettable. Most regrettable. His taste should not be consulted; it is being formed.
                                                        Flannery O'Connor

Education, n: that which discloses to the wise and disguises from the foolish their lack of understanding.   *Ambrose Bierce*

The Romans would never have had time to conquer the world if they had been obliged to learn Latin first of all.   *Heinrich Heine*

John Milton called his school, Christ College, 'a stony-hearted step-mother.'

The ultimate goal of the educational system is to shift to the individual the burden of pursuing his education.   *John W. Gardner*

To make your children capable of honesty is the beginning of education.
                                                        John Ruskin

The antithesis between a technical and a liberal education is fallacious. There can be no adequate technical education which is not liberal, and no liberal education which is not technical.   *Alfred North Whitehead*

Creative minds have always been known to survive any kind of bad training.   *Anna Freud*

Fathers send their sons to college either because they went to college, or because they didn't.   *L.L. Hendren*

Education today, more than ever before, must see clearly the dual objectives: education for living and educating for making a living.
                                                        James Mason Wood

The test and the use of man's education is that he finds pleasure in the exercise of his mind.   *Jacques Barzun*

The Jews have always been students, and their greatest study is themselves.
                                                        Albert Goldman

The most effective kind of education is that a child should play amongst lovely things.   *Plato*

Whenever I'm asked what college I attended, I'm tempted to reply, 'Thornton Wilder.'   *Garson Kanin*

Let the schools teach the nobility of labour and the beauty of human service: but the superstitions of ages past? Never!   *Peter Cooper*

Education is what survives when what has been learnt has been forgotten.
B.F. Skinner

If a man empties his purse into his head, no one can take it from him.
Benjamin Franklin

I find the three major administrative problems on a campus are sex for the students, athletics for the alumni and parking for the faculty.
Clark Kerr, President, University of California

Thus education forms the common mind;
Just as the twig is bent, the tree's inclined.   *Alexander Pope*

All learning has an emotional base.   *Plato*

Whatever is good to know is difficult to learn.   *Greek proverb*

Enemies

A wise man gets more use from his enemies than a fool from his friends.
Baltasar Gracián

He hasn't an enemy in the world, and none of his friends like him.
Oscar Wilde, of Bernard Shaw

Don't think there are no crocodiles because the water is calm.
Malayan proverb

The enemies of the future are always the very nicest people.
Christopher Morley

A man cannot be too careful in the choice of his enemies.   *Oscar Wilde*

You can discover what your enemy fears most by observing the means he uses to frighten you.   *Eric Hoffer*

There is no man so friendless but what he can find a friend sincere enough
to tell him disagreeable truths.   *Edward Bulwer-Lytton*

Enemies could become the best companions. Companionship is based on a
common interest, and the greater the interest the closer the companionship.
What makes enemies of people, if not the eagerness, the passion for the same
thing?   *Bernard Berenson*

Whoever has his foe at his mercy, and does not kill him, is his own enemy.
                                                    Sa'di

The little foxes that spoil the vines.   *Song of Solomon 2:15*

We have met the enemy, and he is us.   *Walt Kelly*

The Lacedemonians do not inquire how many the enemy are, but where they
are.   *Agis*

The space in a needle's eye is sufficient for two friends, but the whole world
is scarcely big enough to hold two enemies.   *Solomon ibn Gabirol*

Whoso sheddeth man's blood, by man shall his blood be shed.
                                                    Genesis 9:6

If we could read the secret history of our enemies, we should find in each
man's life, sorrow and suffering enough to disarm all hostility.
                                   Henry Wadsworth Longfellow

Those who hate you don't win unless you hate them — and then you destroy
yourself.   *Richard Nixon*

There's nothing like the sight of an old enemy down on his luck.
                                                    Euripides

The enemy of my enemy is my friend.   *Arabic proverb*

England and the English

Though I love my country, I do not love my countrymen.   *Lord Byron*

England has forty-two religions and only two sauces.   *Voltaire*

Whatever the rest of the world thinks of the English gentleman, the English lady regards him apprehensively as something between God and a goat and equally formidable on both scores.   *Margaret Halsey*

Deploring change is the unchangeable habit of all Englishmen. If you find any important figures who really like change, such as Bernard Shaw, Keir Hardie, Lloyd George, Selfridge or Disraeli, you will find that they are not really English at all, but Irish, Scotch, Welsh, American or Jewish. Englishmen make changes, sometimes great changes. But, secretly or openly, they always deplore them.   *Raymond Postgate*

Where there is one Englishman there is a garden. Where there are two Englishmen there will be a club. But this does not mean any falling off in the number of gardens. There will be three. The club will have one too.
                    A.W. Smith

The Lord Chief Justice of England recently said that the greater part of his judicial time was spent investigating collisions between propelled vehicles, each on its own side of the road, each sounding its horn and each stationary.
                    Philip Guedalla

No one can be as calculatedly rude as the British, which amazes Americans, who do not understand studied insult and can only offer abuse as a substitute.
                    Paul Gallico

What should they know of England, who only England know?
                    Rudyard Kipling

The English have an extraordinary ability for flying into a great calm.
                    Alexander Woollcott

We are articulate, but we are not particularly conversational. An Englishman won't talk for the sake of talking. He doesn't mind silence. But after the silence, he sometimes says something.   *Robert Morley*

The nice sense of measure is certainly not one of Nature's gifts to her English children . . . we have all of us yielded to infatuation at some moment of our lives.   *Matthew Arnold*

I find the Englishman to be him of all men who stands firmest in his shoes.
                    Ralph Waldo Emerson

It seems to me that you can go sauntering along for a certain period, telling the English some interesting things about themselves, and then all at once it feels as if you had stepped on the prongs of a rake. *Patrick Campbell*

One matter Englishmen don't think in the least funny is their happy consciousness of possessing a deep sense of humour.   *Marshall McLuhan*

The English may not like music, but they absolutely love the noise it makes.
Thomas Beecham

That typically English characteristic for which there is no English name —
esprit de corps.   *Frank Adcock*

The British are just as keen to make money as the Americans, but they prefer hypocrisy to a blatantly commercial attitude.   *Wendy Michener*

Nothing unites the English like war. Nothing divides them like Picasso.
Hugh Mills

The British love permanence more than they love beauty.   *Hugh Casson*

An Englishman thinks he is moral when he is only uncomfortable.
George Bernard Shaw

The British are terribly lazy about fighting. They like to get it over and done with and then set up a game of cricket.   *Stephen Leacock*

A Scotch mist may wet an Englishman to the skin.   *English proverb*

Enjoyment and Pleasure

To be able to use leisure intelligently will be the last product of an intelligent civilization.   *Bertrand Russell*

Speed provides the one genuinely modern pleasure.   *Aldous Huxley*

There are two things to aim at in life: first, to get what you want, and after that to enjoy it.   *Logan Pearsall Smith*

That man is richest whose pleasures are the cheapest.
Henry David Thoreau

All the great pleasures in life are silent.   *Georges Clemenceau*

The only way to entertain some folks is to listen to them.   *Kin Hubbard*

Enthusiasm is the greatest asset in the world. It beats money and power and influence.   *Henry Chester*

Danger and delight grow on one stalk.   *English proverb*

Every luxury must be paid for, and everything is a luxury, starting with being in the world.   *Cesare Pavese*

Enjoyment is not a goal, it is a feeling that accompanies important ongoing activity.   *Paul Goodman*

Most of the luxuries, and many of the so-called comforts, of life are not only not indispensable, but positive hindrances to the elevation of mankind.
Henry David Thoreau

To really enjoy the better things in life, one must first have experienced the things they are better than.   *Oscar Homolka*

If you resolve to give up smoking, drinking and loving, you don't actually live longer; it just seems longer.   *Clement Freud*

We act as though comfort and luxury were the chief requirements of life, when all that we need to make us really happy is something to be enthusiastic about.   *Charles Kingsley*

No one in this world needs a mink coat but a mink.   *Anon.*

One's first book, kiss, home run is always the best.   *Clifton Fadiman*

Let us have Wine and Women, Mirth and Laughter
Sermons and soda-water the day after.   *Lord Byron*

1. If your stomach disputes you, lie down and pacify it with cool thoughts. 2. Keep the juices flowing by jangling around gently as you move. 3. Go very lightly on the vices such as carrying on in society. The social ramble ain't restful.   *Satchel Paige*

Love, and do what you like.   *St. Augustine*

Every good thing that comes is accompanied by trouble.
Maxwell Perkins

All the things I really like to do are either immoral, illegal or fattening.
Alexander Woollcott

The physically fit can enjoy their vices.   *Lloyd Percival*

The superfluous is very necessary.   *Voltaire*

There are three ingredients in the good life; learning, earning and yearning.
Christopher Morley

A sense of wrongdoing is an enhancement of pleasure.
Oliver Wendell Holmes, Jr.

From desire I plunge to its fulfilment, where I long once more for desire.
Goethe

Unsatisfied desire is in itself more desirable than any other satisfaction.
C.S. Lewis

Luxury is more deadly than any foe.   *Juvenal*

Environment

The environment is everything that isn't me.   *Albert Einstein*

The most important thing about Spaceship Earth — an instruction book
didn't come with it.   *Buckminster Fuller*

For the first time in the history of the world, every human being is now subjected to contact with dangerous chemicals, from the moment of conception
until death.   *Rachel Carson*

Air pollution is turning Mother Nature prematurely gray.   *Irv Kupcinet*

The first law of ecology is that everything is related to everything else.
Barry Commoner

The sun, moon and stars would have disappeared long ago had they been
within the reach of predatory human hands.   *Havelock Ellis*

Hurt not the earth, neither the sea, nor the trees.   *Revelation 7:3*

Pity the meek for they shall inherit the earth.   *Don Marquis*

We have forgotten how to be good guests, how to walk lightly on the earth as other creatures do.   *1972 Only One Earth Conference*

Experience

Deep experience is never peaceful.   *Henry James*

Experience is the name so many people give to their mistakes.
          Oscar Wilde

Experience, which destroys innocence, also leads one back to it.
          James Baldwin

You must not think, sir, to catch old birds with chaff.   *Cervantes*

To most men, experience is like the stern lights of a ship, which illumine only the track it has passed.   *Samuel Taylor Coleridge*

The life of the law has not been logic, it has been experience.
          Oliver Wendell Holmes, Jr.

A proverb is no proverb to you till life has illustrated it.   *John Keats*

Today is yesterday's pupil.   *Thomas Fuller*

All that I know I learned after I was thirty.   *Georges Clemenceau*

Life is like playing a violin solo in public, and learning the instrument as one goes on.   *Samuel Butler*

What you really value is what you miss, not what you have.
          Jorge Luis Borges

Everything happens to everybody sooner or later if there is time enough.
          George Bernard Shaw

Experience is a good teacher, but she sends in terrific bills.
          Minna Antrim

Men are wise in proportion, not to their experience, but to their capacity for experience.
George Bernard Shaw

Experience is not what happens to a man. It is what a man does with what happens to him.
Aldous Huxley

To a great experience one thing is essential — an experiencing nature.
Walter Bagehot

Good judgement comes from experience, and experience — well, that comes from poor judgement.
Anon.

When choosing between two evils, I always like to take the one I've never tried before.
Mae West

Age is only a number, a cipher for the records. A man can't retire his experience. He must use it. Experience achieves more with less energy and time.
Bernard Baruch

Experience is the comb that Nature gives us when we are bald.
Belgian proverb

Experience enables you to recognize a mistake when you make it again.
Franklin P. Jones

Experience is the worst teacher; it gives the test before presenting the lesson.
Vernon Law

From error to error one discovers the entire truth.   *Sigmund Freud*

Strange how few
After all's said and done, the things that are
Of moment.
Edna St. Vincent Millay

Any man worth his salt has by the time he is forty-five accumulated a crown of thorns, and the problem is to learn to wear it over one ear.
Christopher Morley

Experience teaches only the teachable.   *Aldous Huxley*

Not to transmit an experience is to betray it.   *Elie Wiesel*

Motives and purposes are in the brain and heart of man. Consequences are in the world of fact.
Henry Geaye

Fame and Celebrities

Fame is the sum of the misunderstanding that gathers about a new name.
Rainer Maria Rilke

What a heavy burden is a name that has become too famous.   *Voltaire*

Now when I bore people at a party, they think it's their fault.
Henry Kissinger

One must choose between Obscurity with Efficiency, and Fame with its inevitable collateral of Bluff.   *William McFee*

One lives in the hope of becoming a memory.   *Antonio Porchia*

After I am dead, I would rather have men ask why Cato has no monument than why he had one.   *Cato the Elder*

Fame usually comes to those who are thinking about something else.
Oliver Wendell Holmes, Jr.

The final test of fame is to have a crazy person imagine he is you.
Anon.

The greatest monarch on the proudest throne is obliged to sit upon his own arse.   *Benjamin Franklin*

All celebrated people lose dignity on a close view.   *Napoleon Bonaparte*

Being well known for their well-knowness, celebrities intensify their celebrity images simply by being well known for relations among themselves. By a kind of symbiosis, celebrities live off each other.
A celebrity is a person known for his well-knowness.
Daniel J. Boorstin

Before such a prodigious career, judgement is torn between blame and admiration.   *Charles de Gaulle on Napoleon*

Famous remarks are very seldom quoted correctly.   *Simeon Strunsky*

It is strange how the memory of a man may float to posterity on what he would have himself regarded as the most trifling of his works.
William Osler

To be somebody you must last. *Ruth Gordon*

The world, like an accomplished hostess, pays most attention to those whom it will soonest forget. *John Churton Collins*

Public opinion: a vulgar, impertinent, anonymous tyrant who deliberately makes life unpleasant for any one of us who is not content to be the average man. *William R. Inge*

Man's attitude toward great qualities in others is often the same as toward high mountains — he admires them but he prefers to walk around them. *Morty Saphir*

All the fame I look for in life is to have lived it quietly. *Montaigne*

A celebrity is one who is known to many persons he is glad he doesn't know. *H.L. Mencken*

Fame is a bee
It has a song —
It has a sting —
Ah, too, it has a wing. *Emily Dickinson*

A sign of a celebrity is often that his name is worth more than his services. *Daniel J. Boorstin*

Martyrdom is the only way a man can become famous without ability. *George Bernard Shaw*

Avoid popularity; it has many snares, and no real benefit. *William Penn*

He that hath the name to be an early riser may sleep till noon. *James Howell*

Some day each of us will be famous for fifteen minutes. *Andy Warhol*

Family and Ancestry

All happy families resemble one another; every unhappy family is unhappy in its own way. *Leo Tolstoy*

The dark, uneasy world of family life — where the greatest can fail and the humblest succeed.   *Randall Jarrell*

Where does the family start? It starts with a young man falling in love with a girl — no superior alternative has yet been found.   *Winston Churchill*

As a general thing, when a woman wears the pants in a family, she has a good right to them.   *Josh Billings*

I am he
As you are me
And we are all together.   *John Lennon and Paul McCartney*

Of all my wife's relations I like myself the best.   *Joe Cook*

There is nothing like staying at home for real comfort.   *Jane Austen*

When family relations are no longer harmonious, we have filial children and devoted parents.   *R.D. Laing*

The family is the American fascism.   *Paul Goodman*

The thing that impresses me most about North America is the way parents obey their children.   *Edward, Duke of Windsor*

Who of us is mature enough for offspring before the offspring themselves arrive? The value of marriage is not that adults produce children but that children produce adults.   *Peter de Vries*

Absence is one of the most useful ingredients of family life, and to do it rightly is an art like any other.   *Freya Stark*

No matter how many communes anybody invents, the family always creeps back.   *Margaret Mead*

There are fathers who do not love their children; there is no grandfather who does not adore his grandson.   *Victor Hugo*

The most important thing a father can do for his children is to love their mother.   *Theodore Hesburgh*

None but a mule deserves his family.   *Moroccan proverb*

Today, while the titular head of the family may still be the father, everyone knows that he is little more than chairman, at most, of the entertainment committee.   *Ashley Montagu*

Fashion

Fashion is that by which the fantastic becomes for a moment universal.
                                                        Oscar Wilde

Art produces ugly things which frequently become beautiful with time. Fashion, on the other hand, produces beautiful things which always become ugly with time.   *Jean Cocteau*

Be not the first by whom the new are tried,
Nor yet the last to lay the old aside.   *Alexander Pope*

Fashion can be bought. Style one must possess.
                                                Edna Woolman Chase

Fashion, which elevates the bad to the level of the good, subsequently turns its back on bad and good alike.   *Eric Bentley*

Even knowledge has to be in fashion and where it is not it is wise to affect ignorance.   *Baltasar Gracián*

The fashion wears out more apparel than the man.
                            Shakespeare, 'Much Ado About Nothing'

Fashions, after all, are only induced epidemics.   *George Bernard Shaw*

When a man is once in fashion, all he does is right.   *Lord Chesterfield*

Fashion condemns us to many follies; the greatest is to make oneself its slave.
                                                Napoleon Bonaparte

I have heard with admiring submission the experience of the lady who declared that the sense of being well-dressed gives a feeling of inward tranquility, which religion is powerless to bestow.   *Ralph Waldo Emerson*

Conformism is so hot on the heels of the mass-produced avant garde that the 'ins' and the 'outs' change places with the speed of mach 3.
                                                    Igor Stravinsky

There goes a man made by the Lord Almighty and not by his tailor.

Andrew Jackson

Fashions fade — style is eternal.   *Yves Saint Laurent*

And by my grave you'd pray to have me back
So I could see how well you look in black.   *Marco Carson*

A man of eighty has outlived probably three new schools of painting, two
of architecture and poetry, and a hundred in dress.   *Joyce Carey*

Fate and Destiny

Heaven is the place where the donkey finally catches up with his carrot: hell
is the eternity while he waits for it.   *Russell Green*

Continuous effort — not strength or intelligence — is the key to unlocking
our potential.   *Liane Cardes*

Faith is the substance of things hoped for, the evidence of things not seen.

St. Paul

Everything passes; everything wears out; everything breaks.(Tout passe, tout
lasse, tout casse.)   *French proverb*

Whatso'er we perpetrate
We do but row, we are steered by fate.   *Samuel Butler*

Whatever limits us we call Fate.   *Ralph Waldo Emerson*

Our destiny rules over us, even when we are not yet aware of it; it is the
future that makes laws for our today.   *Friedrich Nietzsche*

Whatever the universal nature assigns to any man at any time is for the good
of that man at that time.   *Marcus Aurelius*

Certain signs precede certain events.   *Cicero*

See how the Fates their gifts allot.
For A is happy — B is not.
Yet B is worthy, I dare say,
Of more prosperity than A.   *W.S. Gilbert*

Destiny, n: a tyrant's authority for crime and a fool's excuse for failure.
Ambrose Bierce

Fate rules the affairs of mankind with no recognizable order.   *Seneca*

He who does not desire or fear the uncertain day or capricious fate, is equal to the gods above and loftier than mortals.   *Justus Lipsius*

The worst is not always certain but it's very likely.   *French proverb*

It is a long road from conception to completion.   *Molière*

God keeps the wicked to give them time to repent.
Sophie Rostopchine Ségur

Fortune is fickle and soon asks back what he has given.   *Latin proverb*

Destiny is what you are supposed to do in life. Fate is what kicks you in the ass to make you do it.   *Henry Miller*

That which God writes on thy forehead, thou wilt come to it.
The Koran

When its time has come, the prey goes to the hunter.   *Persian proverb*

Fear

Fear is not an unknown emotion to us.   *Neil Armstrong*

So let me assert my firm belief that the only thing we have to fear is fear itself — nameless, unreasoning, unjustified terror which paralyzes needed efforts to convert retreat into advance.   *Franklin D. Roosevelt*

I will show you fear in a handful of dust.   *T.S. Eliot*

Fear of losing is what makes competitors so great. Show me a gracious loser and I'll show you a perennial loser.   *O.J. Simpson*

Nothing in life is to be feared. It is only to be understood.   *Marie Curie*

There's nothing I'm afraid of like scared people.   *Robert Frost*

Nothing is more despicable than respect based on fear. *Albert Camus*

Just as courage imperils life, fear protects it. *Leonardo da Vinci*

The scalded cat fears even cold water. *Thomas Fuller*

Fear comes from uncertainty. When we are absolutely certain, whether of our worth or worthlessness, we are almost impervious to fear. Thus a feeling of utter unworthiness can be a source of courage. *Eric Hoffer*

Where no hope is left, is left no fear. *John Milton*

The human race is a race of cowards; and I am not only marching in that procession but carrying a banner. *Mark Twain*

Men hesitate less to injure a man who makes himself loved than to injure one who makes himself feared, for their love is held by a chain of obligation which, because of men's wickedness, is broken on every occasion for the sake of selfish profit; but their fear is secured by a dread of punishment.
Niccolo Machiavelli

I, a stranger and afraid
In a world I never made. *A.E. Housman*

Fear can be headier than whisky, once man has acquired a taste for it.
Donald Downes

Fear has a smell, as
Love does. *Margaret Atwood*

The suspense is terrible. I hope it will last. *Oscar Wilde*

A good scare is worth more to a man than good advice.
Edgar Watson Howe

How does one kill fear, I wonder? How do you shoot a spectre through the heart, slash off its spectral head, take it by the spectral throat?
Joseph Conrad

In grief we know the worst of what we feel,
But who can tell the end of what we fear? *Hannah More*

The only way to get rid of my fears is to make films about them.
Alfred Hitchcock

To live with fear and not be afraid is the final test of maturity.

Edward Weeks

I would often be a coward, but for the shame of it.   *Ralph Connor*

Horror is a feeling that cannot last long; human nature is incapable of supporting it.   *James de Mille*

Food

Dinner, a time when . . . one should eat wisely but not too well, and talk well but not too wisely.   *W. Somerset Maugham*

There is no such thing as a little garlic.   *Anon.*

Even were a cook to cook a fly, he would keep the breast for himself.

Polish proverb

No man is lonely while eating spaghetti — it requires so much attention.

Christopher Morley

Kissing don't last: cookery do.   *George Meredith*

Hunger is not debatable.   *Harry Hopkins*

A hungry man is not a free man.   *Adlai Stevenson*

A great step toward independence is a good-humoured stomach.   *Seneca*

I feel a recipe is only a theme, which an intelligent cook can play each time with a variation.   *Madame Benoit*

All happiness depends on a leisurely breakfast.   *John Gunther*

Cheese — milk's leap toward immortality.   *Clifton Fadiman*

A gourmet is just a glutton with brains.   *Philip W. Haberman, Jr.*

Vegetarianism is harmless enough, though it is apt to fill a man with wind and self-righteousness.   *Sir Robert Hutchinson*

If you wish to grow thinner, diminish your dinner.   *H.S. Leigh*

To a man with an empty stomach food is god.   *Gandhi*

Hunger is the best sauce.   *Proverb*

A man is in general better pleased when he has a good dinner upon his table,
than when his wife talks Greek.   *Samuel Johnson*

If you ask the hungry man how much is two and two, he replies four loaves.
                                                           Hindu proverb

A good meal makes a man feel more charitable toward the whole world than
any sermon.   *Arthur Pendenys*

More die in the United States of too much food than of too little.
                                                           J.K. Galbraith

A good meal ought to begin with hunger.   *French proverb*

It is a hard matter, my fellow citizens, to argue with the belly, since it has
no ears.   *Plutarch*

The one way to get thin is to re-establish a purpose in life.
                                                          Cyril Connolly

To eat is human, to digest, divine.   *Anon.*

A smiling face is half the meal.   *Latvian proverb*

There is no such thing as a pretty good omelette.   *French proverb*

Fish, to taste right, must swim three times — in water, in butter and in wine.
                                                           Polish proverb

Fools and Foolishness

Every man is a damn fool for at least five minutes every day; wisdom consists in not exceeding the limit.   *Elbert Hubbard*

Nothing is more like a wise man than a fool who holds his tongue.
                                                     St. Francis de Sales

England and America are two countries separated by the same language.
George Bernard Shaw

In England I would rather be a man, a horse, a dog or a woman, in that order. In America I think the order would be reversed.   *Bruce Gould*

England is the paradise of individuality, eccentricity, heresy, anomalies, hobbies and humours.   *George Santayana*

Not only England, but every Englishman is an island.   *Novalis*

The English instinctively admire any man who has no talent and is modest about it.   *James Agate*

In the end it may well be that Britain will be more honoured by the historians for the way she disposed of an empire than for the way in which she acquired it.   *David Ormsby Gore*

Oh, it's a snug little island!
A right little, tight little island!   *Thomas Dibdin*

I regard England as my wife and America as my mistress.
Cedric Hardwicke

The Englishman respects your opinions, but he never thinks of your feelings.   *Wilfrid Laurier*

The Englishman has all the qualities of a poker except its occasional warmth.
Daniel O'Connell

The English never draw a line without blurring it.   *Winston Churchill*

I'm an extinct volcano.   *Lady Astor*

Socialism has been preached for so long the British people no longer have any sense of personal responsibility.   *Lord Thomson of Fleet*

Britain's best bulwarks are her wooden walls.   *T. Augustine Arne*

Queen Victoria — a mixture of national landlady and actress.
V.S. Pritchett

I think the British have the distinction above all other nations of being able to put new wine into old bottles without bursting them.   *Clement Atlee*

If fifty million people say a foolish thing, it is still a foolish thing.
Anatole France

There are two kinds of fools: one says, 'This is old, therefore it is good';
the other says, 'This is new, therefore it is better.'   *William R. Inge*

A fool must now and then be right by chance.   *William Cowper*

Let us be thankful for the fools. But for them the rest of us could not succeed.
Mark Twain

Here cometh April again, and as far as I can see the world hath more fools
in it than ever.   *Charles Lamb*

A busy fool is fitter to be shut up than a downright madman.
George, Lord Halifax

With stupidity the gods themselves struggle in vain.
Friedrich von Schiller

There are some people that if they don't know, you can't tell 'em.
Louis Armstrong

A fellow who is always declaring he's no fool usually has his suspicions.
Wilson Mizner

Stupidity is an elemental force for which no earthquake is a match.
Karl Kraus

Every inch that is not fool is rogue.   *John Dryden*

A little nonsense now and then is relished by the wisest men.   *Anon.*

He who lives without folly is not as wise as he thinks.
La Rochefoucauld

The poor schlemiel is a man who falls on his back and breaks his nose.
Jewish proverb

None but a fool worries about things he cannot influence.
Samuel Johnson

Nature never makes any blunders; when she makes a fool she means it.
Josh Billings

Set a beggar on horseback, and he will ride a gallop.   *Robert Burton*

It is said that a wise man who stands firm is a statesman, and a foolish man who stands firm is a catastrophe.   *Adlai Stevenson*

It is hard to free fools from the chains they revere.   *Voltaire*

Hain't we got all the fools in town on our side? And ain't that a big enough majority for any town?   *Mark Twain*

For God's sake give me the young man who has brains enough to make a fool of himself.   *Robert Louis Stevenson*

Who loves not women, wine and song,
Remains a fool his whole life long.   *Attributed to Martin Luther*

What is life but a series of inspired follies? The difficulty is to find them to do.   *George Bernard Shaw*

There is no chance for old fools.   *Cree Indian proverb*

Friends and Friendship

If you press me to say why I loved him, I can say no more than it was because he was he, and I was I.   *Montaigne*

Of my friends I am the only one I have left.   *Terence*

Anybody amuses me for once. A new acquaintance is like a new book. I prefer it, even if bad, to a classic.   *Benjamin Disraeli*

My God, this is a hell of a job. I have no trouble with my enemies. I can take care of my enemies all right. But my damn friends, my goddamn friends. They're the ones that keep me walking the floor nights.
    Warren G. Harding

There are three faithful friends: an old wife, an old dog, and ready money.
    Benjamin Franklin

He makes no friend who never made a foe.   *Alfred, Lord Tennyson*

Give me the avowed, the erect, and manly foe,
Bold I can meet, perhaps may turn the blow;
But of all plagues, good Heaven, thy wrath can send,
Save, save, oh save me from the candid friend! *George Canning*

It is not enough to succeed, a friend must fail. *La Rochefoucauld*

A friend in power is a friend lost. *Henry Adams*

Do not rely completely on any other human being, however dear. We meet
all life's greatest tests alone. *Agnes Macphail*

You cannot be friends upon any other terms than upon the terms of equality.
Woodrow Wilson

How often we find ourselves turning our backs on our actual friends, that
we may go and meet their ideal cousins. *Henry David Thoreau*

We make our friends; we make our enemies; but God makes our next-door
neighbour. *G.K. Chesterton*

You never know till you try to reach them how accessible men are; but you
must approach each man by the right door. *Henry Ward Beecher*

A friend is one before whom I may think aloud.
Ralph Waldo Emerson

She is such a good friend that she would throw all her acquaintances into
the water for the pleasure of fishing them out.
Talleyrand of Mme. de Staël

Without friends no one would choose to live, though he had all other goods.
Aristotle

The more we love our friends, the less we flatter them; it is by excusing nothing
that pure love shows itself. *Molière*

It's important to our friends to believe that we are unreservedly frank with
them, and important to friendship that we are not.
Mignon McLaughlin

In life it is difficult to say who do you the most mischief, enemies with the
worst intentions, or friends with the best. *Edward Bulwer-Lytton*

It is better to be deceived by one's friends than to deceive them. *Goethe*

A friend that ain't in need is a friend indeed. *Kin Hubbard*

We need new friends. Some of us are cannibals who have eaten their old friends up; others must have ever-renewed audiences before whom to re-enact an ideal version of their lives. *Logan Pearsall Smith*

Friendship needs a certain parallelism of life, a community of thought, a rivalry of aim. *Henry Adams*

When my friends lack an eye, I look at them in profile. *Joseph Joubert*

As in political, so in literary action, a man wins friends for himself mostly by the passion of his prejudices. *Joseph Conrad*

God save me from my friends — I can protect myself from my enemies. *Marshall de Villars*

Never exaggerate your faults; your friends will attend to that. *Robert C. Edwards*

Don't tell your friends their social faults; they will cure the fault and never forgive you. *Logan Pearsall Smith*

Iron sharpeneth man; so a man sharpeneth the countenance of his friend. *Proverbs 27:17*

Friendship is almost always the union of a part of one mind with a part of another; people are friends in spots. *George Santayana*

Who friendship with a knave hath made,
Is judged a partner in the trade. *John Gay*

Chance makes our parents, but choice makes our friends. *Jacques Delille*

Love demands infinitely less than friendship. *George Jean Nathan*

If we were all given by magic the power to read each other's thoughts, I suppose the first effect would be to dissolve all friendships. *Bertrand Russell*

There is a magnet in your heart that will attract true friends. That magnet is unselfishness, thinking of others first . . . when you learn to live for others, they will live for you.   *Paramahansa Yogananda*

Never join with your friend when he abuses his horse or his wife unless the one is to be sold, and the other to be buried.   *Charles Caleb Colton*

The Future

Upper classes are a nation's past; the middle-class is its future.
                                                              Ayn Rand

If you can look into the seeds of time and say, which grain will grow, and which will not, speak then to me.   *Shakespeare, 'Macbeth'*

Tomorrow is the most important thing in life. Comes in to us at midnight very clean. It's perfect when it arrives and it puts itself in our hands and hopes we've learnt something from yesterday.   *John Wayne*

Nothing in the world can one imagine beforehand, not the least thing. Everything is made up of so many unique particulars that cannot be foreseen.
                                                     Rainer Maria Rilke

You can never plan the future by the past.   *Edmund Burke*

One must care about a world one will not see.   *Bertrand Russell*

People are afraid of the future, of the unknown. If a man faces up to it, and takes the dare of the future, he can have some control over his destiny. That's an exciting idea to me, better than waiting with everybody else to see what's going to happen.   *John H. Glenn, Jr.*

The future is something which every one reaches at the rate of sixty miles an hour, whatever he does, whoever he is.   *C.S. Lewis*

My interest is in the future because I am going to spend the rest of my life there.   *Charles F. Kettering*

Tomorrow is a satire on today,
And shows its weakness.   *Edward Young*

The future comes one day at a time.   *Dean Acheson*

Never let the future disturb you. You will meet it, if you have to, with the same weapons of reason which today arm you against the present.
Marcus Aurelius

What we look for does not come to pass.
God finds a way for what none foresaw.   *Euripides*

With high hope for the future, no prediction is ventured.
Abraham Lincoln

We can pay our debt to the past by putting the future in debt to ourselves.
John Buchan

The future is not a gift — it is an achievement.   *Harry Lauder*

The world is full of people whose notion of a satisfactory future is, in fact, a return to the idealized past.   *Robertson Davies*

That which is escaped now is pain to come.   *Proverb*

Light tomorrow with today!   *Elizabeth Barrett Browning*

If tomorrow were never to come, it would not be worth living today.
Dagobert Runes

If we lacked imagination enough to foresee something better, life would indeed be a tragedy.   *Laurence J. Peter*

The afternoon knows what the morning never suspected.
Swedish proverb

You can only predict things after they've happened.   *Eugene Ionesco*

I never think of the future. It comes soon enough.   *Albert Einstein*

Life is an irreversible process and for that reason its future can never be a repetition of the past.   *Walter Lippmann*

I believe the future is only the past again, entered through another gate.
Arthur Wing Pinero

The world will be saved by one or two people.   *André Gide*

Genius

Genius, in truth, means little more than the faculty of perceiving in an unhabitual way. *William James*

Genius as such can neither be explained nor treated away; only, at times, its delay and inhibition and its perversion to destructive or self-destructive ends. *Erik Erikson*

To believe your own thought, to believe that what is true for you in your private heart is true for all men — that is genius. *Ralph Waldo Emerson*

Doing easily what others find is difficult is talent; doing what is impossible for talent is genius. *Henri Frédéric Amiel*

It takes immense genius to represent, simply and sincerely, what we see in front of us. *Edmond Duranty*

Results! Why, man, I have gotten a lot of results. I know several thousand things that won't work. *Thomas A. Edison*

The parting genius is with sighing sent. *Anon.*

In the republic of mediocrity, genius is dangerous. *Robert G. Ingersoll*

Every man of genius is considerably helped by being dead. *Robert S. Lund*

We define genius as the capacity for productive reaction against one's training. *Bernard Berenson*

Before I was a genius I was a drudge. *Ignace Jan Paderewski*

In every work of genius we recognize our own rejected thoughts; they come back to us with a certain alienated majesty. *Ralph Waldo Emerson*

Genius develops in quiet places, character out in the full current of human life. *Goethe*

Men of genius are the worst possible models for men of talent. *Murray D. Edwards*

Genius is childhood recaptured.   *Charles Baudelaire*

The public is wonderfully tolerant. It forgives everything except genius.
Oscar Wilde

When a true genius appears in the world you may know him by this sign,
that the dunces are all in confederacy against him.   *Jonathan Swift*

When Professor William Lyon Phelps of Yale said of his student, Thornton
Wilder, 'I believe he is a genius,' Wilder's father replied, 'Oh, tut, tut, Billy,
you're puffing my boy up way beyond his parts.'

Talent is that which is in a man's power; genius is that in whose power a
man is.   *James Russell Lowell*

There is a thin line between genius and insanity. I have erased this line.
Oscar Levant

Improvement makes straight roads; but the crooked roads without improvement are roads of genius.   *William Blake*

Geniuses are the luckiest of mortals because what they must do is the same
as what they most want to do.   *W. H. Auden*

Everyone is a genius at least once a year; a real genius has his original ideas
closer together.   *G. C. Lichtenberg*

Too often we forget that genius . . . depends upon the data within its reach,
that Archimedes could not have devised Edison's inventions.
Ernest Dimnet

The true genius is a mind of large general powers, accidentaly determined
to some particular direction.   *Samuel Johnson*

The mark of genius is an incessant activity of mind. Genius is a spiritual
greed.   *V. S. Pritchett*

Sometimes men come by the name of genius in the same way that certain
insects come by the name of centipede — not because they have a hundred
feet, but because most people can't count above fourteen.
G. C. Lichtenberg

Genius is an African who dreams up snow.   *Vladimir Nabokov*

Goals and Ambition

The significance of a man is not in what he attains but rather in what he longs to attain.
Kahlil Gibran

Once you say you're going to settle for second, that's what happens to you in life, I find.
John F. Kennedy

A successful individual typically sets his next goal somewhat but not too much above his last achievement. In this way he steadily raises his level of aspiration.
Kurt Lewin

The most absurd and reckless aspirations have sometimes led to extraordinary success.
Vauvenargues

All rising to great places is by a winding stair.
Francis Bacon

The only thing to know is how to use your neuroses.
Arthur Adamov

Every ceiling, when reached, becomes a floor, upon which one walks as a matter of course and prescriptive right.
Aldous Huxley

We can always redeem the man who aspires and strives.
Goethe

The world stands aside to let anyone pass who knows where he is going.
David Starr Jordan

I have learned to have very modest goals for society and myself; things like clean air, green grass, children with bright eyes, not being pushed around, useful work that suits one's abilities, plain tasty food, and occasional satisfying nookie.
Paul Goodman

If you would hit the mark, you must aim a little above it:
Every arrow that flies feels the attraction of earth.
Henry Wadsworth Longfellow

Ah, but a man's reach should exceed his grasp, or what's a heaven for?
Robert Browning

Before we set our hearts too much upon anything, let us examine how happy they are, who already possess it.
La Rochefoucauld

Ours is a world where people don't know what they want and are willing to go through hell to get it.
Don Marquis

Accept the place the divine providence has found for you, the society of your contemporaries, the connection of events.   *Ralph Waldo Emerson*

Those who aim at great deeds must also suffer greatly.   *Plutarch*

It is a mistake to look too far ahead. Only one link in the chain of destiny can be handled at a time.   *Winston Churchill*

Do not wish to be anything but what you are, and try to be that perfectly.
St. Francis de Sales

This one thing I do, forgetting those things which are behind, and reaching forth unto those things which are before, I press toward the mark!
Phillipians 3:13

Winning isn't everything. It is the only thing.   *Vince Lombardi*

It is no longer clear which way is up even if one wants to rise.
David Riesman

Ambition is pitiless. Any merit that it cannot use it finds despicable.
Joseph Joubert

Every man is said to have his peculiar ambition.   *Abraham Lincoln*

Well is it known that ambition can creep as well as soar.
Edmund Burke

Make no little plans; they have no magic to stir men's blood . . . Make big plans, aim high in hope and work.   *Daniel H. Burnham*

God

The nature of God is a circle of which the centre is everywhere and the circumference is nowhere.   *Anon.*

By night an atheist half-believes in God.   *Edward Young*

Father expected a good deal of God. He didn't actually accuse God of inefficiency, but when he prayed his tone was loud and angry, like that of a dissatisfied guest in a carelessly managed hotel.   *Clarence Day*

Lord, who art always the same, give that I know myself, give that I know Thee.
St. Augustine

We have no choice but to be guilty,
God is unthinkable if we are innocent.
Archibald MacLeish

Man appoints, and God disappoints.
Cervantes

I am afraid I shall not find Him, but I shall still look for Him. If He exists, He may be appreciative of my efforts.
Jules Renard

God is not a cosmic bellboy for whom we can press a button to get things done.
Harry Emerson Fosdick

God is usually on the side of big squadrons and against little ones.
Roger de Bussy-Rabutin

The more of himself man attributes to God, the less he has left in himself.
Karl Marx

God tempers the wind to the shorn lamb.
Laurence Sterne

God is a comedian whose audience is afraid to laugh.
H. L. Mencken

Every man thinks God is on his side. The rich and powerful know he is.
Jean Anouilh

I could prove God statistically.
George Gallup

Man is a dog's ideal of what God should be.
André Malraux

Christ — an anarchist who succeeded.
Axel Munthe

An honest God is the noblest work of man.
Robert G. Ingersoll

It is left only to God and to the angels to be lookers on.
Francis Bacon

God is really another artist. He invented the giraffe, the elephant and the cat. He has no real style. He just goes on trying other things.
Pablo Picasso

The nearer the church, the further from God.
Bishop Lancelot Andrewes

God'll send the bill to you.   *James Russell Lowell*

I believe there is no god but Allah alone and Muhammed is his prophet.
                                                Muslim Creed

The world is more exacting than God himself.   *Yiddish proverb*

Give God time.   *The Koran*

God will be present, whether asked or not.   *Latin proverb*

If God did not exist, it would be necessary to invent him.   *Voltaire*

We trust, sir, that God is on our side. It is more important to know that
we are on God's side.   *Abraham Lincoln*

Beware of the man whose God is in the skies.   *George Bernard Shaw*

I can't believe that God plays dice with the universe.   *Albert Einstein*

One on God's side is a majority.   *Wendell Phillips*

If triangles had a God, he would have three sides.   *Montesquieu*

The abdomen is the reason why man does not easily take himself for a god.
                                                Friedrich Nietzsche

God does not pay weekly, but he pays at the end.   *Dutch proverb*

The finding of God is the coming to one's own self.   *Meher Baba*

God moves in a mysterious way
His wonders to perform;
He plants his footsteps in the sea
And rides upon the storm.   *William Cowper*

Man proposes; God disposes.   *Thomas à Kempis*

God doth not need
Either man's work or his own gifts; who best
Bear His mild yoke, they serve Him best; His state
Is kingly; thousands at His bidding speed
And post o'er land and ocean without rest —
They also serve who only stand and wait.   *John Milton*

If God lived on earth, people would break his windows.   *Anon.*

If God made us in his image, we have certainly returned the compliment.
Voltaire

God does not die on the day when we cease to believe in a personal deity, but we die on the day when our lives cease to be illuminated by the steady radiance, renewed daily, of a wonder, the source of which is beyond all reason.   *Dag Hammarskjöld*

Learn to see God in all persons, of whatever race or creed. You will know what divine love is when you begin to feel your oneness with every human being, not before. In mutual service we forget the little self and glimpse the one measureless self, the spirit that unifies all men.
Paramahansa Yogananda

Goodness and Giving

If a man wants to be of the greatest possible value to his fellow-creatures, let him begin the long, solitary task of perfecting himself.
Robertson Davies

We'd all like a reputation for generosity and we'd all like to buy it cheap.
Mignon McLaughlin

He who would do good to another, must do it in minute particulars.
Anon.

General good is the plea of the scoundrel, hypocite, flatterer.
William Blake

The word 'good' has many meanings. For example, if a man were to shoot his grandmother at a range of five hundred yards, I should call him a good shot, but not *necessarily* a good man.   *G. K. Chesterton*

I expect to pass though this world but once. Any good therefore that I can do, or any kindness that I can show to my fellow-creature, let me do it now. Let me not defer or neglect it, for I shall not pass this way again.
Attributed to Stephen Grellet

Pity costs nothin' and ain't worth nothin'.   *Josh Billings*

That best portion of a good man's life,
His little, nameless, unremembered acts
Of kindness and of love.   *William Wordsworth*

There is no man so good, who, were he to submit all his thoughts and actions to the laws, would not deserve hanging ten times in his life.
                                                  Montaigne

Should not the giver be thankful that the receiver received? Is not giving a need? Is not receiving, mercy?   *Friedrich Nietzsche*

When thou doest alms, do not let thy left hand know what thy right hand doeth.   *Matthew 6:3*

No good deed ever goes unpunished.   *Brooks Thomas*

Be good, sweet maid, and let who will be clever.   *Charles Kingsley*

Messenger of sympathy and love, servant of parted friends, consoler of the lonely, bond of the scattered family, enlarger of the common life.
                          U.S. Post Office inscription, Washington, D.C.

Good things are not done in a hurry.   *German proverb*

Be charitable and indulgent to every one but thyself.   *Joseph Joubert*

We are all here on earth to help others; what on earth the others are here for I don't know.   *W. H. Auden*

Why is it that when people have no capacity for private usefulness they should be so anxious to serve the public?   *Sara Jeannette Duncan*

I have found men more kind than I expected, and less just.
                                                  Samuel Johnson

Good men need no recommendation and bad men it wouldn't help.
                                                  Jewish proverb

There is so much good in the worst of us and so much bad in the best of us, that it's rather hard to tell which of us ought to reform the rest of us.
                          Sign in Springdale, Connecticut

Real unselfishness consists in sharing the interests of others.
                                                  George Santayana

I hate the giving of the hand unless the whole man accompanies it.
Ralph Waldo Emerson

Is not a patron one who looks with unconcern on a man struggling for life in the water, and, when he has reached ground, encumbers him with help?
Samuel Johnson

If you're naturally kind, you attract a lot of people you don't like.
William Feather

The good should be grateful to the bad — for providing the world with a basis for comparison.   *Sven Halla*

All strangers and beggars are from Zeus, and a gift, though small, is precious.
Homer

Behold! I do not give lectures on a little charity.
When I give, I give myself.   *Walt Whitman*

If a friend is in trouble, don't annoy him by asking if there is anything you can do. Think up something appropriate and do it. *Edgar Watson Howe*

The greatest pleasure I know is to do a good action by stealth, and to have it found out by accident.   *Charles Lamb*

As Charles Lamb says, there is nothing so nice as doing good by stealth and being found out by accident, so I now say it is even nicer to make heroic decisions and to be prevented by 'circumstances beyond your control' from ever trying to execute them.   *William James*

Giving is the highest expression of potency.   *Erich Fromm*

If I knew . . . that a man was coming to my house with the conscious design of doing me good, I should run for my life.   *Henry David Thoreau*

If I've learned anything in my seventy years it's that nothing's as good or as bad as it appears.   *Bushrod H. Campbell*

The Devil himself is good when he is pleased.   *Thomas Fuller*

Wise men appreciate all men, for they see the good in each and know how hard it is to make anything good.   *Baltasar Gracián*

The only gift is a portion of thyself.   *Ralph Waldo Emerson*

Take egotism out, and you would castrate the benefactor.
Ralph Waldo Emerson

It is one of the beautiful compensations of this life that no one can sincerely try to help another without helping himself.   *Charles Dudley Warner*

No man deserves to be praised for his goodness unless he has the strength of character to be wicked. All other goodness is generally nothing but indolence or impotence of will.   *La Rochefoucauld*

We know the good, we apprehend it clearly. But we can't bring it to achievment.   *Euripides*

Generosity is the vanity of giving.   *La Rochefoucauld*

My only policy is to profess evil and do good.   *George Bernard Shaw*

For an inheritance to be really great, the hand of the defunct must not be seen.   *René Char*

Fearful is the seductive power of goodness.   *Bertolt Brecht*

One trouble with a kind of falsely therapeutic and always reassuring attitude that it is easy to fall into with old people, is the tendency to be satisfied with too little.   *Kenneth Koch*

There are bad people who would be less dangerous if they were quite devoid of goodness.   *La Rochefoucauld*

The age of strong belief is over, the good is no longer always very good.   *D. L. Coles*

When you cease to make a contribution you begin to die.
Eleanor Roosevelt

Gossip and Gossips

Gossip is when you hear something you like about someone you don't.
Earl Wilson

Gossip needs no carriage.   *Russian proverb*

Another good thing about gossip is that it is within everybody's reach,
And it is much more interesting than any other form of speech.

Ogden Nash

Hating anything in the way of ill-natured gossip ourselves, we are always
grateful to those who do it for us and do it well.   *Saki*

No gossip ever dies away entirely, if many people voice it: it, too, is a kind
of divinity.   *Hesiod*

Gossip is vice enjoyed vicariously — the sweet, subtle satisfaction without
the risk.   *Kin Hubbard*

The best-loved man or maid in the town would perish with anguish could
they hear all that their friends say in the course of a day.   *John Hay*

If you can't say something good about someone, sit right here by me.

Attributed to Alice Roosevelt Longworth

What some invent, the rest enlarge.   *Jonathan Swift*

Even doubtful accusations leave a stain behind them.   *Thomas Fuller*

What people say behind your back is your standing in the community.

Edgar Watson Howe

Whoever gossips to you will gossip of you.   *Spanish proverb*

A little public scandal is good once in a while — takes the tension out of
the news.   *Beryl Pfizer*

Gossip is the art of saying nothing in a way that leaves practically nothing
unsaid.   *Walter Winchell*

Government and Rule

Any people anywhere, being inclined and having the power, have the right
to rise up and shake off the existing government and form a new one. This
is a most valuable and sacred right — a right which we hope and believe
is to liberate the world.   *Abraham Lincoln*

No man should be in public office who can't make more money in private
life.   *Thomas E. Dewey*

Government is the only institution that can take a valuable commodity like paper, and make it worthless by applying ink. *Ludwig van Moses*

The poorest man may in his cottage bid defiance to all the force of the crown. It may be frail — its roof may shake — the wind may blow through it — the storm may enter — the rain may enter — but the King of England cannot enter! — all his force dares not cross the threshhold of the ruined tenement! *William Pitt the Elder*

The art of government is the organization of idolatry
George Bernard Shaw

Every government is run by liars and nothing they say should be believed.
I. F. Stone

The more the world is specialized the more it will be run by generalists.
Marcel Masse

A friend of mine says that every man who takes office in Washington either grows or swells, and when I give a man an office, I watch him carefully to see whether he is swelling or growing. *Woodrow Wilson*

We are under a Constitution, but the Constitution is what the judges say it is.
Charles Evans Hughes

At certain times of grave national stress, when that rag-bag called the British Constitution is in grave danger of coming unstuck, thank heaven for the big safety-pin at the top that keeps it together.
Anonymous comment on the British monarchy

The majority is the best way, because it is visible, and has strength to make itself obeyed. Yet it is the opinion of the least able. *Blaise Pascal*

The best government is a benevolent tyranny tempered by an occasional assassination. *Voltaire*

No man ever saw a government. I live in the midst of the Government of the United States, but I never saw the Government of the United States.
Woodrow Wilson

The State, that cawing rookery of committees and subcommittees.
V. S. Pritchett

The weak have one weapon — the errors of those who think they are strong.
Georges Bidault

Government in the last analysis is organised opinion. Where there is little or no public opinion, there is likely to be bad government, which sooner or later becomes autocratic government.   *William Lyon Mackenzie King*

Under democracy, one party always devotes its chief energies to trying to prove that the other party is unfit to rule — and both commonly succeed, and are right.   *H. L. Mencken*

Inflation is one form of taxation that can be imposed without legislation.   *Milton Friedman*

Doing what's right isn't the problem. It's knowing what's right.   *Lyndon B. Johnson*

It is the aim of good government to stimulate production, of bad government to encourage consumption.   *Jean Baptiste Say*

Bureaucracy, the rule of no one, has become the modern form of despotism.   *Mary McCarthy*

Be thankful we're not getting all the government we're paying for.   *Will Rogers*

A government that is big enough to give you all you want is big enough to take it all away.   *Barry Goldwater*

Government is the political representative of a natural equilibrium, of custom, of inertia; it is by no means a representative of reason.   *George Santayana*

The best reason why monarchy is a strong government is that it is an intelligible government: the mass of mankind understand it, and they hardly anywhere in the world understand any other.   *Walter Bagehot*

The world is ruled only by consideration of advantages.   *Friedrich von Schiller*

Must a government of necessity be too strong for the liberties of its people or too weak to maintain its own existence?   *Abraham Lincoln*

As I get older . . . I become more convinced that good government is not a substitute for self-government.   *Dwight Morrow*

We hold the power and bear the responsibility.   *Abraham Lincoln*

Every man wishes to pursue his occupation and to enjoy the fruits of his labours and the produce of his property in peace and safety, and with the least possible expense. When these things are accomplished, all the objects for which government ought to be established are answered.

Thomas Jefferson

It is not possible to found a lasting power upon injustice.   *Demosthenes*

A monarchy is a merchantman, which sails well, but will sometimes strike on a rock and go to the bottom, whilst a republic is a raft which will never sink, but then your feet are always in water.   *Fisher Ames*

The state, it cannot too often be repeated, does nothing, and can give nothing, which it does not take from somebody.   *Henry George*

Government is an association of men who do violence to the rest of us.

Leo Tolstoy

Government, even in its best state, is but a necessary evil; in its worst state, an intolerable one.   *Thomas Paine*

Government is not reason, it is not eloquence — it is force.

George Washington

Bureaucracy is a giant mechanism operated by pygmies.

Honoré de Balzac

Whenever by an unfortunate occurrence of circumstances an opposition is compelled to support the government, the support should be given with a kick and not a caress and should be withdrawn at the first available moment.

Randolph Churchill

To govern is to choose.   *Pierre Mendes-France*

For a country to have a great writer is to have another government.

Aleksandr Solzhenitsyn

The state — the great fiction by which everybody tries to live at the expense of everybody else.   *Frédéric Bastiat*

Republics are brought to their ends by luxury; monarchies by poverty.

Montesquieu

The foremost art of kings is the power to endure hatred.   *Seneca*

China has no income tax, no unemployed and not a single soldier outside its own territory.   *Chou En-lai*

In the long run every government is the exact symbol of its people, with their wisdom and unwisdom.   *Thomas Carlyle*

The art of governing consists in not letting men grow old in their jobs.
Napoleon Bonaparte

The worst thing in this world, next to anarchy, is government.
Henry Ward Beecher

The legitimate object of government is to do for a community of people, whatever they need to have done, but cannot do at all, or cannot so well do for themselves, in their separate and individual capacities.
Abraham Lincoln

That government is best which governs the least, because its people discipline themselves.   *Thomas Jefferson*

My movement to the chair of government will be accompanied by feelings not unlike those of a culprit who is going to the place of execution.
George Washington

How can you govern a country with two hundred and forty-six varieties of cheese?   *Charles de Gaulle*

There is but one way for a president to deal with the Congress, and that is continuously, incessantly, and without interruption. If it's really going to work, the relationship between the president and the Congress has got to be almost incestuous.   *Lyndon B. Johnson*

The illegal we do immediately. The unconstitutional takes a little longer.
Henry Kissinger

To make certain that crime does not pay, the government should take it over and try to run it.   *G. Norman Collie*

The average man that I encounter all over the country regards government as a sort of great milk cow, with its head in the clouds eating air, and growing a full teat for everybody on earth.   *Clarence C. Manion*

The strongest pressure in the world can be friendly pressure.
Lester Pearson

The vices of monarchs can never remain hidden.   *Claudian*

The art of putting the right men in the right places is first in the science of government; but that of finding places for the discontented is the most difficult.   *Talleyrand*

It is common sense to take a method and try it. If it fails, admit it frankly and try another, but above all, try something.   *Franklin D. Roosevelt*

The government is becoming the family of last resort.   *Jerry Brown*

All this will not be finished in the first one hundred days. Nor will it be finished in the first one thousand days, nor in the life of this administration, nor even perhaps in our lifetime on this planet.   *John F. Kennedy*

Governments last as long as the undertaxed can defend themselves against the overtaxed.   *Bernard Berenson*

The impersonal hand of government can never replace the helping hand of a neighbour.   *Hubert Humphrey*

Too bad that all the people who know how to run the country are busy driving taxicabs and cutting hair.   *George Burns*

When we got into office, the thing that surprised me most was to find that things were just as bad as we'd been saying they were. *John F. Kennedy*

No government can be long secure without a formidable opposition.
                                                     Benjamin Disraeli

The dogmas of the quiet past are inadequate to the stormy present. As our case is new, so we must think anew and act anew. We must disenthrall ourselves, and then we shall save our country.   *Abraham Lincoln*

The people's right to change what does not work is one of the greatest principles of our system of government.   *Richard Nixon*

No intelligence system can predict what a government will do if it doesn't know itself.   *J. K. Galbraith*

When I am abroad, I always make it a rule never to criticize or attack the government of my own country. I make up for lost time when I come home.
                                                    Winston Churchill

The U.S. Senate — an old scow which doesn't move very fast, but never sinks.   *Everett Dirksen*

The supply of government exceeds the demand.   *Lewis H. Lapham*

Tyranny is yielding to the lust of governing.   *Lord Moulton*

Greatness

One can build the Empire State Building, discipline the Prussian army, make a state hierarchy mightier than God, yet fail to overcome the unaccountable superiority of certain human beings.   *Aleksandr Solzhenitsyn*

We are all worms, but I do believe that I am a glow-worm.
                                                        Winston Churchill

To do great things is difficult, but to command great things is more difficult.
                                                        Friedrich Nietzsche

Greatness is a zigzag streak of lightning in the brain.   *Herbert Asquith*

If you want to know your true opinion of someone, watch the effect produced in you by the first sight of a letter from him.
                                                        Arthur Schopenhauer

The banalities of a great man pass for wit.   *Alexander Chase*

True perfection is achieved only by those who are prepared to destroy it. It is a by-product of greatness.   *Kenneth Clark*

Few great men could pass Personnel.   *Paul Goodman*

Clever men are impressed in their differences from their fellows. Wise men are conscious of their resemblance to them.   *R. H. Tawney*

His eminence was due to the flatness of the surrounding landscape.
                                                        John Stuart Mill

The heights by great men reached and kept
Were not attained by sudden flight,
But they, while their companions slept,
Were toiling upward in the night.   *Henry Wadsworth Longfellow*

Each honest calling, each walk of life, has its own elite, its own aristocracy based on excellence of performance.   *James Bryant Conant*

Only great men may have great faults.   *French proverb*

He (Turgenev) had the air of his own statue erected by national subscription.   *Oliver Wendell Holmes*

The world knows nothing of its greatest men.   *Henry Taylor*

Every age needs men who will redeem the time by living with a vision of things that are to be.   *Adlai Stevenson*

Not a day passes over the earth, but men and women of no note do great deeds, speak great words and suffer noble sorrows.   *Charles Reude*

Some are born great, some achieve greatness, and some hire public relations officers.   *Daniel J. Boorstin*

Do continue to believe that with your feeling and your work you are taking part in the greatest; the more strongly you cultivate in yourself this belief, the more will reality and the world go forth from it. *Rainer Maria Rilke*

It is not the strength, but the duration, of great sentiments that makes great men.   *Friedrich Nietzsche*

Greatness is a road leading towards the unknown.   *Charles de Gaulle*

A great ship asks deep water.   *George Herbert*

Great men too often have greater faults than little men can find room for.   *Walter Savage Landor*

Great and good are seldom the same man.   *Thomas Fuller*

The highest and most lofty trees have the most reason to dread the thunder.   *Charles Rollin*

Born of the sun they travelled a short while towards the sun
And left the vivid air signed with their honour.   *Stephen Spender*

If I am a great man, then a good many of the great men of history are frauds.   *Bonar Law*

Great men hallow a whole people, and lift up all who live in their time.
Sydney Smith

The greatest truths are the simplest, and so are the greatest men.
J.C. and A.W. Hare

The dullard's envy of brilliant men is always assuaged by the suspicion that they will come to a bad end.   *Max Beerbohm*

Of what is great, one must either be silent, or speak with greatness — that means cynically and with innocence.   *Friedrich Nietszche*

The perfection preached in the Gospels never yet built up an Empire. Every man of action has a strong dose of optimism, pride, hardness and cunning. But all these things will be forgiven him, indeed they will be regarded as high qualities, if he can make of them the means to achieve great ends.
Charles de Gaulle

The mind reaches great heights only by spurts.   *Vauvenargues*

When you're as great as I am, it's hard to be humble.   *Muhammad Ali*

No sadder proof can be given by a man of his own littleness, than disbelief in great men.   *Thomas Carlyle*

A tomb now suffices him for whom the whole world was not sufficient.
Anonymous epitaph for Alexander the Great

If my theory of relativity is proven successful, Germany will claim me as a German, and France will declare that I am a citizen of the world. Should my theory prove untrue, France will say that I am a German, and Germany will declare that I am a Jew.   *Albert Einstein*

Most of the trouble in the world is caused by people wanting to be important.
T. S. Eliot

What makes a nation great is not primarily its great men, but the stature of its innumerable mediocre ones.   *José Ortega y Gasset*

You cannot fly like an eagle with the wings of a wren.
William Henry Hudson

The biggest dog has been a pup.   *Joaquin Miller*

There's a pinch of the madman in every great man.   *French proverb*

It is unavoidable that if we learn more about a great man's life, we shall also hear of occasions on which he has done no better than we, and has in fact come nearer to us as a human being.   *Sigmund Freud*

Happiness

We have no more right to consume happiness without producing it than to consume wealth without producing it.   *George Bernard Shaw*

Man's real life is happy, chiefly because he is ever expecting that it soon will be so.   *Edgar Allan Poe*

Unquestionably, it is possible to do without happiness; it is done involuntarily by nineteen-twentieths of mankind.   *John Stuart Mill*

When one door of happiness closes, another opens; but often we look so long at the closed door that we do not see the one which has been opened for us.   *Helen Keller*

Many persons have a wrong idea of what constitutes true happiness. It is not attained through self-gratification but through fidelity to a worthy purpose.   *Helen Keller*

A man should always consider how much he has more than he wants, and how much more unhappy he might be than he really is. *Joseph Addison*

If a man has important work, and enough leisure and income to enable him to do it properly, he is in possession of as much happiness as is good for any of the children of Adam.   *R. H. Tawney*

The greatest happiness you can have is knowing that you do not necessarily require happiness.   *William Saroyan*

Existence is a strange bargain. Life owes us little; we owe it everything. The only true happiness comes from squandering ourselves for a purpose.
William Cowper

Even if we can't be happy, we must always be cheerful.   *Irving Kristol*

New Year's Day is every man's birthday.   *Charles Lamb*

Happiness is the perpetual possession of being well deceived.

Lytton Strachey

To be without some of the things you want is an indispensable part of happiness.

Bertrand Russell

For the rational, psychologically healthy man, the desire for pleasure is the desire to celebrate his control over reality. For the neurotic, the desire for pleasure is the desire to escape from reality.

Nathaniel Branden

What is a demanding pleasure? A pleasure that demands the use of one's mind; not in the sense of problem solving, but in the sense of exercising discrimination, judgement, awareness.

Ayn Rand

If thou workest at that which is before thee, following right reason seriously, vigorously, calmly, without allowing anything else to distract thee, but keeping thy divine part pure, as if thou shouldst be bound to give it back immediately; if thou holdest to this, expecting nothing, fearing nothing, but satisfied with thy present activity according to Nature, and with heroic truth in every word and sound which thou utterest, thou wilt live happy. And there is no man who is able to prevent this.

Marcus Aurelius

We act as though comfort and luxury were the chief requirements of life, when all that we need to make us really happy is something to be enthusiastic about.

Charles Kingsley

One thing I know: the only ones among you who will be really happy are those who will have sought and found how to serve.

Albert Schweitzer

It has never been given to a man to attain at once his happiness and his salvation.

Charles Péguy

Happiness is the light on the water. The water is cold and dark and deep.

William Maxwell

There is no duty we so much underrate as the duty of being happy.

Robert Louis Stevenson

Happiness: a good bank account, a good cook and a good digestion.

Jean-Jacques Rousseau

Knowledge of what is possible is the beginning of happiness.

George Santayana

Happiness is the interval between periods of unhappiness. *Don Marquis*

Behold, we count them happy which endure. Ye have heard of the patience
of Job. *James 5:3*

The will of man is his happiness. *Friedrich von Schiller*

There is only one way to happiness and that is to cease worrying about things
which are beyond the power of our will. *Epictetus*

The secret of happiness is not in doing what one likes, but in liking what
one has to do. *James M. Barrie*

True happiness is of a retired nature and an enemy to pomp and noise; it
arises, in the first place, from the enjoyment of one's self; and, in the next,
from the friendship and conversations of a few select companions.
Joseph Addison

It is nonsense to speak of 'higher' and 'lower' pleasures. To a hungry man
it is, rightly, more important that he eat than that he philosophize.
W. H. Auden

Man's happiness springs mainly from moderate troubles, which afford the
mind a healthful stimulus, and are followed by a reaction which produces
a cheerful flow of spirits. *E. Wigglesworth*

I have known some quite good people who were unhappy, but never an interested person who was unhappy. *A. C. Benson*

My creed is that: Happiness is the only good.
          The place to be happy is here.
          The time to be happy is now.
          The way to be happy is to make others so.
Robert G. Ingersoll

My life has no purpose, no direction, no aim, no meaning, and yet I'm happy.
I can't figure it out. What am I doing right? *Charles M. Schulz*

Happiness to a dog is what lies on the other side of a door.
Charleton Ogburn, Jr.

Happiness comes fleetingly now and then,
To those who have learned to do without it
And to them only. *Don Marquis*

I believe in the possibility of happiness, if one cultivates intuition and outlives
the grosser passions, including optimism. *George Santayana*

Happiness is brief
It will not stay.
God batters at its sails.   *Euripides*

To be happy, we must not be too concerned with others.   *Albert Camus*

For each ecstatic instant
We must an anguish pay
In keen and quivering ratio
To the ecstasy   *Emily Dickinson*

At rare moments in history, by a series of accidents never to be repeated,
arise flower societies in which the cult of happiness is paramount, hedonistic,
mindless, intent upon the glorious physical instant.   *Colm MacInnes*

Man is that he might have joy.   *Joseph Smith*

The formula for complete happiness is to be very busy with the unimportant.
A. Edward Newton

. . . the little hills rejoice on every side. The pastures are clothed with flocks;
the valleys also are covered over with corn; they shout for joy, they also sing.
Psalms 65:12 and 13

Make happy those who are near, and those who are far will come.
Chinese proverb

Remember that happiness is a way of travel — not a destination.
Roy M. Goodman

If we cannot live so as to be happy, let us at least live so as to deserve it.
Immanuel Hermann von Fichte

I never admired another's fortune so much that I became dissatisfied with
my own.   *Cicero*

Happiness is essentially a state of going somewhere, wholeheartedly, one-
directionally, without regret or reservation.   *William H. Sheldon*

Happiness? That's nothing more than health and a poor memory.
Albert Schweitzer

Happiness is the only sanction of life; where happiness fails, existence remains a mad and lamentable experiment.   *George Santayana*

Happiness makes up in height for what it lacks in length.   *Robert Frost*

It is not easy to find happiness in ourselves, and it is not possible to find it elsewhere.   *Agnes Repplier*

Happiness depends, as Nature shows,
Less on exterior things than most suppose.   *William Cowper*

Happiness is a small and unworthy goal for something as big and fancy as a whole lifetime, and should be taken in small doses.   *Russell Baker*

Hatred

Hatred is the coward's revenge for being intimidated.
George Bernard Shaw

Hatred comes from the heart; contempt from the head; and neither feeling is quite within our control.   *Arthur Schopenhauer*

Hatred seems to operate on the same glands as love; it even produces the same actions. If we had not been taught how to interpret the story of the Passion, would we have been able to say from their actions alone whether it was the jealous Judas or the cowardly Peter who loved Christ?
Graham Greene

I do desire we may be better strangers.   *Shakespeare, 'As You Like It'*

Psychiatrists today . . . see the irrational hostility that people everywhere vent upon one another as chiefly projected self-hate.   *Bonaro Overstreet*

Don't hate, it's too big a burden to bear.   *Martin Luther King, Sr.*

A hateful act is the transference to others of the degradation we bear in ourselves.   *Simone Weil*

The worst, the least curable hatred is that which has superseded deep love.
Euripides

Hatred is settled anger.   *Cicero*

Passionate hatred can give meaning and purpose to an empty life.
Eric Hoffer

Hate is the consequence of fear; we fear something before we hate it; a child who fears noises becomes a man who hates noise.   *Cyril Connolly*

Hatred is self-punishment.   *Hosea Ballou*

Hatreds are the cinders of affection.   *Walter Raleigh*

I never hated a man enough to give him his diamonds back.
Zsa Zsa Gabor

It does not matter much what a man hates, provided he hates something.
Samuel Butler

Whom they have injured, they also hate.   *Seneca*

We love without reason, and without reason we hate.
Jean-François Regnard

If you hate a person, you hate something in him that is part of yourself. What isn't part of ourselves doesn't disturb us.   *Hermann Hesse*

Hate is such a luxurious emotion, it can only be spent on one we love.
Bob Udkoff

Hell and the Devil

The safest road to Hell is the gradual one — the gentle slope, soft underfoot, without sudden turnings, without milestones, without signposts.
C. S. Lewis

The Devil's boots don't creak.   *Scottish proverb*

Man can hardly even recognize the devils of his own creation.
Albert Schweitzer

What is hell? I maintain that it is the suffering of being unable to love.
Fyodor Dostoevsky

Hell, madame, is to love no longer.   *Georges Bernanos*

Hell is more bearable than nothingness.   *P. J. Bailey*

Hell is truth seen too late.   *Anon.*

A perpetual holiday is a good working definition of hell.
George Bernard Shaw

Be sober, be vigilant; because your adversary the devil, as a roaring lion, walketh about, seeking whom he may devour.   *1 Peter 5:8*

Heaven for climate, hell for company.   *James M. Barrie*

We may not pay Satan reverence, for that would be indiscreet, but we can at least respect his talents.   *Mark Twain*

An apology for the Devil — it must be remembered that we have only heard one side of the case. God has written all the books.   *Samuel Butler*

When you first learn to love hell, you will be in heaven.
Thaddeus Golas

The devil's name is Dullness.   *Robert E. Lee*

Hell is indefinite.   *Charles Williams*

It has been more wittily than charitably said that hell is paved with good intentions. They have their place in heaven also.   *Robert Southey*

Heredity

Heredity is nothing but stored environment.   *Luther Burbank*

One of the best things people could do for their descendants would be to sharply limit the number of them.   *Olin Miller*

A man's rootage is more important than his leafage.   *Woodrow Wilson*

Nothing is so soothing to our self-esteem as to find our bad traits in our forebears. It seems to absolve us.   *Van Wyck Brooks*

Heredity is an omnibus in which all our ancestors ride, and every now and then one of them puts his head out and embarrasses us.
Oliver Wendell Holmes

It is indeed a desirable thing to be well descended, but the glory belongs to our ancestors.
Plutarch

With him for a sire, and her for a dam
What should I be, but just what I am?
Edna St. Vincent Millay

The child is father to the man.
William Wordsworth

Gentility is what is left over from rich ancestors after the money is gone.
John Ciardi

Whoever serves his country well has no need of ancestors.
Voltaire

The best blood will sometimes get into a fool or a mosquito.
Austin O'Malley

The man who has not anything to boast of but his illustrious ancestors is like a potato — the only good belonging to him is underground.
Thomas Overbury

A genealogist is one who traces your family back as far as your money will go.
Anon.

The pedigree of honey
Does not concern the bee;
A clover, anytime, to him
Is aristocracy.
Emily Dickinson

A hen is only an egg's way of making another egg.
Samuel Butler

When I want a peerage, I shall buy one like an honest man.
Lord Northcliffe

Heroes and Heroism

Being a hero is about the shortest-lived profession on earth. *Will Rogers*

Every hero becomes a bore at last.
Ralph Waldo Emerson

Heroes are created by popular demand, sometimes out of the scantiest materials . . . such as the apple that William Tell never shot, the ride that Paul Revere never finished, the flag that Barbara Frietchie never waved.
Gerald Johnson

A hero is a man who stands up manfully against his father and in the end victoriously overcomes him.   *Sigmund Freud*

When the heroes go off the stage, the clowns come on.   *Heinrich Heine*

A hero is no braver than an ordinary man, but he is brave five minutes longer.
Ralph Waldo Emerson

One of the forms of psychological heroism is the willingness to tolerate anxiety and uncertainty in the pursuit of our values — whether these values be work goals, the love of another human being, the raising of a family or personal growth.   *Samuel Branden*

Don't be so humble. You're not that great.   *Golda Meir*

Ezra Pound — idiosyncrasy on a monument.   *Randall Jarrell*

All these were honoured in their generations and were the glory of their times.
Ecclesiasticus 44:7
Engraved on a government building, Ottawa

This thing of being a hero, about the main thing to it is to know when to die.   *Will Rogers*

One murder makes a villain, millions a hero.   *Bishop Beilby Porteus*

The savage bows down to idols of wood and stone, the civilized man to idols of flesh and blood.   *George Bernard Shaw*

An efficiency-regime cannot be run without a few heroes stuck about it to carry off the dullness — much as plums have to be put into a bad pudding to make it palatable.   *E.M. Forster*

In a truly heroic life there is no peradventure. It is always doing or dying.
R.D. Hitchcock

It is said that no man is a hero to his valet. That is because a hero can be recognized only by a hero.   *Goethe*

History and Historians

History doesn't pass the dishes again.   *Louis-Ferdinand Celine*

The past is a foreign country; they do things differently there.   *Anon.*

Very few things happen at the right time, and the rest do not happen at all; the conscientious historian will correct these defects.   *Herodotus*

Most history is a record of the triumphs, disasters and follies of top people. The black hole in it is the way of life of mute, inglorious men and women who made no nuisance of themselves in the world.   *Philip Howard*

Nostalgia is a seductive liar.   *George W. Ball*

It has been said that though God cannot alter the past, historians can; it is perhaps because they can be useful to Him in this respect that He tolerates their existence.   *Samuel Butler*

It is pleasant to be transferred from an office where one is afraid of a sergeant-major into an office where one can intimidate generals, and perhaps this is why history is so attractive to the more timid among us.   *E. M. Forster*

History never looks like history when you are living through it. It always looks confusing and messy, and it always feels uncomfortable.   *John W. Gardner*

History is philosophy learned from examples.   *Dionysius of Halicarnassus*

History teaches us that men and nations behave wisely once they have exhausted all other alternatives.   *Abba Eban*

Noble acts and momentous events happen in the same way and produce the same impression as the ordinary facts.   *Roberto Rossellini*

Don't brood on what's past, but never forget it either.   *Thomas H. Raddall*

Those who cannot remember the past are condemned to repeat it.   *George Santayana*

Most of us spend too much time on the last twenty-four hours and too little on the last six thousand years.   *Will Durant*

I never realized that there was history, close at hand, beside my very own home. I did not realize that the old grave that stood among the brambles at the foot of our farm was *history*.   *Stephen Leacock*

All history is but the lengthened shadow of a great man.
Ralph Waldo Emerson

The history of the world is the record of a man in quest of his daily bread and butter.   *Hendrik Willem van Loon*

The historian looks backward. In the end he also believes backward.
Friedrich Nietzsche

Biography is history seen through the prism of a person.   *Louis Fischer*

The past is a work of art, free of irrelevancies and loose ends.
Max Beerbohm

Any event, once it has occurred, can be made to appear inevitable by a competent historian.   *Lee Simonson*

History is not another name for the past, as many people imply. It is the name for stories about the past.   *A. J. P. Taylor*

History is:
Fables agreed upon — *Voltaire*
The biography of a few stout and earnest persons — *Ralph Waldo Emerson*
A vast Mississippi of falsehood — *Matthew Arnold*
A confused heap of facts — *Lord Chesterfield*
A cyclic poem written by time upon the memories of man —
Percy Bysshe Shelley

With malice toward none, with charity for all, with firmness in the right as God gives us to see the right, let us strive on to finish the work we are in, to bind up the nation's wounds.
Abraham Lincoln, Second Inaugural Address

Give the historians something to write about.   *Propertius*

Societies that do not eat people are fascinated by those that do.
Ronald Wright

War makes rattling good history; but Peace is poor reading.
Thomas Hardy

The history of almost every civilization furnishes examples of geographical expansion coinciding with deterioration in quality.   *Arnold Toynbee*

History is past politics; and politics present history.   *John Seeley*

The first qualification for a historian is to have no ability to invent.
Stendhal

Whosoever, in writing a modern history, shall follow truth too near the heels,
it may haply strike out his teeth.   *Walter Raleigh*

One of the lessons of history is that nothing is often a good thing to do and
always a clever thing to say.   *Will Durant*

When great changes occur in history, when great principles are involved, as
a rule the majority are wrong.   *Eugene V. Debs*

More history's made by secret handshakes than by battles, bills and proclama-
tions.   *John Barth*

History: an account mostly false, of events, mostly unimportant, which are
brought about by rulers, mostly knaves, and soldiers, mostly fools.
Ambrose Bierce

The historical sense involves a perception, not only of the pastness of the
past, but of its presence.   *T. S. Eliot*

Truth is the only merit that gives dignity and worth to history.
Lord Acton

History is more or less bunk.   *Henry Ford*

I have no history but the length of my bones.   *Robin Skelton*

History is a pact between the dead, the living, and the yet unborn.
Edmund Burke

A people without history is like wind on the buffalo grass.
Sioux proverb

The function of posterity is to look after itself.   *Dylan Thomas*

The world's history is constant, like the laws of nature, and simple, like the
souls of men. The same conditions continually produce the same results.
Friedrich von Schiller

History is just the portrayal of crimes and misfortunes.   *Voltaire*

We should keep the Panama Canal. After all we stole it fair and square.
S. I. Hayakawa

The history of things that didn't happen has never been written.
Henry Kissinger

The memories of men are too frail a thread to hang history from.
John Still

All the ancient histories, as one of our wits has said, are but fables that have been agreed upon.
Voltaire

The rich experience of history teaches that up to now not a single class has voluntarily made way for another class.
Joseph Stalin

History is the science of what never happens twice.
Paul Valéry

Dictators ride to and fro on tigers from which they dare not dismount. And the tigers are getting hungry.
Winston Churchill

The Home

Home is not where you live but where they understand you.
Christian Morgenstern

Where thou art, that, is Home.
Emily Dickinson

Home is the place where, when you have to go there,
They have to take you in.
Robert Frost

A man builds a fine house; and now he has a master, and a task for life; he is to furnish, watch, show it, and keep it in repair the rest of his life.
Ralph Waldo Emerson

The strength of a nation, especially of a republican nation, is in the intelligent and well-ordered homes of the people.
Lydia Sigourney

Justice was born outside the home and a long way from it; and it has never been adopted there.
Walter Cronkite

The home of everyone is to him his castle and fortress, as well for his defence against injury and violence, as for his repose.
Edward Coke

Pride, avarice and envy are in every home.   *Thornton Wilder*

Of all modern notions, the worst is this: that domesticity is dull. Inside the home, they say, is dead decorum and routine; outside is adventure and variety. But the truth is that the home is the only place of liberty, the only spot on earth where a man can alter arrangements suddenly, make an experiment or indulge in a whim. The home is not the one tame place in a world of adventure; it is the one wild place in a world of rules and set tasks.

G. K. Chesterton

I have come back again to where I belong; not an enchanted place, but the walls are strong.   *Dorothy H. Rath*

To mankind in general Macbeth and Lady Macbeth stand out as the supreme type of all that a host and hostess should not be.   *Max Beerbohm*

The fellow that owns his own home is always just coming out of a hardware store.   *Kin Hubbard*

Homo Sapiens

We are only cave men who have lost their cave.   *Christopher Morley*

Every man is to be respected as an absolute end in himself: and it is a crime against the dignity that belongs to him as a human being, to use him as a mere means for some external purpose.   *Immanuel Kant*

The race of man, while sheep in credulity, are wolves for conformity.

Carl van Doren

Men are cruel, but man is kind.   *Rabindranath Tagore*

In this world, a man must either be anvil or hammer.

Henry Wadsworth Longfellow

I believe I've found the missing link between animal and civilized man. It is us.   *Konrad Lorenz*

A human being isn't an orchid, he must draw something from the soil he grows in.   *Sara Jeannette Duncan*

He was a man, take him for all in all, I shall not look upon his life again.
Shakespeare, 'Hamlet'

I am a member of the rabble in good standing.   *Westbrook Pegler*

The strongest human instinct is to impart information, the second strongest
is to resist it.   *Kenneth Graham*

Who is wise? He that learns from everyone.
Who is powerful? He that governs his passions.
Who is rich? He that is content.
Who is that? Nobody.   *Benjamin Franklin*

God made him, and therefore let him pass for a man.
Shakespeare, 'The Merchant of Venice'

Darwinian Man, though well-behaved,
At best is only a monkey shaved!   *W. S. Gilbert*

Each man is his own absolute lawgiver and dispenser of glory or gloom to
himself, the maker of his life, his reward, his punishment.   *Anon.*

Man is the only animal whose desires increase as they are fed; the only animal
that is never satisfied.   *Henry George*

Most people in action are not worth very much; and yet every human being
is an unprecedented miracle.   *James Baldwin*

People are too durable, that's their main trouble. They can do too much
to themselves, they last too long.   *Bertolt Brecht*

I believe that man will not merely endure: he will prevail. He is immortal,
not because he alone among creatures has an inexhaustible voice, but because
he has a soul, a spirit capable of compassion and sacrifice and endurance.
William Faulkner

A man is a kind of inverted thermometer, the bulb uppermost, and the column
of self-valuation is all the time going up and down.
Oliver Wendell Holmes

To be reborn is a constantly recurring human need.   *Henry Hewes*

Man's most valuable trait
Is a judicious sense of what not to believe.   *Euripides*

The natural man has only two primal passions: to get and to beget.
William Osler

A humanist is anyone who rejects the attempt to describe or account for man wholly on the basis of physics, chemistry or animal behaviour.
Joseph Wood Krutch

Man is a wanting animal — as soon as one of his needs is satisfied, another appears in its place. This process is unending. It continues from birth to death.
Douglas McGregor

The forgotten man. He is the clean, quiet, virtuous domestic citizen who pays his debts and his taxes and is never heard of outside his little circle. . . . He works, he votes, generally he prays, but his chief business in life is to pay.
William Graham Sumner

Limited in his nature, infinite in his desires, man is a fallen god who remembers heaven.
Alphonse de Lamartine

Man is a make-believe animal — he is never so truly himself as when he is acting a part.
William Hazlitt

Men must endure their going hence, even as their coming hither; ripeness is all.
Shakespeare, 'King Lear'

Every man in the world is better than someone else and not as good as someone else.
William Saroyan

The voice is a second signature.
R.I. Fitzhenry

It would hardly be possible to exaggerate man's wretchedness if it were not so easy to overestimate his sensibility.
George Santayana

Know then thyself, presume not God to scan:
The proper study of mankind is man.
Alexander Pope

Man, an animal that makes bargains.
Adam Smith

Man will ever stand in need of man.
Theocritus

Man is a reasoning, rather than a reasonable animal.
Robert B. Hamilton

We are members one of another.
Ephesians 4:25

Man is only a reed, the weakest thing in nature, but he is a thinking reed.
Blaise Pascal

Man is the only animal that laughs and weeps; for he is the only animal that is struck by the difference between what things are and what they might have been.   *William Hazlitt*

To her fair works did Nature link
The human soul that through me ran;
And much it grieved my heart to think
What Man has made of Man.   *William Wordsworth*

Admire, exult, despise, laugh, weep — for here
There is such matter for all feelings: — Man!
Thou pendulum betwixt a smile and tear.   *Lord Byron*

The dignity of man lies in his ability to face reality in all its meaninglessness.
Martin Esslin

If heaven made him, earth can find some use for him.   *Chinese proverb*

Everything in space obeys the laws of physics. If you know these laws, and obey them, space will treat you kindly. And don't tell me man doesn't belong out there. Man belongs wherever he wants to go — and he'll do plenty well when he gets there.   *Wernher von Braun*

An unlearned carpenter of my acquaintance once said in my hearing: 'There is very little difference between one man and another, but what there is is *very important.*'   *William James*

One of the laws of paleontology is that an animal which must protect itself with thick armour is degenerate. It is usually a sign that the species is on the road to extinction.   *John Steinbeck*

The Family of Man is more than three billion strong. It lives in more than one hundred nations. Most of its members are not white. Most of them are not Christians. Most of them know nothing about free enterprise, or due process of law, or the Australian ballot.   *John F. Kennedy*

Man is as full of potentiality as he is of impotence.   *George Santayana*

That man is an aggressive creature will hardly be disputed. With the exception of certain rodents, no other vertebrate habitually destroys members of its own species.   *Anthony Storr*

Every man is more than just himself; he also represents the unique, the very special and always significant and remarkable point at which the world's phenomena intersect, only once in this way, and never again.

Hermann Hesse

Every man is an impossibility until he is born.   *Ralph Waldo Emerson*

Man is a gaming animal. He must be always trying to get the better in something or other.   *Charles Lamb*

Man makes holy what he believes, as he makes beautiful what he loves.

Ernest Renan

Man is an abyss, and I turn giddy when I look down into it.

Georg Büchner

Honesty

It's better to be quotable than to be honest.   *Tom Stoppard*

Everybody has a little bit of Watergate in him.   *Billy Graham*

Of all feats of skill, the most difficult is that of being honest.

Comtesse Diane (Marie de Beausacq)

To be honest, one must be inconsistent.   *H.G. Wells*

He that resolves to deal with none but honest men, must leave off dealing.

Thomas Fuller

'Tis my opinion every man cheats in his way, and he is only honest who is not discovered.   *Susannah Centlivre*

There is one way to find out if a man is honest — ask him. If he says 'yes,' you know he is crooked.   *Groucho Marx*

The honester the man, the worse luck.   *John Ray*

Let none of us delude himself by supposing that honesty is always the best policy. It is not.   *William R. Inge*

Barring that natural expression of villainy which we all have, the man looked honest enough.   *Mark Twain*

Honesty's praised, then left to freeze.   *Juvenal*

Wealth makes everything easy — honesty most of all.
                    Comtesse Diane (Marie de Beausacq)

Honesty is as rare as a man without self-pity.   *Stephen Vincent Benét*

Every man has his fault, and honesty is his.
                    Shakespeare, 'Timon of Athens'

One must not cheat anybody, not even the world of one's triumph.
                    Franz Kafka

People who are brutally honest get more satisfaction out of the brutality than
out of the honesty.   *Richard J. Needham*

Anger cannot be dishonest.   *George R. Bach*

I'm frank, brutally frank. And even when I'm not frank, I look frank.
                    Lord Thomson of Fleet

The young man turned to him with a disarming candour, which instantly
put him on his guard.   *Saki*

A man should be careful never to tell tales of himself to his own disadvantage. People may be amused at the time, but they will be remembered, and
brought out against him upon some subsequent occasion.
                    Samuel Johnson

Being entirely honest with oneself is a good exercise.   *Sigmund Freud*

Honour

It is better to deserve honours and not have them than to have them and
not deserve them.   *Mark Twain*

A man has honour if he holds himself to an ideal of conduct though it is
inconvenient, unprofitable or dangerous to do so.   *Walter Lippmann*

The louder he talked of his honour, the faster we counted our spoons.
                    Ralph Waldo Emerson

Honour follows those who flee it.   *Anon.*

God sells knowledge for labour — honour for risk.   *Arabic proverb*

Fame is something which must be won; honour is something which must not be lost.   *Arthur Schopenhauer*

Dignity does not consist in possessing honours, but in deserving them.
                                                                    Aristotle

I could not love thee, dear, so much,
Loved I not honour more.   *Richard Lovelace*

Honour pricks me on. Yea, but how if honour prick me off when I come on? How then? Can honour set to a leg? No. Or an arm? No. Or take away the grief of a wound? No. Honour hath no skill in surgery, then? No. What is honour? A word.   *Shakespeare, 'Henry IV' Part I*

Would that . . . a sense of the true aim of life might elevate the tone of politics and trade till public and private honour become identical.
                                                              Margaret Fuller

No revenge is more honorable than the one not taken.   *Spanish proverb*

Hope

For what human ill does not dawn seem to be an alleviation?
                                                            Thornton Wilder

Hope is itself a species of happiness, and, perhaps, the chief happiness which this world affords.   *Samuel Johnson*

Hope, deceitful as it is, serves at least to lead us to the end of life along an agreeable road.   *La Rochefoucauld*

One need not hope in order to undertake; nor succeed in order to persevere.
                                                            William the Silent

Hope! of all ills that men endure
The only cheap and universal cure.   *Abraham Cowley*

Hope is the poor man's bread.   *George Herbert*

Hope springs eternal in the human breast;
Man never is, but always *to be* blest.   *Alexander Pope*

I suppose it can be truthfully said that hope is the only universal liar who
never loses his reputation for veracity.   *Robert G. Ingersoll*

Every thing that is done in the world is done by hope.   *Martin Luther*

Hope is a good breakfast, but it is a bad supper.   *Francis Bacon*

Man's many desires are like the small metal coins he carries about in his
pocket. The more he has the more they weight him down.
                                                      Satya Sai Baba

One of the best safeguards of our hopes, I have suggested, is to be able to
mark off the areas of hopelessness and to acknowledge them, to face them
directly, not with despair but with the creative intent of keeping them from
polluting all the areas of possibility.   *William F. Lynch*

The human body experiences a powerful gravitational pull in the direction
of hope. That is why the patient's hopes are the physician's secret weapon.
They are the hidden ingredients in any prescription.   *Norman Cousins*

Some one once said to me, 'Reverend Schuller, I hope you live to see all
your dreams fulfilled.' I replied, 'I hope not, because if I live and all my
dreams are fulfilled, I'm dead,' It's unfulfilled dreams that keep you alive.
                                                      Robert Schuller

The slow compromise, or even surrender, of our fondest hopes is a regular
feature of normal human life.   *Leston L. Havens*

Hope is an echo, hope ties itself yonder, yonder.   *Carl Sandburg*

'Hope' is the thing with feathers
That perches in the soul —
And sings the tune without words
And never stops — at all.   *Emily Dickinson*

Human Relations

Almost all of our relationships begin, and most of them continue, as forms
of mutual exploitation, a mental or physical barter, to be terminated when
one or both parties run out of goods.   *W. H. Auden*

When you meet anyone in the flesh you realize immediately that he is a human being and not a sort of caricature embodying certain ideas. It is partly for this reason that I don't mix much in literary circles, because I know from experience that once I have met and spoken to anyone I shall never again be able to feel any intellectual brutality towards him, even when I feel I ought to — like the Labour M.P.s who get patted on the back by dukes and are lost forever more.   *George Orwell*

The wisest man I have ever known once said to me: 'Nine out of every ten people improve on acquaintance,' and I have found his words true.
                                                   Frank Swinnerton

I am a part of all that I have met.   *Alfred, Lord Tennyson*

At the heart of our friendly or purely social relations, there lurks a hostility momentarily cured but recurring in fits and starts.   *Marcel Proust*

The worst sin towards our fellow creatures is not to hate them, but to be indifferent to them; that's the essence of inhumanity.
                                              George Bernard Shaw

We rarely confide in those who are better than we are.   *Albert Camus*

A sense of duty is useful in work, but offensive in personal relations. People wish to be liked, not be endured with patient resignation.
                                                   Bertrand Russell

The fact is that the possession of a highly social conscience about large-scale issues is no guarantee whatever of reasonable conduct in private relations.
                                                   Lewis Hastings

With three or more people there is something bold in the air: direct things get said which would frighten two people alone and conscious of each inch of their nearness to one another. To be three is to be in public — you feel safe.   *Elizabeth Bowen*

Acquaintance, n: a person whom we know well enough to borrow from, but not well enough to lend to.   *Ambrose Bierce*

In any relationship we feel an unconscious need to create, as it were, a new picture, a new edition of ourselves to present to the fresh person who claims our interest; for them, we in a strange sense wish to, and do, start life anew.
                                                   Ann N. Bridge

Make yourself necessary to somebody.   *Ralph Waldo Emerson*

Only the person who has faith in himself is able to be faithful to others.
Erich Fromm

We accept every person in the world as that for which he gives himself out only he must give himself out for something. We can put up with the unpleasant more easily than we can endure the insignificant.   *Goethe*

If someone below us does not treat us politely, we don't like anything he does. If, instead, we take a liking to someone, we forgive him anything he does.   *St. Francis de Sales*

Each of us keeps, battened down inside himself, a sort of lunatic giant — impossible socially, but full-scale. It's the knockings and batterings we sometimes hear in each other that keep our intercourse from utter banality.
Elizabeth Bowen

We should ever conduct ourselves towards our enemy as if he were one day to be our friend.   *Cardinal Newman*

We wander through this life together in a semi-darkness in which none of us can distinguish exactly the features of his neighbour. Only from time to time, through some experience that we have of our companion, or through some remark that he passes, he stands for a moment close to us, as though illuminated by a flash of lightning. Then we see him as he really is.
Albert Schweitzer

A loving person lives in a loving world. A hostile person lives in a hostile world: everyone you meet is your mirror.   *Ken Keyes, Jr.*

It is always safe to assume that people are more subtle and less sensitive than they seem.   *Eric Hoffer*

I was born modest; not all over, but in spots.   *Mark Twain*

A modest man is usually admired — if people ever hear of him.
Edgar Watson Howe

When the Quaker Penn kept his hat on in the royal presence, Charles (King Charles II) politely removed his, explaining that it was the custom in that place for only one person at a time to remain covered.   *Arthur Bryant*

If you treat men the way they are you never improve them. If you treat them the way you want them to be, you do.   *Goethe*

See everything: overlook a great deal: correct a little.   *Pope John XXIII*

The more you let yourself go, the less others let you go.
Friedrich Nietzsche

Do not do unto others as you would that they should do unto you. Their tastes may not be the same.   *George Bernard Shaw*

A hundred times every day I remind myself that my inner and outer life depend on the labours of other men, living and dead, and that I must exert myself in order to give in the same measure as I have received.
Albert Einstein

At bottom the world isn't a joke. We only joke about it to avoid an issue with someone, to let someone know that we know he's there with his questions; to disarm him by seeming to have heard and done justice to his side of the standing argument.   *Robert Frost*

I reckon there's as much human nature in some folks as there is in others, if not more.   *Edward Noyes Westcott*

If only there were evil people somewhere, insidiously committing evil deeds, and it were necessary only to separate them from the rest of us and destroy them. But the line dividing good and evil cuts through the heart of every human being. And who is willing to destroy a piece of his own heart?
Aleksandr Solzhenitsyn

Science may have found a cure for most evils: but it has found no remedy for the worst of them all — the apathy of human beings.   *Helen Keller*

The go-between wears out a thousand sandals.   *Japanese proverb*

Life is livable because we know that wherever we go most of the people we meet will be restrained in their actions toward us by an almost instinctive network of taboos.   *Havelock Ellis*

I was taught when I was young that if people would only love one another, all would be well with the world. This seemed simple and very nice; but I found when I tried to put it in practice not only that other people were seldom lovable, but that I was not very lovable myself.   *George Bernard Shaw*

It is well to remember that the entire population of the universe, with one trifling exception, is composed of others.   *John Andrew Holmes*

Our concern is not how to worship in the catacombs but how to remain human in the skyscrapers.   *Abraham J. Heschel*

Humour and Humorists

He that jokes confesses.
                                                        Italian proverb

There are things of deadly earnest that can only be safely mentioned under cover of a joke.
                                                        J. J. Procter

Humour is the only test of gravity, and gravity of humour, for a subject which will not bear raillery is suspicious, and a jest which will not bear serious examination is false wit.
                                                        Aristotle

The sadness in legitimate humour consists in the fact that honestly, and without deceit, it reflects in a purely human way upon what it is to be a child.
                                                        Søren Kierkegaard

Everything is funny as long as it is happening to somebody else.
                                                        Will Rogers

A satirist is a man who discoves unpleasant things about himself and then says them about other people.
                                                        Peter McArthur

Humour is emotional chaos remembered in tranquillity.   *James Thurber*

The best definition of humour I know is: humour may be defined as the kindly contemplation of the incongruities of life, and the artistic expression thereof. I think this is the best I know because I wrote it myself.
                                                        Stephen Leacock

A humorist is a man who feels bad but who feels good about it.
                                                        Don Herold

Humour plays close to the big, hot fire, which is the truth, and the reader feels the heat.
                                                        E.B. White

Wit is the only wall
Between us and the dark.
                                                        Mark Van Doren

Look at Jewish history. Unrelieved lamenting would be intolerable. So, for every ten Jews beating their breasts, God designated one to be crazy and amuse the breast-beaters. By the time I was five I knew I was that one.
                                                        Mel Brooks

Mirthfulness is in the mind and you cannot get it out. It is just as good in its place as conscience or veneration.   *Henry Ward Beecher*

Novelist Peter de Vries, like Adlai Stevenson and Mark Twain, has suffered from the American assumption that anyone with a sense of humour is not to be taken seriously.   *Timothy Foote*

Humour can be dissected, as a frog can, but the thing dies in the process.
E.B. White

Humour is the contemplation of the finite from the point of view of the infinite.   *Christian Morgenstern*

The total absence of humour from the Bible is one of the most singular things in all literature.   *Alfred North Whitehead*

Laughter is the closest thing to the grace of God.   *Karl Barth*

Humour is richly rewarding to the person who employs it. It has some value in gaining and holding attention. But it has no persuasive value at all.
J.K. Galbraith

Humour is the most engaging cowardice. With it myself I have been able to hold some of my enemy in play far out of gunshot.   *Robert Frost*

A comedian is a fellow who finds other comedians too humorous to mention.
Jack Herbert

It it's sanity you're after
There's no recipe like
Laughter.
Laugh it off.   *Henry Rutherford Elliot*

Humour is an affirmation of dignity, a declaration of man's superiority to all that befalls him.   *Romain Gary*

Comedy is simply a funny way of being serious.   *Peter Ustinov*

Comedy is tragedy — plus time.   *Carol Burnett*

Caricature: putting the face of a joke upon the body of a truth.
Joseph Conrad

The ability to laugh at life is right at the top, with love and communication, in the hierarchy of our needs. Humour has much to do with pain; it exaggerates the anxieties and absurdities we feel, so that we gain distance and through laughter, relief.   *Sara Davidson*

He deserves paradise who makes his companions laugh.   *The Koran*

Laughter is the shortest distance between two people.   *Victor Borge*

You encourage a comic man too much, and he gets silly.
Stephen Leacock

Any man will admit if need be that his sight is not good, or that he cannot swim or shoots badly with a rifle, but to touch upon his sense of humour is to give him mortal affront.   *Stephen Leacock*

Anything awful makes me laugh. I misbehaved once at a funeral.
Charles Lamb

Wit is far more often a shield than a lance.   *Anon.*

If there's anything I hate it's the word humorist — I feel like countering with the word seriousist.   *Peter de Vries*

A jest's prosperity lies in the ear
Of him that hears it, never in the tongue
Of him that makes it.   *Shakespeare, 'Love's Labour's Lost'*

Nonsense is an assertion of man's spiritual freedom in spite of all the oppressions of circumstance.   *Aldous Huxley*

Humour is just another defence against the universe.   *Mel Brooks*

The great humorist forgets himself in his delighted contemplation of other people.   *Douglas Bush*

The role of a comedian is to make the audience laugh, at a minimum of once every fifteen seconds.   *Lenny Bruce*

Laughter is the sensation of feeling good all over, and showing it principally in one spot.   *Josh Billings*

He who laughs, lasts.   *Anon.*

We are all here for a spell, get all the good laughs you can.   *Will Rogers*

No one is more profoundly sad than he who laughs too much.
Jean Paul Richter

A joke is an epigram on the death of a feeling.   *Friedrich Nietzsche*

One loses so many laughs by not laughing at oneself.
                                                  Sara Jeannette Duncan

Charles Dickens' creation of Mr. Pickwick did more for the elevation of the human race — I say it in all seriousness — than Cardinal Newman's *Lead Kindly Light Amid the Encircling Gloom*. Newman only cried out for light in the gloom of a sad world. Dickens gave it.   *Stephen Leacock*

The love of truth lies at the root of much humour.   *Robertson Davies*

You can pretend to be serious, but you can't pretend to be witty.
                                                              Sacha Guitry

Hypocrisy

Hypocrisy is the homage which vice pays to virture.   *La Rochefoucauld*

He that hath the name to be an early riser may sleep till noon.
                                                              James Howell

We are not hypocrites in our sleep.   *William Hazlitt*

No man is a hypocrite in his pleasures.   *Samuel Johnson*

The wolf was sick, he vowed a monk to be;
But when he got well, a wolf once more was he.   *Walter Bower*

Remember this: If you work for a man, in Heaven's name, work for him. If he pays you wages which supply you bread and butter, work for him; speak well of him; stand by the institution he represents. If put to a pinch, an ounce of loyalty is worth a pound of cleverness. If you must vilify, condemn and eternally disparage — resign your position, and when you are on the outside, damn to your heart's content, but as long as you are part of the institution do not condemn it.   *Elbert Hubbard*

For neither man nor angel can discern hypocrisy, the only evil that walks invisible.   *John Milton*

The teeth are smiling, but is the heart?   *Congo proverb*

Affectation is a greater enemy to the face than smallpox.
                                                            English proverb

It is a trick among the dishonest to offer sacrifices that are not needed, or not possible, to avoid making those that are required.   *Ivan Goncharov*

When you say that you agree to a thing in principle, you mean that you have not the slightest intention of carrying it out.   *Otto von Bismarck*

An appeaser is one who feeds a crocodile — hoping it will eat him last.
Winston Churchill

There is luxury in self-reproach. When we blame ourselves we feel that no one else has the right to blame us.   *Oscar Wilde*

Extremes meet, and there is no better example than the naughtiness of humility.   *Ralph Waldo Emerson*

Hypocrite — mouth one way, belly 'nother way.
Australian Aboriginal proverb

When the fox preaches, look to your geese.   *German proverb*

I hope you have not been leading a double life, pretending to be wicked and being really good all the time. That would be hypocrisy.   *Oscar Wilde*

Reasons are whores.   *Leonard Michaels*

Ideas

To say that an idea is fashionable is to say, I think, that it has been adulterated to a point where it is hardly an idea at all.   *Murray Kempton*

Great ideas are not charitable.   *Henry de Montherlant*

You cannot put a rope around the neck of an idea: you cannot put an idea up against a barrack-square wall and riddle it with bullets: you cannot confine it in the strongest prison cell that your slaves could ever build.
Sean O'Casey

For an idea ever to be fashionable is ominous, since it must afterwards be always old-fashioned.   *George Santayana*

Every man with an idea has at least two or three followers.
Brooks Atkinson

An idea is a feat of association, and the height of it is a good metaphor.
Robert Frost

Every time a man puts a new idea across he finds ten men who thought of it before he did — but they only thought of it. *Anon.*

There is no adequate defence, except stupidity, against the impact of a new idea. *Percy W. Bridgman*

No army can withstand the strength of an idea whose time has come.
Victor Hugo

Man's mind stretched to a new idea never goes back to its original dimensions.
Oliver Wendell Holmes

Ideas won't keep: something must be done about them.
Alfred North Whitehead

I played with an idea, and grew wilful; tossed it into the air and transformed it; let is escape and recaptured it; made it iridescent with fancy, and winged it with paradox. *Oscar Wilde*

Ideas, as distinguished from events, are never unprecedented.
Hannah Arendt

What's a cult? It just means not enough people to make a minority.
Robert Altman

A cold in the head causes less suffering than an idea. *Jules Renard*

Very simple ideas lie within the reach only of complex minds.
Remy de Gourmont

An idea is salvation by imagination. *Frank Lloyd Wright*

Only the wise possess ideas; the greater part of mankind are possessed by them. *Samuel Taylor Coleridge*

Big ideas are so hard to recognize, so fragile, so easy to kill. Don't forget that, all of you who don't have them. *John Elliott, Jr.*

Idleness

It is no rest to be idle.   *Paul Peel*

It is impossible to enjoy idling thoroughly unless one has plenty of work to do.   *Jerome K. Jerome*

There is less leisure now than in the Middle Ages, when one third of the year consisted of holidays and festivals.   *Ralph Borsodi*

Any fool can be fussy and rid himself of energy all over the place, but a man has to have something in him before he can settle down to do nothing.
J.B. Priestley

Extreme busyness, whether at school, or college, kirk or market, is a symptom of deficient vitality; and a faculty for idleness implies a catholic appetite and a strong sense of personal identity.   *Robert Louis Stevenson*

The hardest work is to go idle.   *Jewish proverb*

Of all our faults, the one that we excuse most easily is idleness.
La Rochefoucauld

Idleness, like kisses, to be sweet must be stolen.   *Jerome K. Jerome*

With enough 'ifs' we could put Paris into a bottle.   *French proverb*

We are lazier in our minds than in our bodies.   *La Rochefoucauld*

Nothing is so intolerable to man as being fully at rest, without passion, without business, without entertainment, without care. It is then that he recognizes that he is empty, insufficient, dependent, ineffectual. From the depths of his soul now comes at once boredom, gloom, sorrow, chagrin, resentment and despair.   *Blaise Pascal*

He is idle that might be better employed.   *Thomas Fuller*

Nine-tenths of the miseries and vices of mankind proceed from idleness.
Thomas Carlyle

Even if a farmer intends to loaf, he gets up in time to get an early start.
Edgar Watson Howe

Did nothing in particular, and did it very well.   *W. S. Gilbert*

If a soldier or labourer complains of the hardship of his lot, set him to do nothing.   *Blaise Pascal*

How beautiful it is to do nothing, and then rest afterward.
                                                          Spanish proverb

Ignorance

The trouble ain't that people are ignorant: it's that they know so much that ain't so.   *Josh Billings*

There is nothing more frightening than ignorance in action.   *Goethe*

When an idea is wanting, a word can always be found to take its place.
                                                          Goethe

If ignorance is indeed bliss, it is a very low grade of the article.
                                                          Tehyi Hsieh

Not ignorance, but ignorance of ignorance is the death of knowledge.
                                                          Alfred North Whitehead

Ignoramus: a person unacquainted with certain kinds of knowledge familiar to yourself, and having certain other kinds that you know nothing about.
                                                          Ambrose Bierce

Ignorance is no excuse, it's the real thing.   *Irene Peter*

The good Lord set definite limits on man's wisdom, but set no limits on his stupidity — and that's just not fair.   *Konrad Adenauer*

Everybody is ignorant, only on different subjects.   *Will Rogers*

A weak mind does not accumulate force enough to hurt itself; stupidity often saves a man from going mad.   *Oliver Wendell Holmes*

Idiot, n: a member of a large and powerful tribe whose influence in human affairs has always been dominant and controlling.   *Ambrose Bierce*

Little wit in the head makes much work for the feet.   *Anon.*

I am not ashamed to confess that I am ignorant of what I do not know.
                                                          Cicero

all ignorance toboggans into know
and trudges up to ignorance again. *e. e. cummings*

The little I know, I owe to my ignorance. *Sacha Guitry*

It is a blind goose that cometh to the fox's sermon. *John Lyly*

And here, poor fool, with all my lore,
I stand no wiser than before. *Goethe*

Illusion

Nothing is more sad than the death of an illusion. *Arthur Koestler*

As I was going up the stair
I met a man who wasn't there.
He wasn't there again today.
I wish, I wish, he'd stay away. *Hughes Mearns*

The task of the real intellectual consists of analyzing illusions in order to discover their causes. *Arthur Miller*

An illusion which makes me happy is worth a verity which drags me to the ground. *Christoph Martin-Wieland*

We must select the illusion which appeals to our temperament, and embrace it with passion, if we want to be happy. *Cyril Connolly*

Winston Churchill is always expecting rabbits to come out of an empty hat. *Field Marshall Lord Wavell*

Reputation is an idle and most false imposition; oft got without merit, and lost without deserving. *Shakespeare, 'Othello'*

Every real object must cease to be what it seemed and none could ever be what the whole soul desired. *George Santayana*

Aspects are within us, and who seems most kingly is king. *Thomas Hardy*

Those who lose dreaming are lost. *Australian Aboriginal proverb*

It is dangerous to let the public behind the scenes. They are easily disillusioned and then they are angry with you, for it was the illusion they loved.
W. Somerset Maugham

Imagination

Were it not for imagination, a man would be as happy in the arms of a chambermaid as of a duchess.   *Samuel Johnson*

Imagination grows by exercise, and contrary to common belief, is more powerful in the mature than in the young.   *W. Somerset Maugham*

The imagination of a boy is healthy, and the mature imagination of a man is healthy, but there is a space of life between, in which the soul is in ferment, the character undecided, the way of life uncertain.   *John Keats*

His imagination resembled the wings of an ostrich. It enabled him to run, though not to soar.   *Thomas Babington Macaulay (of John Dryden)*

Imagination is the eye of the soul.   *Joseph Joubert*

Imagination is a poor substitute for experience.   *Havelock Ellis*

Imagination frames events unknown,
In wild, fantastic shapes of hideous ruin,
And what it fears, creates.   *Hannah More*

Reason respects the differences, and imagination the similitudes of things.
Percy Bysshe Shelley

The sky is the daily bread of the eyes.   *Ralph Waldo Emerson*

Let us leave pretty women to men without imagination.   *Marcel Proust*

To make a prairie it takes clover and one bee
one clover, and a bee,
and revery
The revery alone will do,
if bees are few.   *Emily Dickinson*

The value of a sentiment is the amount of sacrifice you are prepared to make for it.   *John Galsworthy*

It is good to know the truth, but it is better to speak of palm trees.
Arabic proverb

Imitation

When people are free to do as they please, they usually imitate each other.
Eric Hoffer

Almost all absurdity of conduct arises from the imitation of those whom we cannot resemble.   *Samuel Johnson*

There is a difference between imitating a good man and counterfeiting him.
Benjamin Franklin

Every man is a borrower and a mimic; life is theatrical and literature a quotation.   *Ralph Waldo Emerson*

We do not imitate, but are a model to others.   *Pericles*

The crow that mimics a cormorant gets drowned.   *Japanese proverb*

We love in others what we lack ourselves, and would be everything but what we are.   *R.H. Stoddard*

Immature poets imitate: mature poets steal.   *Philip Massinger*

Agesilaus, the Spartan king, was once invited to hear a mimic imitate the nightingale, but declined with the comment that he had heard the nightingale itself.   *Plutarch*

Fewer things are harder to put up with than the annoyance of a good example.
Mark Twain

Indifference and Apathy

Lack of something to feel important about is almost the greatest tragedy a man may have.   *Arthur E. Morgan*

There is nothing harder than the softness of indifference.
Juan Montalvo

Communists have committed great crimes, but at least they have not stood aside, like an established society, and been indifferent. I would rather have blood on my hands than water, like Pilate. *Graham Greene*

Hate is not the opposite of love; apathy is. *Rollo May*

The hottest places in hell are reserved for those who, in time of great moral crisis, maintain their neutrality. *Dante*

What makes life dreary is want of motive. *George Eliot*

Once conform, once do what others do because they do it, and a kind of lethargy steals over all the finer senses of the soul. *Montaigne*

Not to he who is offensive to us are we most unfair, but to he who does not concern us at all. *Friedrich Nietzsche*

Most of us have no real loves and no real hatreds. Blessed is love, less blessed is hatred, but thrice accursed is that indifference which is neither one nor the other. *Mark Rutherford*

The only menace is inertia. *St. John Perse*

Tolerance is a tremendous virtue, but the immediate neighbours of tolerance are apathy and weakness. *Sir James Goldsmith*

The true opposite of love is not hate but indifference. Hate, bad as it is, at least treats the neighbour as a thou, whereas indifference turns the neighbour into an it, a thing. This is why we may say that there is actually one thing worse than evil itself and that is indifference to evil. In human relations the nadir of morality, the lowest point as far as Christian ethics is concerned, is manifest in the phrase, 'I couldn't care less.' *Joseph Fletcher*

If moderation is a fault, then indifference is a crime. *G.C. Lichtenberg*

Indifference may not wreck a man's life at any one turn, but it will destroy him with a kind of dry-rot in the long run. *Bliss Carman*

Innocence

The truly innocent are those who not only are guiltless themselves, but who think others are. *Josh Billings*

The innocent is the person who explains nothing.   *Albert Camus*

Whoever blushes is already guilty; true innocence is ashamed of nothing.
Jean-Jacques Rousseau

Through our own recovered innocence we discern the innocence of our
neighbours.   *Henry David Thoreau*

As innocent as a new-laid egg.   *W. S. Gilbert*

Had laws not been, we never had been blam'd;
For not to know we sinn'd is innocence.   *William Davenant*

Good is when I steal other people's wives and cattle; bad is when they steal
mine.   *Hottentot proverb*

Insults and Calumny

Be thou as chaste as ice, as pure as snow, thou shalt not escape calumny.
Shakespeare, 'Hamlet'

A fly, Sir, may sting a stately horse and make him wince; but one is but
an insect, and the other a horse still.   *Samuel Johnson*

Calumny is only the noise of madmen.   *Diogenes*

To persevere in one's duty and be silent, is the best answer to calumny.
George Washington

Woe unto you, when all men shall speak well of you.   *Luke 6:26*

Young men soon give, and soon forget affronts,
Old age is slow in both.   *Joseph Addison*

As long as there are readers to be delighted with calumny, there will be found
reviewers to calumniate.   *Samuel Taylor Coleridge*

He that flings dirt at another dirtieth himself most.   *Thomas Fuller*

It takes your enemy and your friend, working together to hurt you to the heart; the one to slander you and the other to get the news to you.

Mark Twain

Calumny requires no proof. The throwing out of malicious imputations against any character leaves a stain which no after-refutation can wipe out. To create an unfavourable impression, it is not necessary that certain things should be true, but that they have been said.   *William Hazlitt*

It is often better not to see an insult, than to avenge it.   *Seneca*

Abuse a man unjustly, and you will make friends for him.

Edgar Watson Howe

One of the surest signs of the Philistine is his reverence for the superior tastes of those who put him down.   *Pauline Kael*

Alive, ridiculous, and dead forgot?   *Alexander Pope*

Intellect

All zeal runs down. What replaces it? Intellectualism.

Arthur R.M. Lower

Will and intellect are one and the same thing.   *Benedict Spinoza*

We should take care not to make the intellect our god; it has, of course, powerful muscles, but no personality.   *Albert Einstein*

The highest intellects, like the tops of mountains, are the first to catch and to reflect the dawn.   *Thomas Babington Macaulay*

An intellectual is someone whose mind watches itself.   *Albert Camus*

I hate intellectuals. They are from the top down. I am from the bottom up.

Frank Lloyd Wright

Think sideways!   *Edward de Bono*

A conclusion is the place where you got tired of thinking.   *Arthur Bloch*

The brain is the citadel of sense perception.   *Pliny the Elder*

My body has certainly wandered a good deal, but I have an uneasy suspicion that my mind has not wandered enough. *Noel Coward*

There are innumerable instances suggesting that modern intellectuals do not believe themselves, that they don't really believe what they say, that they say certain things only in order to asure themselves that they possess opinions and ideas that are different from those that are entertained by the common herd of men. *John Lukacs*

Intuition is a spiritual faculty and does not explain, but simply points the way. *Florence Scovel Shinn*

The intellect of man is forced to choose
Perfection of the life or of the work. *William Butler Yeats*

An intellectual is a man who takes more words than necessary to tell more than he knows. *Dwight D. Eisenhower*

The common sense is that which judges the things given to it by other senses. *Leonardo da Vinci*

Intelligence

Time has a way of demonstrating . . . the most stubborn are the most intelligent. *Yevgeny Yevtushenko*

Intelligence must follow faith, never precede it, and never destroy it. *Thomas à Kempis*

Intelligence is derived from two words — *inter* and *legere* — *inter* meaning 'between' and *legere* meaning 'to choose.' An intelligent person, therefore, is one who has learned 'to choose between.' He knows that good is better than evil, that confidence should supersede fear, that love is superior to hate, that gentleness is better than cruelty, forbearance than intolerance, compassion than arrogance, and that truth has more virtue than ignorance. *J. Martin Klotsche*

One of the functions of intelligence is to take account of the dangers that come from trusting solely to the intelligence. *Lewis Mumford*

The intelligent man who is proud of his intelligence is like the condemned man who is proud of his large cell. *Simone Weil*

The sign of an intelligent people is their ability to control emotions by the application of reason.   *Marya Mannes*

Intelligence is quickness in seeing things as they are.   *George Santayana*

Never tell people how to do things. Tell them what to do and they will surprise you with their ingenuity.   *George S. Patton*

I not only use all the brains I have, but all I can borrow.
                                                            Woodrow Wilson

Intelligence is not all that important in the exercise of power and is often, in point of fact, useless. Just as a leader doesn't need intelligence, a man in my job doesn't need too much of it either.   *Henry Kissinger*

The cuckoo who is on to himself is halfway out of the clock.
                                                            Wilson Mizner

I've had a lot of experience with people smarter than I am. *Gerald Ford*

Justice

Injustice is relatively easy to bear; what stings is justice. *H. L. Mencken*

Men are not hanged for stealing horses, but that horses may not be stolen.
                                                        George, Lord Halifax

A fox should not be on the jury at a goose's trial.   *Thomas Fuller*

Thwackum was for doing justice, and leaving mercy to heaven.
                                                            Henry Fielding

The Court's authority — possessed of neither the purse nor the sword — ultimately rests on substantial public confidence in its moral sanctions.
                                                            Felix Frankfurter

Charity is no substitute for justice withheld.   *St. Augustine*

I would remind you that extremism in the defence of liberty is no vice. And let me remind you also that moderation in the pursuit of justice is no virtue.   *Barry Goldwater*

Ne'er of the living can the living judge —
Too blind the affection, or too fresh the grudge.   *Anon.*

I always felt from the beginning that you had to defend people you disliked
and feared as well as those you admired.   *Roger Baldwin*

This is a court of law, young man, not a court of justice.
Oliver Wendell Holmes, Jr.

The whole history of the world is summed up in the fact that, when nations
are strong, they are not always just, and when they wish to be just, they are
no longer strong.   *Winston Churchill*

Nobody is poor unless he stand in need of justice.   *Lactantius*

The hungry judges soon the sentence sign,
And wretches hang that jurymen may dine.   *Alexander Pope*

There is no such thing as justice — in or out of court. *Clarence Darrow*

Justice is too good for some people, and not good enough for the rest.
Norman Douglas

Injustice never rules forever.   *Seneca*

Acquittal of the guilty damns the judge.   *Horace*

Knowledge

Our knowledge is a receding mirage in an expanding desert of ignorance.
Will Durant

Knowledge is of two kinds; we know a subject ourselves, or we know where
we can find information upon it.   *Samuel Johnson*

As we acquire more knowledge, things do not become more comprehensi-
ble, but more mysterious.   *Albert Schweitzer*

A man must carry knowledge with him, if he would bring home knowledge.
Samuel Johnson

Grace is given of God, but knowledge is bought in the market.
Arthur Hugh Clough

If a little knowledge is dangerous — where is the man who has so much as to be out of danger?
Thomas Huxley

We owe almost all our knowledge not to those who have agreed, but to those who have differed.
Charles Caleb Colton

Sit down before fact as a little child, be prepared to give up every preconceived notion, follow humbly wherever and to whatever abyss nature leads, or you shall learn nothing.
Thomas Huxley

The learned is happy, nature to explore,
The fool is happy, that he knows no more.
Alexander Pope

One of the greatest joys known to man is to take a flight into ignorance in search of knowledge.
Robert Lynd

I do not pretend to know what many ignorant men are sure of.
Clarence Darrow

A man only understands what is akin to something already existing in himself.
Henri Frédéric Amiel

Everybody gets so much common information all day long that they lose their common sense.
Gertrude Stein

Anyone who stops learning is old, whether at twenty or eighty. Anyone who keeps learning stays young. The greatest thing in life is to keep your mind young.
Henry Ford

The first problem for all of us, men and women, is not to learn, but to unlearn.
Gloria Steinem

We should live and learn; but by the time we've learned, it's too late to live.
Carolyn Wells

The specialist is a man who fears the other subjects.
Martin H. Fisher

All that men really understand is confined to a very small compass; to their daily affairs and experience; to what they have an opportunity to know; and motives to study or practise. The rest is affectation and imposture.
William Hazlitt

There is much pleasure to be gained from useless knowledge.

Bertrand Russell

Every great advance in natural knowledge has involved the absolute rejection of authority.

Thomas Huxley

Many shall run to and fro, and knowledge shall be increased.

Daniel 12:4

It isn't what we don't know that gives us trouble, it's what we know that ain't so.

Will Rogers

In all affairs, love, religion, politics or business, it's a healthy idea, now and then, to hang a question mark on things you have long taken for granted.

Bertrand Russell

Knowledge is power.

Francis Bacon

Man is not weak — knowledge is more than equivalent to force. The master of mechanics laughs at strength.

Samuel Johnson

I have taken all knowledge to be my province.

Francis Bacon

To know that we know what we know, and that we do not know what we do not know, that is true knowledge.

Henry David Thoreau

The simplest questions are the hardest to answer.

Northrop Frye

They know enough who know how to learn.

Henry Adams

Law and Lawyers

Law . . . begins when someone takes to doing something someone else does not like.

Karl Llewellyn

Any fool can make a rule, and every fool will mind it.

Anon.

Show me the man and I'll show you the law.

David Ferguson

A man may as well open an oyster without a knife, as a lawyer's mouth without a fee.

Barten Holyday

When you have no basis for an argument, abuse the plaintiff.   *Cicero*

No matter whether the Constitution follows the flag or not, the Supreme Court follows the election returns.   *Finley Peter Dunne*

The adversary system is a kind of warfare in mufti.   *R. I. Fitzhenry*

A jury consists of twelve persons chosen to decide who has the better lawyer.
Robert Frost

Lawyers are men who hire out their words and anger.   *Martial*

Litigant: a person about to give up his skin for the hope of retaining his bone.
Ambrose Bierce

In America, an acquittal doesn't mean you're innocent, it means you beat the rap. My clients lose even when they win.   *F. Lee Bailey*

Law and order is one of the steps taken to maintain injustice.
Edward Bond

Whatever is enforced by command is more imputed to him who exacts than to him who performs.   *Montaigne*

The life of the law has not been logic: it has been experience.
Oliver Wendell Holmes, Jr.

Every new time will give its law.   *Maxim Gorky*

Lawyers and painters can soon change white to black.
Danish proverb

No man is above the law and no man is below it: nor do we ask any man's permission when we ask him to obey it.   *Theodore Roosevelt*

Fragile as reason is and limited as law is as the institutionalized medium of reason, that's all we have standing between us and the tyranny of mere will and the cruelty of unbridled, undisciplined feeling.   *Felix Frankfurter*

A lawyer's dream of heaven — every man reclaimed his property at the resurrection, and each tried to recover it from all his forefathers.
Samuel Butler

A vague uneasiness; the police. It's like when you suddenly understand you have to undress in front of the doctor.   *Ugo Betti*

Those who are too lazy and comfortable to think for themselves and be their own judges obey the laws. Others sense their own laws within them.

Hermann Hesse

Every skilled person is to be believed with reference to his own art.

Legal maxim

An excess of law inescapably weakens the rule of law.

Laurence H. Tribe

A judge is a law student who marks his own examination papers.

H. L. Mencken

A successful lawsuit is the one worn by a policeman. *Robert Frost*

I understand you undertake to overthrow my undertaking.

Gertrude Stein

The law locks up both man and woman
Who steals the goose from off the common,
But lets the great felon loose
Who steals the common from the goose. *Anon.*

I know of no method to secure the repeal of bad or obnoxious laws so effective as their stringent execution. *Ulysses S. Grant*

Law school taught me one thing: how to take two situations that are exactly the same and show how they are different. *Hart Pomerantz*

To some lawyers, all facts are created equal. *Felix Frankfurter*

And whether you're an honest man, or whether you're a thief,
Depends on whose solicitor has given me my brief. *W. S. Gilbert*

The law, in its majestic equality, forbids the rich as well as the poor to sleep under bridges, to beg in the streets, and to steal bread. *Anatole France*

In cross-examination, as in fishing, nothing is more ungainly than a fisherman pulled into the water by his catch. *Louis Nizer*

Well, I don't know as I want a lawyer to tell me what I cannot do. I hire him to tell me how to do what I want to do. *J. P. Morgan*

The law must be stable and yet it must not stand still. *Roscoe Pound*

An appeal is when ye ask wan court to show its contempt for another court.
Finley Peter Dunne

Law is nothing unless close behind it stands a warm, living public opinion.
Wendell Phillips

If there were no bad people, there would be no good lawyers.
Charles Dickens

The aim of law is the maximum gratification of the nervous system of man.
Learned Hand

Laws, like the spider's web, catch the fly and let the hawk go free.
Spanish proverb

Laziness

The lazy man gets round the sun as quickly as the busy one.
R. T. Wombat

It is the just doom of laziness and a gluttony to be inactive without ease, and drowsy without tranquillity.　*Samuel Johnson*

Tomorrow is often the busiest day of the year.　*Spanish proverb*

The lazy are always wanting to do something.　*Vauvenargues*

Some folks can look so busy doing nothin' that they seem indispensable.
Kin Hubbard

Indolence is a delightful but distressing state. We must be doing something to be happy.　*William Hazlitt*

Failure is not our only punishment for laziness: there is also the success of others.　*Jules Renard*

Leaders and Leadership

Achilles absent, was Achilles still.　*Homer*

To lead the people, walk behind them.　*Lao-Tzu*

When you come into the presence of a leader of men, you know that you have come into the presence of fire — that it is best not uncautiously to touch that man — that there is something that makes it dangerous to cross him.
Woodrow Wilson

I've got to follow them — I am their leader. *Alexandre Ledru-Rollin*

The reward of a general is not a bigger tent — but command.
Oliver Wendell Holmes, Jr.

A leader may symbolize and express what is best in his people, like Pericles, or what is worst, like Hitler, but he cannot successfully express what is only in his heart and not in theirs. *Charles Yost*

A true leader always keeps an element of surprise up his sleeve, which others cannot grasp but which keeps his public excited and breathless.
Charles de Gaulle

If I advance, follow me! If I retreat, kill me! If I die, avenge me!
La Rochejaquelin

If I advance, follow me! If I retreat, cut me down! If I die, avenge me!
Mussolini

Follow me, if I advance; kill me if I retreat; revenge me if I die!
Ngo Dinh Diem (on becoming President of Vietnam)

I suppose leadership at one time meant muscles; but today it means getting along with people. *Indira Gandhi*

A frightened captain makes a frightened crew. *Lister Sinclair*

As for the best leaders, the people do not notice their existence. The next best, the people honour and praise. The next, the people fear, and the next the people hate. When the best leader's work is done, the people say, 'we did it ourselves!' *Lao-Tzu*

The slave begins by demanding justice and ends by wanting to wear a crown. He must dominate in his turn. *Albert Camus*

A leader is a dealer in hope. *Napoleon Bonaparte*

To lead means to direct and to exact, and no man dares do either — he might be unpopular. What authority we are given now is a trinity: the grin, the generality, and God (the Word). *Marya Mannes*

Dictators are rulers who always look good until the last ten minutes.
Jan Masaryk

A chief is a man who assumes responsibility. He says, 'I was beaten,' he does not say 'My men were beaten.' *Antoine de Saint-Exupéry*

Every man of action has a strong dose of egotism, pride, hardness and cunning. But all those things will be forgiven him, indeed, they will be regarded as high qualities, if he can make them the means to achieve great ends.
Charles de Gaulle

Why don't you show us a statesman who can rise up to the emergency, and cave in the emergency's head? *Artemus Ward*

Dictators ride to and fro upon tigers from which they dare not dismount.
Hindu proverb

I have no family. My only responsibility is the welfare of Quebec. I belong to the province. *Maurice Duplessis*

It is better to have a lion at the head of an army of sheep, than a sheep at the head of an army of lions. *Daniel Defoe*

Where there are no tigers, a wildcat is very self-important. *Korean proverb*

'Ah, John A., John A., how I love you! How I wish I could trust you!
Liberal politician

I really believe my greatest service is in the many unwise steps I prevent.
William Lyon Mackenzie King

I have nothing to offer but blood, toil, sweat and tears. *Winston Churchill*

I have never accepted what many people have kindly said, namely that I have inspired the nation. It was the nation and the race dwelling all around the globe that had the lion heart. I had the luck to be called upon to give the roar. *Winston Churchill*

Winston has written four volumes about himself and called it 'World Crisis.'
Arthur Balfour

Winston Churchill — fifty per cent genius, fifty per cent bloody fool.
Clement Atlee

If you shoot at a king you must kill him. *Ralph Waldo Emerson*

The final test of a leader is that he leaves behind in other men the conviction and the will to carry on.   *Walter Lippmann*

In Pierre Elliott Trudeau, Canada has at last produced a political leader worthy of assassination.   *Irving Layton*

Every woman's man, and every man's woman.
            Said to be the elder Curio's description of Julius Caesar

Liars and Lying

Truth is the safest lie.   *Jewish proverb*

All men are born truthful, and die liars.   *Vauvenargues*

The lie is a condition of life.   *Friedrich Nietzsche*

It takes a wise man to handle a lie. A fool had better remain honest.
                                                          Norman Douglas

We pay a person the compliment of acknowledging his superiority whenever we lie to him.   *Samuel Butler*

Who lies for you will lie against you.   *Bosnian proverb*

The cruellest lies are often told in silence.   *Robert Louis Stevenson*

I deny the lawfulness of telling a lie to a sick man for fear of alarming him; you have no business with consequences, you are to tell the truth.
                                                          Samuel Johnson

I do not mind lying, but I hate inaccuracy.   *Samuel Butler*

A little inaccuracy sometimes saves tons of explanations.   *Saki*

A half-truth is a whole lie.   *Jewish proverb*

A liar should have a good memory.   *Quintilian*

Oh, don't tell me of facts — I never believe in facts; you know Canning said nothing was so fallacious as facts, except figures.   *Sydney Smith*

Liberty and Human Rights

These are the times that try men's souls. The summer soldier and the sunshine patriot will, in this crisis, shrink from the service of their country, but he that stands it now, deserves the love and thanks of man and woman. Tyranny, like hell, is not easily conquered; yet we have this consolation with us, that the harder the conflict, the more glorious the triumph.

Thomas Paine

It is a fair summary of history to say that the safeguards of liberty have frequently been forged in cases involving not very nice people.

Felix Frankfurter

The spirit of liberty is the spirit which is not too sure that it is right.

Learned Hand

Liberty is always dangerous — but it is the safest thing we have.

Harry Emerson Fosdick

None can love freedom heartily, but good men; the rest love not freedom, but licence. *John Milton*

One should never put on one's best trousers to go out to battle for freedom and truth. *Henrik Ibsen*

I understand by 'freedom of spirit' something quite definite — the unconditional will to say No, where it is dangerous to say No.

Friedrich Nietzsche

Man was born free and everywhere he is in shackles.

Jean-Jacques Rousseau

Liberty means responsibility. That is why most men dread it.

George Bernard Shaw

My definition of a free society is a society where it is safe to be unpopular.

Adlai Stevenson

For two decades the state has been taking liberties, and these liberties were once ours. *E. P. Thompson*

By physical liberty I mean the right to do anything which does not interfere with the happiness of another. By intellectual liberty I mean the right to think wrong. *Robert G. Ingersoll*

There can be no real freedom without the freedom to fail.   *Eric Hoffer*

Liberty, as it is conceived by current opinion, has nothing inherent about it; it is a sort of gift or trust bestowed on the individual by the state pending good behaviour.   *Mary McCarthy*

The right to be heard does not automatically include the right to be taken seriously.   *Hubert Humphrey*

If liberty has any meaning it means freedom to improve.   *Philip Wylie*

Those who expect to reap the blessings of freedom must, like men, undergo the fatigue of supporting it.   *Thomas Paine*

Let every nation know, whether it wishes us well or ill, that we shall pay any price, bear any burden, meet any hardship, support any friend, oppose any foe, in order to assure the survival and the success of liberty.
John F. Kennedy

The most stringent protection of free speech would not protect a man in falsely shouting fire in a theatre and causing a panic... The question in every case is whether the words used are used in such circumstances and are of such a nature as to create a clear and present danger that they will bring about the substantive evils that Congress has a right to prevent.
Oliver Wendell Holmes, Jr.

Send these, the homeless, tempest toss'd, to me.
I lift my lamp beside the golden door.
Emma Lazarus (Inscription on the Statue of Liberty)

To be truly free, it takes more determination, courage, introspection and restraint than to be in shackles.   *Pietro Bellusch*

Equality of opportunity is an equal opportunity to prove unequal talents.
Viscount Samuel

The greatest right in the world is the right to be wrong. *Harry Weinberger*

We who lived in concentration camps can remember the men who walked through the huts comforting others, giving away their last piece of bread. They may have been few in number, but they offer sufficient proof that everything can be taken from a man but one thing: the last of human freedoms — to choose one's attitude in any given set of circumstances — to choose one's own way.   *Viktor Frankl*

The world must be made safe for democracy. Its peace must be planted upon the tested foundations of political liberty. We have no selfish ends to serve. We desire no conquest, no domination. We seek no indemnities for ourselves, no material compensation for the sacrifices we shall freely give. We are but one of the champions of the rights of mankind. We shall be satisfied when those rights have been made as secure as the faith and freedom of nations can make them.   *Woodrow Wilson*

A free man is as jealous of his responsibilities as he is of his liberties.
                                                            Cyril James

All free men, wherever they may live, are citizens of Berlin. And therefore, as a free man, I take pride in the words 'Ich bin ein Berliner.'
                                                        John F. Kennedy

Liberty is the right to do what the law permits.   *Montesquieu*

Once freedom lights its beacon in a man's heart, the gods are powerless against him.   *Jean-Paul Sartre*

Equality is the result of human organization. We are not born equal.
                                                          Hannah Arendt

When you have robbed a man of everything, he is no longer in your power. He is free again.   *Aleksandr Solzhenitsyn*

The effect of liberty on individuals is that they may do what they please: we ought to see what it will please them to do, before we risk congratulations.   *Edmund Burke*

We are in bondage to the law in order that we may be free.   *Cicero*

The most certain test by which we judge whether a country is really free is the amount of security enjoyed by minorities.   *John, Lord Acton*

People hardly ever make use of the freedom they have, for example, freedom of thought; instead they demand freedom of speech as a compensation.
                                                      Søren Kierkegaard

Life

Life only demands from the strength you possess. Only one feat is possible — not to have run away.   *Dag Hammarskjöld*

In three words I can sum up everything I've learned about life. It goes on.
Robert Frost

Life is ours to be spent, not to be saved. *D. H. Lawrence*

Life is a luminous halo, a semi-transparent envelope surrounding us from
the beginning. *Virginia Woolf*

Life is ever
Since man was born,
Licking honey
From a thorn. *Louis Ginsberg*

Life would be infinitely happier if we could only be born at the age of eighty
and gradually approach eighteen. *Mark Twain*

Life is like playing a violin in public and learning the instrument as one goes
on. *Samuel Butler*

The first half of our lives is ruined by our parents and the second half by
our children. *Clarence Darrow*

The great pleasure in life is doing what people say you cannot do.
Walter Bagehot

Life consists in what a man is thinking of all day.
Ralph Waldo Emerson

Life is action and passion; therefore, it is required of a man that he should
share the passion and action of the time, at peril of being judged not to have
lived. *Oliver Wendell Holmes, Jr.*

May you live all the days of your life. *Jonathan Swift*

I have measured out my life with coffee spoons. *T. S. Eliot*

If there is a sin against life, it consists perhaps not so much in despairing
of life as in hoping for another, and in eluding the implacable grandeur of
this life. *Albert Camus*

Life can only be understood backwards; but it must be lived forwards.
Søren Kierkegaard

The joy of life is variety; the tenderest love requires to be renewed by inter-
vals of absence. *Samuel Johnson*

O Life! thou art a galling load,
Along a rough, a weary road,
To wretches such as I.   *Robert Burns*

I am on the side of the unregenerate who affirm the worth of life as an end
in itself, as against the saints who deny it.   *Oliver Wendell Holmes, Jr.*

The natural rhythm of human life is routine punctuated by orgies.
                                          Aldous Huxley

Were the offer made true, I would engage to run again, from beginning to
end, the same career of life. All I would ask should be the privilege of an
author, to correct, in a second edition, certain errors of the first.
                                          Benjamin Franklin

Life is what happens to us while we are making other plans.
                                          Thomas la Mance

The man who has no inner life is the slave of his surroundings.
                                          Henri Frédéric Amiel

People in the West are always getting ready to live.   *Chinese proverb*

You've got to keep fighting — you've got to risk your life every six months
to stay alive.   *Elia Kazan*

Unless you can find some sort of loyalty, you cannot find unity and peace
in your active living.   *Josiah Royce*

Life, as it is called, is for most of us one long postponement.
                                          Henry Miller

Life is a progress from want to want, not from enjoyment to enjoyment.
                                          Samuel Johnson

Life as we find it is too hard for us; it entails too much pain, too many disappointments, impossible tasks. We cannot do without palliative remedies.
                                          Sigmund Freud

Be intent upon the perfection of the present day.   *William Law*

Life is a long preparation for something that never happens.
                                          William Butler Yeats

You only live once — but if you work it right, once is enough.
Joe E. Lewis

Growth is the only evidence of life.   *Cardinal Newman*

Life is a stranger's sojourn, a night at an inn.   *Marcus Aurelius*

If you're on the merry-go-round, you have to go round.
Kent Thompson

Most people get a fair amount of fun out of their lives, but on balance life is suffering and only the very sound or the very foolish imagine otherwise.
George Orwell

The whole of what we know is a system of compensations. Each suffering is rewarded; each sacrifice is made up; every debt is paid.
Ralph Waldo Emerson

The truth that many people never understand, until it is too late, is that the more you try to avoid suffering the more you suffer because smaller and more insignificant things begin to torture you in proportion to your fear of being hurt.   *Thomas Merton*

The tragedy of life is not so much what men suffer, but rather what they miss.   *Thomas Carlyle*

He who despairs of the human condition is a coward, but he who has hope for it is a fool.   *Albert Camus*

Basically, I'm interested in friendship, sex and death.   *Sharon Riis*

Such as we are made of, such we be.   *Shakespeare*

Measurement of life should be proportioned rather to the intensity of the experience than to its actual length.   *Thomas Hardy*

Life is seldom as unendurable as, to judge by the facts, it logically ought to be.   *Brooks Atkinson*

Birth, copulation and death. That's all the facts when you come to brass tacks.   *T. S. Eliot*

Life is an offensive, directed against the repetitious mechanism of the universe.   *Alfred North Whitehead*

There is no cure for birth and death, save to enjoy the interval.

George Santayana

The art of living is more like that of wrestling than of dancing. The main thing is to stand firm and be ready for an unforeseen attack.

Marcus Aurelius

We never live, but we are always in the expectation of living.   *Voltaire*

Life, we learn too late, is in the living, in the tissue of every day and hour.

Stephen Leacock

There is time for work. And time for love. That leaves no other time.

Coco Chanel

It is not the years in your life but the life in your years that counts.

Adlai Stevenson

A single event can awaken within us a stranger totally unknown to us. To live is to be slowly born.   *Antoine de Saint-Exupéry*

One hour of life, crowded to the full with glorious action, and filled with noble risks, is worth whole years of those mean observances of paltry decorum.   *Walter Scott*

The good life, as I conceive it, is a happy life. I do not mean that if you are good you will be happy — I mean that if you are happy you will be good.

Bertrand Russell

One man in his time plays many parts.   *Shakespeare, 'As You Like It'*

He alone deserves liberty and life who daily must win them anew.

Goethe

One returns to the place one came from.   *Jean de la Fontaine*

The true meaning of life is to plant trees, under whose shade you do not expect to sit.   *Nelson Henderson*

It is now life and not art that requires the willing suspension of disbelief.

Lionel Trilling

The great use of life is to spend it for something that will outlast it.

William James

Life is painting a picture, not doing a sum.   *Oliver Wendell Holmes, Jr.*

Go placidly amid the noise and the haste, and remember what peace there may be in silence. As far as possible without surrender, be on good terms with all persons. Speak your truth quietly and clearly, and listen to others, even the dull and ignorant; they too have their story. Be yourself. Especially do not feign affection. Neither be cynical about love; for in the face of all aridity and disenchantment it is as perennial as the grass. Take kindly the counsel of the years, gracefully surrendering the things of youth. Nurture strength of spirit to shield you in sudden misfortune. But do not distress yourself with imaginings. Many fears are born of fatigue and loneliness. Beyond a wholesome discipline, be gentle with yourself. You are a child of the universe no less than the trees and the stars; you have a right to be here. And whether or not it is clear to you, no doubt the universe is unfolding as it should. Therefore be at peace with God, whatever you conceive Him to be, and whatever your labours and aspirations, in the noisy confusion of life keep peace with your soul. With all its sham, drudgery and broken dreams, it is still a beautiful world.   *From the works of Max Ehrmann*

At any given moment, life is completely senseless. But viewed over a period, it seems to reveal itself as an organism existing in time, having a purpose, tending in a certain direction.   *Aldous Huxley*

Without a measureless and perpetual uncertainty, the drama of human life would be destroyed.   *Winston Churchill*

Life begins on the other side of despair.   *Jean-Paul Sartre*

For he who lives more lives than one,
More deaths than one must die.   *Oscar Wilde*

It is better to wear out than to rust out.   *George Whitefield*

My advice to those who are about to begin, in earnest, the journey of life, is to take their heart in one hand and a club in the other.   *Josh Billings*

One must choose in life between boredom and suffering.   *Madame de Staël*

All of life is more or less what the French would call 's'imposer' — to be able to create one's own terms for what one does.   *Kenneth Tynan*

The power of habit and the charm of novelty are the two adverse forces which explain the follies of mankind.   *Comtesse Diane (Marie de Beausacq)*

Real life seems to have no plots.   *Ivy Compton-Burnett*

There are two ways to slide easily through life; to believe everything or doubt everything. Both ways save us from thinking.   *Alfred Korzybski*

Life is one long process of getting tired.   *Samuel Butler*

He who has a why to live can bear with almost anyhow.
                                                     Friedrich Nietzsche

Oh, how daily life is. (Ah, que la vie est quotidienne.)   *Jules Laforgue*

Death and taxes and childbirth. There's never any convenient time for any of them.   *Margaret Mitchell*

We're all in this together — by ourselves.   *Lily Tomlin*

Normal day, let me be aware of the treasure you are. Let me learn from you, love you, savour you, bless you before you depart. Let me not pass you by in quest of some rare and perfect tomorrow. Let me hold you while I may for it will not always be so. One day I shall dig my nails into the earth, or bury my face in the pillow, or stretch myself taut, or raise my hands to the sky, and want, more than all the world, your return.   *Mary Jean Irion*

Sloppy, raggedy-assed old life. I love it. I never want to die.
                                                     Dennis Trudell

A proverb is no proverb to you till life has illustrated it.   *John Keats*

It is not true that life is one damn thing after another — it's one damn thing over and over.   *Edna St. Vincent Millay*

Literature

Literature is the effort of man to indemnify himself for the wrongs of his condition.   *Walter Savage Landor*

The short story is the art form that deals with the individual when there is no longer a society to absorb him, and when he is compelled to exist, as it were, by his own inner light.   *Frank O'Connor*

A novel is a mirror carried along a main road.   *Stendhal*

A novel is never anything but a philosophy put into images.   *Albert Camus*

Biographies are but the clothes and buttons of the man — the biography of the man himself cannot be written.   *Mark Twain*

What is an epigram? A dwarfish whole,
Its body brevity, and wit its soul.   *Samuel Taylor Coleridge*

A literary movement consists of five or six people who live in the same town and hate each other cordially.   *George Moore*

Fiction reveals truth that reality obscures.   *Jessamyn West*

Literature is a power to be possessed, not a body of objects to be studied.   *Anon.*

A perfect judge will read each word of wit with the same spirit that its author writ.   *Alexander Pope*

In literary history, generation follows generation in a rage.   *Annie Dillard*

To be a good diarist, one must have a little snouty, sneaky mind.   *Harold Nicolson*

Published memoirs indicate the end of a man's activity, and that he acknowledges the end.   *George Meredith*

It has come to be practically a sort of rule in literature that a man, having once shown himself capable of original writing, is entitled thenceforth to steal from the writings of others at discretion.   *Ralph Waldo Emerson*

The novel is a prose narrative of some length that has something wrong with it.   *Randall Jarrell*

All that non-fiction can do is answer questions. It's fiction's business to ask them.   *Richard Hughes*

Contemporary literature can be classified under three headings: the neurotic, the erotic and the tommy-rotic.   *W. Giese*

Literature is the orchestration of platitudes.   *Thornton Wilder*

Medicine is my lawful wife. Literature is my mistress.   *Anton Chekhov*

One hears about life all the time from different people with very different narrative gifts.
Anthony Powell

The essay is a literary device for saying almost everything about almost anything.
Aldous Huxley

The answers you get from literature depend upon the questions you pose.
Margaret Atwood

The classics are only primitive literature. They belong to the same class as primitive machinery and primitive music and primitive medicine.
Stephen Leacock

A biography is considered complete if it merely accounts for six or seven selves, whereas a person may well have as many as a thousand.
Virginia Woolf

In literature as in love we are astounded by what is chosen by others.
André Maurois

Biography is one of the new terrors of death.
John Arbuthnot

Good children's literature appeals not only to the child in the adult, but to the adult in the child.
Anon.

Literature flourishes best when it is half a trade and half an art.
William R. Inge

Loneliness

Loneliness is and always has been the central and inevitable experience of every man.
Thomas Wolfe

One may have a blazing hearth in one's soul, and yet no one ever comes to sit by it.
Vincent van Gogh

So lonely 'twas that God himself
Scarce seemed there to be.
Samuel Taylor Coleridge

The lonely one offers his hand too quickly to whomever he encounters.
Friedrich Nietszche

Man's loneliness is but his fear of life.
Eugene O'Neill

No man is an Island intire of it self; every man is a peece of the Continent, a part of the maine; if a Clod be washed away by the sea, Europe is the lesse, as well as if a Promontorie were, as well as if a manor of thy friends or thine own were. Any man's death diminishes me because I am involved in Mankinde, and therefore never send to know for whom the bell tolls; it tolls for thee.   *John Donne*

Who knows what true loneliness is — not the conventional word but the naked terror? To the lonely themselves it wears a mask. The most miserable out-cast hugs some memory or some illusion.   *Joseph Conrad*

Little do men perceive what solitude is, and how far it extendeth. For a crowd is not company, and faces are but a gallery of pictures, and talk but a tinkl-ing cymbal, where there is no love.   *Francis Bacon*

Where you used to be, there is a hole in the world, which I find myself con-stantly walking around in the daytime, and falling into at night. I miss you like hell.   *Edna St. Vincent Millay*

The eternal quest of the individual human being is to shatter his loneliness.
                                                              Norman Cousins

Language has created the word 'loneliness' to express the pain of being alone, and the word 'solitude' to express the glory of being alone. *Paul Tillich*

If I'm such a legend, then why am I so lonely? Let me tell you, legends are all very well if you've got somebody around who loves you.
                                                                Judy Garland

Loneliness and the feeling of being unwanted is the most terrible poverty.
                                                              Mother Teresa

Love

Love consists in this, that two solitudes protect and touch and greet each other.   *Rainer Maria Rilke*

No one has ever loved anyone the way everyone wants to be loved.
                                                          Mignon McLaughlin

We always deceive ourselves twice about the people we love — first to their advantage, then to their disadvantage.   *Albert Camus*

Human love is often but the encounter of two weaknesses.

François Mauriac

I am two fools, I know, for loving, and saying so.   *John Donne*

The supreme happiness of life is the conviction that we are loved.

Victor Hugo

What dire offence from am'rous causes springs.
What mighty contests rise from trivial things.   *Alexander Pope*

From success you get a lot of things, but not that great inside thing that love
brings you.   *Sam Goldwyn*

He who loves the more is the inferior and must suffer.   *Thomas Mann*

Love, you know, seeks to make happy rather than to be happy.

Ralph Connor

Love is a spendthrift, leaves its arithmetic at home, is always 'in the red.'

Paul Scherer

The loving are the daring.   *Bayard Taylor*

The porcupine, whom one must handle gloved,
May be respected, but is never loved.   *Arthur Guiterman*

Little privations are easily endured when the heart is better treated than the
body.   *Jean-Jacques Rousseau*

No love, no friendship can cross the path of our destiny without leaving some
mark on it forever.   *François Mauriac*

There is no fear in love; but perfect love casteth out fear.   *1 John 4:18*

I no longer cared about survival — I merely loved.   *Loren Eiseley*

You can always get someone to love you — even if you have to do it yourself.

Tom Masson

You've got to love what's lovable, and hate what's hateable. It takes brains
to see the difference.   *Robert Frost*

Romance without finance is no good.   *Willie 'The Lion' Smith*

To live is like to love — all reason is against it, and all healthy instinct for it. *Samuel Butler*

People who throw kisses are hopelessly lazy. *Bob Hope*

Wine comes in at the mouth
And love comes in at the eye;
That's all we shall know for truth
Before we grow old and die. *William Butler Yeats*

Love lives on propinquity, but dies on contact. *Thomas Hardy*

The heart that has truly loved never forgets
But as truly loves on to the close. *Thomas More*

When the satisfaction or the security of another person becomes as significant to one as one's own satisfaction or security, then the state of love exists. *Henry Stack Sullivan*

At the end of what is called the 'sexual life' the only love which has lasted is the love which has everything, every disappointment, every failure and every betrayal, which has accepted even the sad fact that in the end there is no desire so deep as the simple desire for companionship. *Graham Greene*

When love and skill work together expect a masterpiece. *John Ruskin*

The greater love is a mother's; then comes a dog's; then a sweetheart's. *Polish proverb*

Selfishness is one of the qualities apt to inspire love. *Nathaniel Hawthorne*

There can be no peace of mind in love, since the advantage one has secured is never anything but a fresh starting-point for further desires. *Marcel Proust*

Love does not consist in gazing at each other, but in looking together in the same direction. *Antoine de Saint-Exupéry*

The magic of first love is our ignorance that it can ever end. *Benjamin Disraeli*

What we can do for another is the test of powers; what we can suffer is the test of love. *Brooke Foss Westcott*

They gave each other a smile with a future in it. *Ring Lardner*

Many a man in love with a dimple makes the mistake of marrying the whole girl. *Stephen Leacock*

There is one who kisses, and the other who offers a cheek.
French proverb

The irony of love is that is guarantees some degree of anger, fear and criticism.
Harold H. Bloomfield

It has been wisely said that we cannot really love anybody at whom we never laugh. *Agnes Repplier*

The entire sum of existence is the magic of being needed by just one person.
Vi Putnam

A lady of forty-seven who has been married twenty-seven years and has six children knows what love really is and once described it for me like this: 'Love is what you've been through with somebody.' *James Thurber*

And if I loved you Wednesday,
Well, what is that to you?
I do not love you Thursday —
So much is true. *Edna St. Vincent Millay*

Happiness comes more from loving than being loved; and often when our affection seems wounded it is only our vanity bleeding. To love, and to be hurt often, and to love again — this is the brave and happy life.
J. E. Buckrose

If you cannot inspire a woman with love of you, fill her above the brim with love of herself; all that runs over will be yours. *Charles Caleb Colton*

Respect is love in plain clothes. *Frankie Byrne*

Love is a gross exaggeration of the difference between one person and everybody else. *George Bernard Shaw*

No one can do me any good by loving me; I have more love than I need, or could do any good with; but people do me good by making me love them — which isn't easy. *John Ruskin*

A man is only as good as what he loves. *Saul Bellow*

In the act of loving someone you arm them against you.   *Anon.*

If you want to be loved, be lovable.   *Ovid*

The one thing we can never get enough of is love. And the one thing we never give enough of is love.   *Henry Miller*

Love makes of the wisest man a fool, and of the most foolish woman, a sage.   *Moritz G. Saphir*

In how many lives does Love really play a dominant part? The average tax-payer is no more capable of a 'grand passion' than of a grand opera.
        Israel Zangwill

Love, all love of other sights controls.
And makes one little room an everywhere.   *John Donne*

If we are to judge of love by its consequences, it more nearly resembles hatred than friendship.   *La Rochefoucauld*

Love cannot accept what it is. Everywhere on earth it cries out against kind-ness, compassion, intelligence, everything that leads to compromise. Love demands the impossible, the absolute, the sky on fire, inexhaustible springtime, life after death, and death itself transfigured into eternal life.
        Albert Camus

unlove's the heavenless hell and homeless home . . . lovers alone wear sunlight.   *e. e. cummings*

Marriage

Marriage is our last, best chance to grow up.   *Joseph Barth*

As a general thing, people marry most happily with their own kind. The trou-ble lies in the fact that people usually marry at an age when they do not real-ly know what their own kind is.   *Robertson Davies*

Often the difference between a successful marriage and a mediocre one con-sists of leaving about three or four things a day unsaid.   *Harlan Miller*

Marriage is the deep, deep peace of the double bed after the hurly-burly of the chaise longue.   *Mrs. Patrick Campbell*

A good marriage is that in which each appoints the other guardian of his solitude. Once the realization is accepted that even between the closest human beings infinite distances continue to exist, a wonderful living side by side can grow up, if they succeed in loving the distance between them which makes it possible for each to see the other whole and against a wide sky.

Rainer Maria Rilke

Nothing flatters a man as much as the happiness of his wife; he is always proud of himself as the source of it. *Samuel Johnson*

Pains do not hold a marriage together. It is threads, hundreds of tiny threads which sew people together through the years. That's what makes a marriage last — more than passion or even sex. *Simone Signoret*

Marriage; a job. Happiness or unhappiness has nothing to do with it.
Kathleen Norris

A wife encourages her husband's egoism in order to exercise her own.
Russell Green

A man and a woman marry because both of them don't know what to do with themselves. *Anton Chekhov*

Marriage is neither heaven nor hell; it is simply purgatory.
Abraham Lincoln

Every marriage tends to consist of an aristocrat and a peasant, of a teacher and a learner. *John Updike*

Marriage is one long conversation checkered by disputes.
Robert Louis Stevenson

Husband and wife come to look alike at last.
Oliver Wendell Holmes

There is a radicalism in all getting, and a conservatism in all keeping. Love-making is radical, while marriage is conservative. *Eric Hoffer*

The young man who wants to marry happily should pick out a good mother and marry one of her daughters — any one will do. *J. Ogden Armour*

His designs were strictly honourable, as the phrase is: that is, to rob a lady of her fortune by way of marriage. *Henry Fielding*

If thee marries for money, thee surely will earn it. *Ezra Bowen*

Only two things are necessary to keep one's wife happy. One is to let her think she is having her own way, and the other, to let her have it.
Lyndon B. Johnson

Henry VIII had so many wives because his dynastic sense was very strong whenever he saw a maid of honour.   *Will Cuppy*

A simple enough pleasure, surely, to have breakfast alone with one's husband, but how seldom married people in the midst of life achieve it.
Anne Morrow Lindbergh

Marriages would in general be as happy, and often more so, if they were all made by the Lord Chancellor.   *Samuel Johnson*

No man is regular in his attendance at the House of Commons until he is married.   *Benjamin Disraeli*

Love is a fever which marriage puts to bed and cures.
Richard J. Needham

An ideal wife is one who remains faithful to you but tries to be just as if she weren't.   *Sacha Guitry*

No labourer in the world is expected to work for room, board, and love — except the housewife.   *Letty Cottin Pogrebin*

What is instinct? It is the natural tendency in one when filled with dismay to turn to his wife.   *Finley Peter Dunne*

A husband always prefers his wife's mother-in-law to his own.   *Anon.*

Woe to the house where the hen crows and the rooster keeps still.
Spanish proverb

Married couples who love each other tell each other a thousand things without talking.   *Chinese proverb*

Marriage is not a finished affair. No matter to what age you live, love must be continuously consolidated. Being considerate, thoughtful and respectful without ulterior motives is the key to a satisfactory marriage.
Pamphlet from Chinese Family Planning Centre

Seldom, or perhaps never, does a marriage develop into an individual relationship smoothly and without crises; there is no coming to consciousness without pain.   *Carl Jung*

I never married because I have three pets at home that answer the same purpose as a husband. I have a dog that growls every morning, a parrot that swears all afternoon, and a cat that comes home late at night.

Marie Corelli

Let there be spaces in your togetherness.   *Kahlil Gibran*

Any marriage, happy or unhappy, is infinitely more interesting and significant than any romance, however passionate.   *W. H. Auden*

One of the best things about marriage is that it gets young people to bed at a decent hour.   *M. M. Musselman*

The majority of husbands remind me of an orangutan trying to play the violin.

Honoré de Balzac

Polygamy: an endeavour to get more out of life than there is in it.

Elbert Hubbard

Marriage, n: the state or condition of a community consisting of a master, a mistress, and two slaves, making, in all, two.   *Ambrose Bierce*

Marriage is a great institution, and no family should be without it.

Channing Pollock

No matter how happily a woman may be married, it always pleases her to discover that there is a nice man who wishes she were not.

H. L. Mencken

Any married man should forget his mistakes — no use two people remembering the same thing.   *Duane Dewel*

Marriage is three parts love and seven parts forgiveness of sins.

Langdon Mitchell

I married beneath me — all women do.   *Nancy Astor*

One of the best hearing aids a man can have is an attentive wife.

Groucho Marx

A good husband should always bore his wife.   *Fred Jacob*

There isn't a wife in the world who has not taken the exact measure of her husband, weighed him and settled him in her own mind, and knows him as well as if she had ordered him after designs and specifications of her own.
Charles Dudley Warner

A woman is not a whole woman without the experience of marriage. In the case of a bad marriage, you win if you lose. Of the two alternatives — bad marriage or none — I believe bad marriage would be better. It is a bitter experience and a high price to pay for fulfillment, but it is the better alternative.
Fannie Hurst

Maturity

Growing up is after all only the understanding that one's unique and incredible experience is what everyone shares.
Doris Lessing

A mark of maturity seems to be the range and extent of one's feeling of self-involvement in abstract ideals.
Gordon Wallport

The mark of a mature man is the ability to give love and receive it joyously and without guilt.
Leo Baeck

My poetry doesn't change from place to place — it changes with the years. It's very important to be one's age. You get ideas you have to turn down — 'I'm sorry, no longer' 'I'm sorry, not yet.'
W. H. Auden

Maturity is the capacity to endure uncertainty.
John Finley

I believe that the sign of maturity is accepting deferred gratification.
Peggy Cahn

You don't learn to hold your own by standing on guard, but by attacking, and getting well hammered yourself.
George Bernard Shaw

Our judgements about things vary according to the time left us to live — that we think is left us to live.
André Gide

Grown up, and that is a terribly hard thing to do. It is much easier to skip it and go from one childhood to another.
F. Scott Fitzgerald

How many really capable men are children more than once during the day?
Napoleon Bonaparte

The immature mind hops from one thing to another; the mature mind seeks to follow through.   *Harry A. Overstreet*

One of the signs of passing youth is the birth of a sense of fellowhip with other human beings as we take our place among them.   *Virginia Woolf*

It is unjust to claim the privileges of age and retain the playthings of childhood.   *Samuel Johnson*

Medicine and Sickness

It is much more important to know what sort of a patient has a disease than what sort of a disease a patient has.   *William Osler*

The desire to take medicine is perhaps the greatest feature which distinguishes man from animals.   *William Osler*

The doctor, if he forgets he is only the assistant to nature and zealously takes over the stage, may so add to what nature is already doing well that he actually throws the patient into shock by the vigour he adds to nature's forces.
                                                   Herbert Ratner

There are worse occupations in this world than feeling a woman's pulse.
                                                   Laurence Sterne

God heals, and the doctor takes the fees.   *Benjamin Franklin*

The history of medicine is a story of amazing foolishness and amazing intelligence.   *Jerome Tarshis*

If men could get pregnant, abortion would be a sacrament.
                                                   Florynce Kennedy

Abortion is advocated only by persons who have themselves been born.
                                                   Ronald Reagan

Man should not strive to eliminate his complexes, but to get in accord with them; they are legitimately what directs his contact in the world.
                                                   Sigmund Freud

The body never lies.   *Martha Graham*

All that is really necessary for survival of the fittest, it seems, is an interest in life, good, bad or peculiar. *Grace Paley*

The only thing to know is how to use your neurosis. *Arthur Adamov*

If every man would mend a man, then all the world would be mended. *Anon.*

Common sense is in medicine the master workman. *Peter Latham*

The prime goal is to alleviate suffering, and not to prolong life. And if your treatment does not alleviate suffering, but only prolongs life, that treatment should be stopped. *Christian Barnard*

As long as men are liable to die and are desirous to live, a physician will be made fun of, but he will be well paid. *Jean de la Bruyère*

A doctor wastes no time with patients; and if you have to die, he will put the business through quicker than anybody else. *Molière*

After dinner, rest a while, after supper walk a mile. *Arabic proverb*

Imprisoned in every fat man, a thin one is wildly signalling to be let out. *Cyril Connolly*

Wherever a doctor cannot do good, he must be kept from doing harm. *Hippocrates*

The student is to collect and evaluate facts. The facts are locked up in the patient. *Abraham Flexner*

Every surgeon carries about him a little cemetery, in which from time to time he goes to pray, a cemetery of bitterness and regret, of which he seeks the reason for certain of his failures. *René Leriche*

The practice of medicine is a thinker's art, the practice of surgery a plumber's. *Martin H. Fisher*

Symptoms, then, are in reality nothing but the cry from suffering organs. *Jean-Martin Charcot*

I observe the physician with the same diligence as the disease. *John Donne*

The very first requirement in a hospital is that it should do the sick no harm.
Florence Nightingale

There are some remedies worse than the disease. *Publilius Syrus*

To avoid delay, please have all your symptoms ready.
Notice in an English doctor's waiting-room

Sickness is a sort of early old age; it teaches us a diffidence in our earthly state. *Alexander Pope*

To be sick is to enjoy monarchal prerogatives. *Charles Lamb*

Every invalid is a physician. *Irish proverb*

'Tis healthy to be sick sometimes. *Henry David Thoreau*

Our doctor would never really operate unless it was necessary. He was just that way. If he didn't need the money, he wouldn't lay a hand on you.
Herb Shriner

Physicians of the Utmost Fame
Were called at once, but when they came
They answered, as they took their fees,
'There is no cure for this disease.' *Hillaire Belloc*

A good gulp of hot whisky at bedtime — it's not very scientific, but it helps.
Alexander D. Fleming

I enjoy convalescence. It is the part that makes the illness worthwhile.
George Bernard Shaw

A general flavour of mild decay,
But nothing local, as one may say. *Oliver Wendell Holmes*

One of the first duties of the physician is to educate the masses not to take medicine. *William Osler*

I was sick, and ye visited me. *Matthew 25:36*

There is a great difference between a good physician and a bad one; yet very little between a good one and none at all. *Arthur Young*

Nature, time and patience are the three great physicians. *Proverb*

So many come to the sickroom thinking of themselves as men of science fighting disease and not as healers with a little knowledge helping nature to get a sick man well.   *Sir Auckland Geddes*

No doctor takes pleasure in the health even of his friends.   *Montaigne*

It requires a great deal of faith for a man to be cured by his own placebos.
John L. McClenahan

It is very difficult to slow down. The practice of medicine is like the heart muscle's contraction — it's all or none.   *Bela Schick*

Those in the United States who, by and large, have the best medical care and advice readily available to them at the least expense are the families of the specialists in internal medicine. These families use less medicine and undergo less surgery on the whole than any other group, rich or poor.
Edward C. Lambert

Nothing is more fatal to health than an overcare of it.
Benjamin Franklin

Doctor, feel my purse.   *Jane Ace*

The sorrow which has no vent in tears may make other organs weep.
Henry Maudsley

In my youth, once, when I had a really exquisite toothache, I suddenly realized that my tooth had temporarily become the centre of the universe, that its outcries were more important than anything else, and that I would do absolutely anything to placate it. And as one gets older and starts worrying about cancer, one becomes more and more conscious of the fragility of the whole body, and with that consciousness comes a new and degrading kind of fear. It is degrading because it strengthens the desire to survive on any terms, and the desire to survive on any terms is the most base of all our instincts.   *Otto Friedrich*

There is some reason to believe there is greater safety in this branch of medicine from modest, unassuming ignorance, than from a meddling presumption which frequently accompanies a little learning. *Samuel Bard*

If a man thinks about his physical or moral state, he usually discovers that he is ill.   *Goethe*

A person seldom falls sick but the bystanders are animated with a faint hope that he will die.   *Ralph Waldo Emerson*

I reckon being ill is one of the greatest pleasures of life, provided one is not too ill and is not obliged to work till one is better.   *Samuel Butler*

We are usually the best men when in the worst health.   *English proverb*

Some of the papers presented at today's medical meeting tell us what we already know, but in a much more complicated manner.
                                                   Alphonse Raymond Dochez

A human being who is first of all an invalid is all body; therein lies his inhumanity and his debasement.   *Thomas Mann*

Invalids live longest.   *German proverb*

A vigorous five-mile walk will do more good for an unhappy but otherwise healthy adult than all the medicine and psychology in the world.
                                                         Paul Dudley White

We firmly believe that therapy is education rather than healing; that it is growth rather than treatment.   *Arnold Lazarus and Alan Fay*

As long as we incorrectly blame outside sources for our miseries, it remains impossible to do much about them. However, if we realize that we upset ourselves over the things that happen to us, we can work at changing. The first step is to ask: 'Exactly how did I manage to upset myself?' We then obtain the clues about how to avoid upsetting ourselves.
                                                Arnold Lazarus and Alan Fay

Ask many of us who are disabled what we would like in life and you would be surprised how few would say, 'Not to be disabled.' We accept our limitations.   *Itzhak Perlman*

What is dangerous about tranquillizers is that whatever peace of mind they bring is packaged peace of mind. Where you buy a pill and buy peace with it, you get conditioned to cheap solutions instead of deep ones.
                                                              Max Lerner

So long as the body is affected through the mind, no audacious device, even of the most manifestly dishonest character, can fail of producing occasional good to those who yield to it an implicit or even a partial faith.
                                                     Oliver Wendell Holmes

Tranquillizers do not change our environment, nor do they change our personalities. They merely reduce our responsiveness to stimuli. They dull the keen edge of the angers, fears, or anxiety with which we might otherwise react to the problems of living. Once the response has been dulled, the irritating surface noise of living muted or eliminated, the spark and brilliance are also gone.   *Indra Devi*

I am in a moment of pretty wellness.   *Horace Walpole*

Health is the thing that makes you feel that now is the best time of the year.
                                                        Franklin Pierce Adams

When you hear hoofbeats, think of horses before zebras.
                                        Medical maxim quoted by Harley S. Smyth

The American Medical Association operating from a platform of negative vigilance presents no solutions but busily fights each change and then loudly supports it against the next proposal.   *John H. Knowles*

The tongue ever turns to the aching tooth.   *Proverb*

When we are sick our virtues and our vices are in abeyance.
                                                              Vauvenargues

Most things get better by themselves. Most things, in fact, are better by morning.   *Lewis Thomas*

In medicine, sins of commission are mortal, sins of omission venial.
                                                         Théodore Tronchin

It is the duty of a doctor to prolong life and it is not his duty to prolong the act of dying.   *Thomas, Lord Horder*

I came, I saw, I concurred.   *Irvine H. Page*

Disease often tells its secrets in a casual parenthesis.   *Wilfred Trotter*

Meetings and Partings

Man's feelings are always purest and most glowing in the hour of meeting and of farewell.   *Jean Paul Richter*

Visits always give pleasure — if not the arrival, the departure.
                                                          Portuguese proverb

There's a kind of release
And a kind of torment in every goodbye for every man.   *C. Day Lewis*

Parting is all we know of heaven
And all we need of hell.   *Emily Dickinson*

The joys of meeting pay the pangs of absence;
Else who could bear it?   *Nicholas Rowe*

We only part to meet again.   *John Gay*

Departure should be sudden.   *Benjamin Disraeli*

Memory

Memory, of all the powers of the mind, is the most delicate and frail.
Ben Jonson

Gratitude is the heart's memory.   *French proverb*

The true art of memory is the art of attention.   *Samuel Johnson*

A man must get a thing before he can forget it.   *Oliver Wendell Holmes*

It isn't so astonishing, the number of things that I can remember, as the
number of things I can remember that aren't so.   *Mark Twain*

For the sense of smell, almost more than any other, has the power to recall
memories and it is a pity that we use it so little.   *Rachel Carson*

I have a remarkable memory; I forget everything. It is wonderfully convenient. It is as though the world were constantly renewing itself for me.
Jules Renard

Nostalgia ain't want it used to be.   *Anon.*

It is commonly seen by experience that excellent memories do often accom-
pany weak judgements.   *Montaigne*

There must be at least 500 million rats in the United States; of course, I am
speaking only from memory.   *Edgar Wilson Nye*

Nostalgia is a seductive liar. *George W. Ball*

The past is a work of art, free of irrelevancies and loose ends.
Max Beerbohm

Quite literally, a man's memory is what he forgets with. *Odell Shepard*

'The horror of that moment,' the King went on, 'I shall never, never forget!'
'You will, though,' the Queen said, 'if you don't make a memorandum of
it.' *Lewis Carroll*

If, after I depart this vale, you ever remember me and have thought to please
my ghost, forgive some sinner and wink your eye at some homely girl.
H. L. Mencken

If a man can remember what he worried about last week, he has a very good
memory. *Anon.*

That which we remember of our conduct is ignored by our closest neighbour;
but that which we have forgotten having said, or even what we never said,
will cause laughter even into the next world. *Marcel Proust*

Oh longing for places that were not
Cherished enough in that fleeting hour
How I long to make good from afar
The forgotten gesture, the additional act. *Rainer Maria Rilke*

That which is bitter to endure may be sweet to remember. *Thomas Fuller*

Not the power to remember, but its very opposite, the power to forget, is
a necessary condition for our existence. *Sholem Asch*

Memory is the thing you forget with. *Alexander Chase*

The palest ink is better than the best memory. *Chinese proverb*

The advantage of a bad memory is that one enjoys several times the same
good thing for the first time. *Friedrich Nietzsche*

We forget because we must
And not because we will. *Matthew Arnold*

Everyone complains of his lack of memory, but nobody of his want of judgement. *La Rochefoucauld*

What was hard to endure is sweet to recall.   *Old saying*

Our memories are independent of our wills. It is not so easy to forget.
                                    Richard Brinsley Sheridan

God gave us memories that we might have roses in December.
                                              James M. Barrie

To want to forget something is to think of it.   *French proverb*

What is forgiven is usually well-remembered.   *Louis Dudek*

Men

The beauty of stature is the only beauty of men.   *Montaigne*

Men become old, but they never become good.   *Oscar Wilde*

Men are what their mothers made them.   *Ralph Waldo Emerson*

Men's men: be they gentle or simple, they're much of a muchness.
                                              George Eliot

To be a man will continue to demand a heroic heart as long as mankind is
not quite human.
                    Julius Fucik (before he was beheaded)

A gentleman does things no gentleman should do in a way only a gentleman
can.   *Luigi Banzini*

The right man is the one that seizes the moment.   *Goethe*

Every man in the world is better than someone else, and not as good as someone else.   *William Saroyan*

This is the worst pain a man can suffer: to have insight into much and power
over nothing.   *Herododus*

The world is my country,
The human race is my race.
The spirit of man is my god,
The future of man is my heaven.   *F. R. Scott*

The only things that distinguish us from the rest of the animals, Madam, is our habit of drinking when we are not thirsty and making love at any time.
Beaumarchais

There was never any reason to believe in any innate superiority of the male, except his superior muscle. *Bertrand Russell*

I like men to behave like men. I like them strong and childish.
Françoise Sagan

Celibacy bestows on a man the qualified freedom of a besieged city where one sometimes has to eat rats. *Sean O'Faolain*

Men build bridges and throw railroads across deserts, and yet they contend successfully that the job of sewing on a button is beyond them. Accordingly, they don't have to sew buttons. *Heywood Broun*

As vivacity is the gift of women, gravity is that of men.
Joseph Addison

The desire of a man for a woman is not directed at her because she is a human being, but because she is a woman. That she is a human being is of no concern to him. *Immanuel Kant*

I am mortal, born to love and to suffer. *Friedrich Hölderlin*

Two things control man's nature: instinct and experience. *Blaise Pascal*

In his private heart no man much respects himself. *Mark Twain*

When I was young, I used to have successes with women because I was young. Now I have successes with women because I am old. Middle age was the hardest part. *Artur Rubinstein*

A man who has been the indisputable favourite of his mother keeps for life the feeling of a conqueror. *Sigmund Freud*

We love women in proportion to their degree of strangeness to us.
Charles Beaudelaire

At twenty a man is a peacock, at thirty a lion, at forty a camel, at fifty a serpent, at sixty a dog, at seventy an ape, at eighty, nothing at all.
Baltasar Gracián

Inconsistency is the only thing in which men are consistent.*Horatio Smith*

There are three classes of men — lovers of wisdom, lovers of honour, lovers of gain.

Plato

I am a man; nothing human is alien to me.

Terence

Men and Women

Breathes there a man with hide so tough
Who says two sexes aren't enough?

Samuel Hoffenstein

If men and women are to understand each other, to enter into each other's nature with mutual sympathy, and to become capable of genuine comradeship, the foundation must be laid in youth.

Havelock Ellis

American women expect to find in their husbands a perfection that English women only hope to find in their butlers.

W. Somerset Maugham

A man's idee in a card game is war — crool, devastatin' and pitiless. A lady's idee iv it is a combynation iv larceny, embezzlement an' burglary.

Finley Peter Dunne

Women have one great advantage over men. It is commonly thought that if they marry they have done enough, and need career no further. If a man marries, on the other hand, public opinion is all against him if he takes this view.

Rose Macaulay

What is most beautiful in virile men is something feminine; what is most beautiful in feminine women is something masculine.

Susan Sontag

In our civilization, men are afraid that they will not be men enough and women are afraid that they might be considered only women.

Theodor Reik

A woman knows how to keep quiet when she is in the right, whereas a man, when he is in the right, will keep on talking.

Chazai

A woman means by unselfishness chiefly taking trouble for others; a man means not giving trouble to others. Thus each sex regards the other as basically selfish.

C. S. Lewis

Failing to be there when a man wants her is a woman's greatest sin, except to be there when he doesn't want her.

Helen Rowland

There is probably nothing like living together for blinding people to each other.   *Ivy Compton-Burnett*

I wish Adam had died with all his ribs in his body.   *Dion Boucicault*

Behind every great man there is a surprised woman.   *Maryon Pearson*

Behind every successful man you'll find a woman who has nothing to wear.
                                                                                              Harold Goffin

If a man hears much that a woman says, she is not beautiful.
                                                                                          Henry S. Haskins

God has given you one face, and you make yourselves another.
                                                                                Shakespeare, 'Hamlet'

Men have a much better time of it than women. For one thing, they marry later. For another thing, they die earlier.   *H. L. Mencken*

There is no word equivalent to 'cuckold' for women.   *Joseph Epstein*

He and I had an office so tiny that an inch smaller and it would have been adultery.   *Dorothy Parker*

A man is a person who will pay two dollars for a one-dollar item he wants. A woman will pay one dollar for a two-dollar item she doesn't want.
                                                                                            William Binger

There is more difference within the sexes than between them.
                                                                                Ivy Compton-Burnett

A woman may very well form a friendship with a man, but for this to endure, it must be assisted by a little physical antipathy.
                                                                                        Friedrich Nietzsche

When I was very young, I kissed my first woman, and smoked my first cigarette on the same day. Believe me, never since have I wasted any more time on tobacco.   *Arturo Toscanini*

The double standard of morality will survive in this world so long as the woman whose husband has been lured away is favoured with the sympathetic tears of other women, and a man whose wife has made off is laughed at by other men.   *H. L. Mencken*

Flirtation — attention without intention.   *Max O'Neil*

All women become like their mothers. That is their tragedy. No man does. That's his.   *Oscar Wilde*

As the faculty of writing has chiefly been a masculine endowment, the reproach of making the world miserable has always been thrown upon the women.   *Samuel Johnson*

Though statisticians in our time
Have never kept the score
Man wants a great deal here below
And Woman even more.   *James Thurber*

A good cigar is as great a comfort to a man as a good cry is to a woman.
                                                                 Edward Bulwer-Lytton

A man should be taller, older, heavier, uglier and hoarser than his wife.
                                                                    Edgar Watson Howe

Even the wisest men make fools of themselves about women, and even the most foolish women are wise about men.   *Theodor Reik*

I love men, not because they are men, but because they are not women.
                                                              Christina, Queen of Sweden

The Mind

One man who has a mind and knows it can always beat ten men who haven't and don't.   *George Bernard Shaw*

When the mind is thinking, it is talking to itself.   *Plato*

I am not absent-minded. It is the presence of mind that makes me unaware of everything else.   *G. K. Chesterton*

Our unconsciousness is like a vast subterranean factory with intricate machinery that is never idle, where work goes on day and night from the time we are born until the moment of our death.   *Milton R. Sapirstein*

Only an incompetent mind is content to express itself incompetently.
                                                                          J. M. Barker

A great many open minds should be closed for repairs.   *Toledo Blade*

If you keep your mind sufficiently open, people will throw a lot of rubbish into it.

William A. Orton

Merely having an open mind is nothing. The object of opening the mind, as of opening the mouth, is to shut it again on something solid.

G. K. Chesterton

The perversion of the mind is only possible when those who should be heard in its defence are silent.

Archibald MacLeish

Our minds are lazier than our bodies.

La Rochefoucauld

Strength is a matter of the made-up mind.

John Beecher

What we think and feel and are is to a great extent determined by the state of our ductless glands and our viscera.

Aldous Huxley

The feeling of inferiority rules the mental life and can be clearly recognized as the sense of incompleteness and unfulfillment, and in the uninterrupted struggle both of individuals and of humanity.

Alfred Adler

Discipline does not mean suppression and control, nor is it adjustment to a pattern or ideology. It means a mind that sees 'what is' and learns from 'what was.'

Jiddu Krishnamurti

That which enters the mind through reason can be corrected. That which is admitted through faith, hardly ever.

Santiago Ramón y Cajal

Minorities

The nations which have put mankind and posterity most in their debt have been small states — Israel, Athens, Florence, Elizabethan England.

William R. Inge

How a minority,
Reaching majority,
Seizing authority,
Hates a minority!

Leonard H. Robbins

In the country of the blind, the one-eyed man is king.

Erasmus

By gnawing through a dyke, even a rat may drown a nation.

Edmund Burke

The thing we have to fear in this country, to my way of thinking, is the influence of the organized minorities, because somehow or other the great majority does not seem to organize. They seem to feel that they are going to be effective because of their own strength, but they give no expression of it.   *Alfred E. Smith*

We must indeed all hang together, or most assuredly we shall all hang separately.   *Benjamin Franklin*

A minority may be right, and a majority is always wrong. *Henrik Ibsen*

Governments exist to protect the rights of minorities. The loved and the rich need no protection — they have many friends and few enemies.
                                                                      Wendell Phillips

It is always the minorities that hold the key of progess; it is always through those who are unafraid to be different that advance comes to human society.
                                                                    Raymond B. Fosdick

A minority group has 'arrived' only when it has the right to produce some fools and scoundrels without the entire group paying for it.
                                                                          Carl T. Rowan

Shall we judge a country by the majority, or by the minority? By the minority, surely.   *Ralph Waldo Emerson*

Never in the field of human conflict was so much owed by so many to so few.   *Winston Churchill*

One dog barks at something, the rest bark at him.   *Chinese proverb*

The nail that sticks out is hammered down.   *Japanese proverb*

Mistakes and Blunders

Great services are not canceled by one act or by one single error.
                                                                      Benjamin Disraeli

Any man whose errors take ten years to correct, is quite a man.
                                                  J. Robert Oppenheimer (of Albert Einstein)

There is nothing wrong with making mistakes. Just don't respond with encores.   *Anon.*

I beseech you, in the bowels of Christ, think it possible you may be mistaken.

Oliver Cromwell

There is no error so monstrous that it fails to find defenders among the ablest men. Imagine a congress of eminent celebrities such as More, Bacon, Grotius, Pascal, Cromwell, Bossuet, Montesquieu, Jefferson, Napoleon, Pitt, etc. The result would be an Encyclopedia of Errors.   *Lord Acton*

Men are men, they needs must err.   *Euripides*

A clever man commits no minor blunders.   *Goethe*

Most men would rather be charged with malice than with making a blunder.

Josh Billings

It is very easy to forgive others their mistakes. It takes more gut and gumption to forgive them for having witnessed your own.   *Jessamyn West*

Things could be worse. Suppose your errors were counted and published every day, like those of a baseball player.   *Anon.*

It's over, and can't be helped, and that's one consolation, as they always say in Turkey, when they cut the wrong man's head off.

Charles Dickens

A man can believe a considerable deal of rubbish, and yet go about his daily work in a rational and cheerful manner.   *Norman Douglas*

Don't ever take a fence down until you know why it was put up.

Robert Frost

Money

Money is the poor people's credit card.   *Marshall McLuhan*

A man is rich in proportion to the things he can afford to let alone.

Henry David Thoreau

Money is like a sixth sense, and you can't make use of the other five without it.   *W. Somerset Maugham*

Money swore an oath that nobody who did not love it should ever have it.

Irish proverb

I'm so happy to be rich, I'm willing to take all the consequences.
Howard Ahmanson

I haven't heard of anybody who wants to stop living on account of the cost.
Kin Hubbard

It isn't enough for you to love money — it's also necessary that money should love you.
Baron Rothschild

Philanthropist: a rich (and usually bald) old gentleman who has trained himself to grin while his conscience is picking his pocket.
Ambrose Bierce

The darkest hour of any man's life is when he sits down to plan how to get money without earning it.
Horace Greeley

The petty economies of the rich are just as amazing as the silly extravagances of the poor.
William Feather

Money is human happiness in the abstract.   *Arthur Schopenhauer*

Money is the most egalitarian force in society. It confers power on whoever holds it.
Roger Starr

Bankruptcy is a legal proceeding in which you put your money in your pants pocket and give your coat to your creditors.
Joey Adams

There are plenty of good five-cent cigars in the country. The trouble is they cost a quarter. What the country really needs is a good five-cent nickle.
Franklin P. Adams

I don't like money actually, but it quiets my nerves.   *Joe Louis*

Money isn't everything — but it'a a long way ahead of what comes next.
Edmund Stockdale

In the bad old days, there were three easy ways of losing money — racing being the quickest, women the pleasantest and farming the most certain.
William Pitt Amherst

We forget that money gives its value — that someone exchanged work for it.
Neal O'Hara

Money is something you got to make in case you don't die.   *Max Asnas*

If you would know what the Lord God thinks of money, you have only to look at those to whom he gives it.

Maurice Baring

Making money is fun, but it's pointless if you don't use the power it brings.

John Bentley

Make money and the whole world will conspire to call you a gentleman.

Mark Twain

I never been in no situation where havin' money made it any worse.

Clinton Jones

Money is the wise man's religion.

Euripides

Money, it turned out, was exactly like sex; you thought of nothing else if you didn't have it and thought of other things if you did.

James Baldwin

A feast is made for laughter, and wine maketh merry: but money answereth all things.

Ecclesiastes 10:19

Neither a borrower nor a lender be
For loan oft loses both itself and friend,
And borrowing dulls the edge of husbandry.

Shakespeare, 'Hamlet'

Never invest your money in anything that eats or needs repairing.

Billy Rose

Money is always there but the pockets change; it is not in the same pockets after a change, and that is all there is to say about money.

Gertrude Stein

Men are more often bribed by their loyalties and ambitions than by money.

Robert H. Jackson

Money dignifies what is frivolous if unpaid for.

Virginia Woolf

How do you make a million?
You start with $900,000.

Stephen Lewis to Morton Shulman

When you have told anyone you have left him a legacy, the only decent thing to do is to die at once.

Samuel Butler

He that maketh haste to be rich shall not be innocent.

Proverbs 28:20

Money is good for bribing yourself through the inconveniences of life.
Gottfried Reinhardt

There's nothing an economist should fear so much as applause.
Herbert Marshall

You can't force anyone to love you or to lend you money. *Jewish proverb*

With money in your pocket, you are wise, and you are handsome, and you sing well too. *Jewish proverb*

If the rich could hire other people to die for them, the poor would make a wonderful living. *Jewish proverb*

The farmer's way of saving money: to be owed by someone he trusted.
Hugh MacLennan

Gentlemen prefer bonds. *Andrew Mellon*

When you want really big money, you usually find yourself talking to people who didn't go to Eton. *An English banker*

A good mind possesses a kingdom: a great fortune is a great slavery.
Seneca

When it is a question of money, everybody is of the same religion.
Voltaire

Money is like muck — not good unless it be spread. *Francis Bacon*

Morality and Ethics

To act without rapacity, to use knowledge with wisdom, to respect interdependence, to operate without hubris and greed are not simply moral imperatives. They are an accurate scientific description of the means of survival. *Barbara Ward*

If some great power would agree to make me always think what is true and do what is right, on condition of being some sort of clock and wound up every morning before I got out of bed, I should close instantly with the offer. *Thomas Huxley*

We have two kinds of morality side by side: one which we preach but do not practice, and the other which we practice but seldom preach.

Bertrand Russell

There are ten commandments, right? Well, it's like an exam. You get eight out of ten, you're just about top of the class.   *Mordecai Richler*

A man does not have to be an angel in order to be a saint.*Albert Schweitzer*

No man is so exquisitely honest or upright in living but that ten times in his life he might not lawfully be hanged.   *Montaigne*

It is often easier to fight for principles than to live up to them.

Adlai Stevenson

Only that which does not teach, which does not cry out, which does not condescend, which does not explain, is irresistible.   *William Butler Yeats*

Quality — in its classic Greek sense — how to live with grace and intelligence, with bravery and mercy.   *Theodore H. White*

What is morality in any given time or place? It is what the majority then and there happen to like and immorality is what they dislike.

Alfred North Whitehead

No morality can be founded on authority, even if the authority were divine.

A. J. Ayer

In any assembly the simplest way to stop transacting business and split the ranks is to appeal to a principle.   *Jacques Barzun*

He who would do good to another must do it in minute particulars: general good is the plea of the scoundrel, hypocrite and flatterer. For art and science cannot exist but in minutely organized particulars.   *William Blake*

You've got to be brave and you've got to be bold. Brave enough to take your chance on your own discrimination — what's right and what's wrong, what's good and what's bad.   *Robert Frost*

We have left undone those things which we ought to have done; and we have done those things we ought not to have done; and there is no health in us.

Book of Common Prayer

Most people sell their souls and live with a good conscience on the proceeds.

Logan Pearsall Smith

This world is white no longer, and it will never be white again.
James Baldwin

Below the navel there is neither religion nor truth.   *Italian proverb*

It is customary these days to ignore what should be done in favour of what pleases us.   *Plautus*

What is morality but immemorial custom? Conscience is the chief of conservatives.   *Henry David Thoreau*

What you get free costs too much.   *Jean Anouilh*

You cannot receive a shock unless you have an electric affinity for that which shocks you.   *Henry David Thoreau*

Kindness goes a long way lots o' times when it ought t' stay at home.
Kin Hubbard

Even moderation ought not to be practised to excess.   *Anon.*

When a blind man carries the lame man, both go forward.
Swedish proverb

I have found by experience that they who have spent all their lives in cities, improve their talents but impair their virtues; and strengthen their minds but weaken their morals.   *Charles Caleb Colton*

Shame and guilt are noble emotions essential in the maintenance of civilized society, and vital for the development of some of the most refined and elegant qualities of human potential — generosity, service, self-sacrifice, unselfishness and duty.   *Willard Gaylen*

If your morals make you dreary, depend on it they are wrong.
Robert Louis Stevenson

Do not be too moral. You may cheat yourself out of much life. So aim above morality. Be not simply good; be good for something.
Henry David Thoreau

Moral courage is a more rare commodity than bravery in battle or great intelligence.   *Robert F. Kennedy*

Morality is not respectability.   *George Bernard Shaw*

Moral indignation — jealousy with a halo.   *H. G. Wells*

Nobody does nothing for nobody for naught.   *Peter Lord*

The man who is anybody and who does anything is surely going to be criticized, vilified, and misunderstood. This is part of the penalty for greatness,
and every man understands, too, that it is no proof of greatness.

Elbert Hubbard

Music

After silence, that which comes nearest to expressing the inexpressible is
music.   *Aldous Huxley*

When people hear good music, it makes them homesick for something they
never had, and never will have.   *Edgar Watson Howe*

Light quirks of music, broken and uneven,
Make the soul dance upon a jig of heaven.   *Alexander Pope*

Who hears music, feels his solitude peopled at once.   *Robert Browning*

Richard Wagner, a musician who wrote music which is better than it sounds.

Mark Twain

One cannot judge 'Lohengrin' from a first hearing, and I certainly do not
intend to hear it a second time.   *Gioacchino Antonio Rossini*

He could fiddle all the bugs off a sweet-potato vine.

Stephen Vincent Benét

Opera purges men of those hesitations and worries which make it difficult
for them to acknowledge their importance to themselves. A good performance
of an opera, that is, provides a language for us to speak of ourselves as we
have always known we should speak.   *Hamish Swanston*

No one can any longer write in the fat style of Strauss. That was killed by
Stravinsky. He stripped the body of much of its clothes. Music is the craft
of building structures with sound and that is what Stravinsky represents.

Vladimir Nabokov

A nation creates music — the composer only arranges it.

Mikhail Glinka

Sentimentally I am disposed to harmony; but organically I am incapable of a tune.

Charles Lamb

Music produces a kind of pleasure which human nature cannot do without.

Confucius

Conductors must give unmistakable and suggestive signals to the orchestra, not choreography to the audience.

George Szell

Music is the shorthand of emotion.

Leo Tolstoy

For most singers the first half of the career involves extending one's repertoire, the second half trimming it.

Ethan Mordden

How wonderful opera would be if there were no singers.

Gioacchino Antonio Rossini

Opera in English is, in the main, just about as sensible as baseball in Italian.

H. L. Mencken

Music is only sound expressing certain patterns, so to what extent is that sound architecture and to what extent theatre?

Arthur Brown

A jazz musician is a juggler who uses harmonies instead of oranges.

Benny Green

Music is a language by whose means messages are elaborated, that such messages can be understood by the many but sent out only by few, and that it alone among all the languages unites the contradictory character of being at once intelligible and untranslatable — these facts make the creator of music a being like the gods.

Claude Levi-Strauss

Music is your own experience, your thoughts, your wisdom. If you don't live it, it won't come out of your horn.

Charlie Parker

The good composer is slowly discovered, the bad composer is slowly found out.

Ernest Newman

The function of pop music is to be consumed.

Pierre Boulez

Oboe — an ill woodwind that nobody blows good.

Anon.

Music first and last should sound well, should allure and enchant the ear.
Never mind the inner significance.   *Thomas Beecham*

I am tired before the concert, not afterward.   *Artur Rubinstein*

Music, the greatest good that mortals know,
And all of heaven we have below.   *Joseph Addison*

What we play is life.   *Louis Armstrong*

I know that the twelve notes in each octave and the varieties of rhythm offer
me opportunities that all of human genius will never exhaust.
                                                      Igor Stravinsky

Had I learned to fiddle, I should have done nothing else.
                                                      Samuel Johnson

The notes I handle no better than many pianists. But the pauses between
the notes — ah, that is where the art resides!   *Artur Schnabel*

Without music, life would be a mistake.   *Friedrich Nietzsche*

Chamber music — a conversation between friends.
                                                      Catherine Drinker Bowen

Mozart is the human incarnation of the divine force of creation. *Goethe*

I write as a sow piddles.   *Wolfgang Amadeus Mozart*

I am an arrogant and impatient listener, but in the case of a few composers,
a very few, when I hear a work I do not like, I am convinced that it is my
own fault. Verdi is one of those composers.   *Benjamin Britten*

Music hath charms to soothe a savage breast,
To soften rocks, or bend a knotted oak.   *William Congreve*

Harpists spend half their life tuning and the other half playing out of tune.
                                                      Anon.

She was an aging singer who had to take every note above 'A' with her
eyebrows.   *Montague Glass*

Going to the opera, like getting drunk, is a sin that carries its own punishment with it and that a very severe one.   *Hannah More*

Opera is when a guy gets stabbed in the back and instead of bleeding he sings.
Ed Gardner

I think popular music in this country is one of the few things in the twentieth century that have made giant strides in reverse.   *Bing Crosby*

If a literary man puts together two words about music, one of them will be wrong.   *Aaron Copland*

Music is given to us specifically to make order of things, to move from an anarchic, individualistic state to a regulated, perfectly concious one, which alone insures vitality and durability.   *Igor Stravinsky*

Nature

The universe is not hostile, nor yet is it friendly. It is simply indifferent.
John Hughes Holmes

In nature there are neither rewards nor punishments — there are consequences.   *Robert G. Ingersoll*

Monotony is the law of nature. Look at the monotonous manner in which the sun rises. The monotony of necessary occupations is exhilarating and life-giving.   *Gandhi*

Nature, with equal mind,
Sees all her sons at play,
Sees man control the wind,
The wind sweep man away.   *Mattthew Arnold*

Men argue, nature acts.   *Voltaire*

Nature is usually wrong.   *James McNeill Whistler*

Speak to the earth, and it shall teach thee.   *Job 12:8*

Flowers have an expression of countenance as much as men or animals. Some seem to smile, some have a sad expression, some are pensive and diffident, others again are plain, honest and upright.   *Henry Ward Beecher*

Gie me a spark o' nature's fire,
That's a' the learning I desire.   *Robert Burns*

Nature is reckless of the individual. When she has points to carry, she carries them.   *Ralph Waldo Emerson*

I wanted to say something about the universe. There's God, angels, plants... and horseshit.   *Zero Mostel*

When elephants fight it is the grass that suffers.   *African saying*

The dinosaur's eloquent lesson is that if some bigness is good, an overabundance of bigness is not necessarily better.   *Eric Johnston*

Who are we? We find that we live on an insignificant planet of a humdrum star lost in a galaxy tucked away in some forgotten corner of a universe in which there are far more galaxies than people.   *Carl Sagan*

A vacuum is a hell of a lot better than some of the stuff that nature replaces it with.   *Tennessee Williams*

Talk of mysteries! Think of our life in Nature — daily to be shown matter, to come in contact with it — rocks, trees, wind on our cheeks! The solid earth! The actual world! Common sense! Contact! Contact! Who are we? Where are we?   *Henry David Thoreau*

We cannot command Nature except by obeying her.   *Francis Bacon*

The mastery of nature is vainly believed to be an adequate substitute for self-mastery.   *Reinhold Niebuhr*

Nature thrives on patience; man on impatience.   *Paul Boese*

The soil, in return for her service, keeps the tree tied to her; the sky asks nothing and leaves it free.   *Rabindranath Tagore*

What mighty battles have I seen and heard waged between the trees and the west wind — an Iliad fought in the fields of air.   *Edith M. Thomas*

Grass is the forgiveness of nature — her constant benediction. Forests decay, harvests perish, flowers vanish, but grass is immortal.   *Brian Ingalls*

The whole of nature is a conjugation of the verb to eat, in the active and passive.   *William R. Inge*

The universe is like a safe to which there is a combination, but the combination is locked up in the safe.   *Peter de Vries*

When the oak is felled the whole forest echoes with its fall, but a hundred acorns are sown in silence by an unnoticed breeze.   *Thomas Carlyle*

Deep in their roots,
All flowers keep the light.   *Theodore Roethke*

By nature's kindly disposition, most questions which it is beyond man's power to answer do not occur to him at all.   *George Santayana*

To demand 'sense' is the hallmark of nonsense. Nature does not make sense. Nothing makes sense.   *Ayn Rand*

If allowed to survive this grass will produce enough oxygen for two students to breathe for one semester.   *Lawn sign, University of Iowa*

I frequently tramped eight or ten miles through the deepest snow to keep an appointment with a beech tree, or a yellow birch, or an old acquaintance among the pines.   *Henry David Thoreau*

Like a great poet, Nature is capable of producing the most stunning effects with the smallest means. Nature possesses only the sun, trees, flowers, water and love. But for him who feels no love in his heart, none of these things has any poetic value. To such an individual the sun has a diameter of a certain number of miles, the trees are good for making a fire, the flowers are divided into varieties, and the water is wet.   *Heinrich Heine*

The bluebird carries the sky on his back.   *Henry David Thoreau*

There is nothing in which the birds differ more from man than the way in which they can build and yet leave a landscape as it was before.   *Robert Lynd*

The greatest joy in nature is the absence of man.   *Bliss Carman*

When a man wantonly destroys a work of man we call him a vandal; when a man destroys one of the works of God, we call him a sportsman.   *Joseph Wood Krutch*

Man is a complex being: he makes deserts bloom and lakes die.   *Gil Stern*

Nature never did betray the heart that loved her.   *William Wordsworth*

Newspapers and Journalism

Burke said there were three Estates in Parliament; but in the reporters' gallery yonder, there sat a fourth Estate more important than them all.

Thomas Carlyle

Comfort the afflicted and afflict the comfortable. *Finley Peter Dunne*

Remember, son, many a good story has been ruined by over-verification.

James Gordon Bennett

Don't be afraid to make a mistake, your readers might like it.

William Randolph Hearst

One newspaper a day ought to be enough for anyone who still prefers to retain a little mental balance. *Clifton Fadiman*

Journalism is literature in a hurry. *Matthew Arnold*

The sports page records people's accomplishments, the front page usually records nothing but man's failures. *Earl Warren*

News is the first rough draft of history. *Benjamin Bradlee*

Carelessness is not fatal to journalism, nor are clichés, for the eye rests lightly on them. But what is intended to be read once can seldom be read more than once; a journalist has to accept the fact that his work, by its very todayness, is excluded from any share in tomorrow. *Cyril Connolly*

He had been kicked in the head by a mule when young, and believed everything he read in the Sunday papers. *George Ade*

An editor — a person employed on a newspaper, whose business it is to separate the wheat from the chaff, and to see that the chaff is printed.

Elbert Hubbard

The day you write to please everyone you no longer are in journalism. You are in show business. *Frank Miller, Jr.*

It is a newspaper's duty to print the news and raise hell.

Wilbur F. Storey

If some great catastrophe is not announced every morning, we feel a certain void. 'Nothing in the paper today,' we sigh. *Paul Valéry*

Newspapers have developed what might be called a vested interest in catastrophe. If they can spot a fight, they play up that fight. If they can uncover a tragedy, they will headline that tragedy.   *Harry A. Overstreet*

What you see is news, what you know is background, what you feel is opinion.   *Lester Markel*

Freedom of the press is guaranteed only to those who own one.
     A. J. Liebling

A good newspaper is a nation talking to itself.   *Arthur Miller*

The first essence of journalism is to know what you want to know; the second, is to find out who will tell you.   *John Gunther*

Today's reporter is forced to become an educator more concerned with explaining the news than with being first on the scene.   *Fred Friendly*

A writer who takes up journalism abandons the slow tempo of literature for a faster one and the change will do him harm. By degrees the flippancy of journalism will become a habit and the pleasure of being paid on the nail and more especially of being praised on the nail, grow indispensable.
     Cyril Connolly

Observation

The eyes believe themselves; the ears believe other people.
     German proverb

The lower classes of men, though they do not think it worthwhile to record what they perceive, nevertheless perceive everything that is worth noting; the difference between them and a man of learning often consists in nothing more than the latter's facility for expression.   *G. C. Lichtenberg*

The eye sees only what the mind is prepared to comprehend.
     Robertson Davies

The things we see are the mind's best bet as to what is out front.
     Adelbert Ames

You can observe a lot just by watching.   *Yogi Berra*

The eye is the jewel of the body.   *Henry David Thoreau*

The ear tends to be lazy, craves the familiar and is shocked by the unexpected; the eye, on the other hand, tends to be impatient, craves the novel and is bored by repetition. *W. H. Auden*

The eyes indicate the antiquity of the soul. *Ralph Waldo Emerson*

To become the spectator of one's own life is to escape the suffering of life. *Oscar Wilde*

One must always tell what one sees. Above all, which is more difficult, one must always see what one sees. *Charles Péguy*

A fool sees not the same tree that a wise man sees. *William Blake*

Cultivated men and women who do not skim the cream of life, and are attached to the duties, yet escape the harsher blows, make acute and balanced observers. *George Meredith*

People only see what they are prepared to see. *Ralph Waldo Emerson*

There's none so blind as those who won't see. *English proverb*

Opinion

One should respect public opinion in so far as it is necessary to avoid starvation and to keep out of prison, but anything that goes beyond this is voluntary submission to an unnecessary tyranny. *Bertrand Russell*

Public opinion, a vulgar, impertinent, anonymous tyrant who deliberately makes life unpleasant for anyone who is not content to be the average man. *William R. Inge*

You've no idea what a poor opinion I have of myself — and how little I deserve it. *W. S. Gilbert*

Predominant opinions are generally the opinions of the generation that is vanishing. *Benjamin Disraeli*

To be positive: to be mistaken at the top of one's voice. *Ambrose Bierce*

When I want your opinion I'll give it to you. *Laurence J. Peter*

It is always considered a piece of impertinence in England if a man of less than two or three thousand a year has any opinions at all upon important subjects.
Sydney Smith

The pressure of public opinion is like the pressure of the atmosphere; you can't see it — but all the same, it is sixteen pounds to the square inch.
James Russell Lowell

The right to be heard does not automatically include the right to be taken seriously.
Hubert Humphrey

The world is not run by thought, nor by imagination, but by opinion.
Elizabeth Drew

'No' and 'Yes' are words quickly said, but they need a great amount of thought before you utter them.
Baltasar Gracián

I disapprove of what you say, but I will defend to the death your right to say it.
Voltaire

It is not truth, but opinion that can travel the world without a passport.
Walter Raleigh

There never were two opinions alike in all the world, no more than two hours or two grains: the most universal quality is diversity.
Montaigne

A difference of opinion is what makes horse racing and missionaries.
Will Rogers

All empty souls tend to extreme opinion.
William Butler Yeats

The foolish and the dead alone never change their opinions.
James Russell Lowell

Too often we . . . enjoy the comfort of opinion without the discomfort of thought.
John F. Kennedy

Public opinion is a compound of folly, weakness, prejudice, wrong feeling, right feeling, obstinacy, and newspaper paragraphs.
Robert Peel

Opinions cannot survive if one has no chance to fight for them.
Thomas Mann

There are a great many opinions in this world, and a good half of them are professed by people who have never been in trouble.
Mavis Gallant

Optimism and Pessimism

When I look in the glass I see that every line in my face means pessimism, but in spite of my face — that is my experience — I remain an optimist.
Richard Jefferies

Fit for the sunshine, so, it followed him
A happy-tempered bringer of the best
Out of the worst.   *Robert Browning*

An optimist is a guy
that has never had
much experience.   *Don Marquis*

An optimist is a fellow who believes what's going to be will be postponed.
Kin Hubbard

Pessimist — one who, when he has the choice of two evils, chooses both.
Oscar Wilde

My pessimism goes to the point of suspecting the sincerity of the pessimists.
Jean Rostand

A pessimist is one who has been compelled to live with an optimist.
Elbert Hubbard

Pessimism is only the name that men of weak nerves give to wisdom.
Elbert Hubbard

When it is dark enough, you can see the stars.   *Charles A. Beard*

There is not enough darkness in all the world to put out the light of even one small candle.   *Robert Alden*

When things come to the worst, they generally mend.   *Susanna Moodie*

The optimist claims we live in the best of all possible worlds, and the pessimist fears this is true.   *James Branch Cabell*

Still round the corner there may wait,
A new road, or a secret gate.   *J. R. R. Tolkien*

When Fortune empties her chamberpot on your head, smile and say 'We are going to have a summer shower.'   *John A. Macdonald*

The world gets better every day — then worse again in the evening.
Kin Hubbard

A man he seems of cheerful yesterdays
And confident tomorrows.   *William Wordsworth*

There is a budding morrow in midnight.   *John Keats*

Order and Organization

When liberty destroys order, the hunger for order will destroy liberty.
Will Durant

Those who are fond of setting things to rights have no great objection to
setting them wrong.   *William Hazlitt*

Our laws make law impossible; our liberties destroy all freedom; our property is organized robbery; our morality an impudent hypocrisy; our wisdom
is administered by inexperienced or mal-experienced dupes; our power wielded
by cowards and weaklings; and our honour false in all its points. I am an
enemy of the existing order for good reasons.   *George Bernard Shaw*

Crude classifications and false generalizations are the curse of organized life.
H. G. Wells

To have his path made clear for him is the aspiration of every human being
in our beclouded and tempestuous existence.   *Joseph Conrad*

Timing, degree and conviction are the three wise men in this life.
R. I. Fitzhenry

We put things in order — God does the rest. Lay an iron bar east and west,
it is not magnetized. Lay it north and south and it is.   *Horace Mann*

I must create a system, or be enslaved by another man's. *William Blake*

Out of intense complexities intense simplicities emerge.
Winston Churchill

There is no course of life so weak and sottish as that which is managed by
order, method and discipline.   *Montaigne*

Large organization is loose organization. Nay, it would be almost as true to say that organization is always disorganization.   *G. K. Chesterton*

Originality

Originality is nothing but judicious imitation. The most original writers borrowed one from another. The instruction we find in books is like fire. We fetch it from our neighbours, kindle it at home, communicate it to others, and it becomes the property of all.   *Voltaire*

Originality does not consist in saying what no one has ever said before, but in saying exactly what you think yourself.   *James Stephens*

What a good thing Adam had — when he said a good thing, he knew nobody had said it before.   *Mark Twain*

All cases are unique and very similar to others.   *T. S. Eliot*

I invent nothing. I rediscover.   *Auguste Rodin*

There is nothing new under the sun.   *Ecclesiastes 1:9*

When people are free to do as they please, they usually imitate each other. Originality is deliberate and forced, and partakes of the nature of a protest.   *Eric Hoffer*

All profoundly original work looks ugly at first.   *Clement Greenberg*

Riding hard for glory.   *Irving Layton*

What is originality? Undetected plagiarism.   *William R. Inge*

The dogmas of the quiet past are inadequate to the stormy present. The occasion is piled high with difficulty, and we must rise with the occasion. As our case is new, so we must think anew and act anew. We must disenthrall ourselves.   *Abraham Lincoln*

Ownership and Possession

It is preoccupation with possession, more than anything else, that prevents men from living freely and nobly.   *Bertrand Russell*

Broad acres are a patent of nobility; and no man but feels more of a man in the world if he have a bit of ground that he can call his own. However small it is on the surface, it is 4000 miles deep; and that is a very handsome property.   *Charles Dudley Warner*

The landscape should belong to the people who see it all the time.
                                                                    Le Roi Jones

Whatever it not nailed down is mine. Whatever I can pry loose is not nailed down.   *Collis P. Huntington*

I don't want to own anything that won't fit into my coffin.   *Fred Allen*

Lives based on having are less free than lives based either on doing or on being.   *William James*

The possession of gold has ruined fewer men than the lack of it.
                                                            Thomas Bailey Aldrich

The want of a thing is perplexing enough, but the possession of it is intolerable.   *John Vanbrugh*

Our life on earth is, and ought to be, material and carnal. But we have not yet learned to manage our materialism and carnality properly; they are still entangled with the desire for ownership.   *E. M. Forster*

Keep a thing seven years and you will find a use for it.   *Anon.*

You must lose a fly to catch a trout.   *George Herbert*

He who wants a rose must respect the thorn.   *Persian proverb*

A man never feels the want of what it never occurs to him to ask for.
                                                            Arthur Schopenhauer

I feel when people say 'bigger and better' they should say 'bigger and badder.'   *Marie Elizabeth Kane, thirteen years old*

People are so overwhelmed with the prestige of their instruments that they consider their personal judgement of hardly any account.
                                                                 Wyndham Lewis

Can anything be so elegant as to have few wants, and to serve them one's self?   *Ralph Waldo Emerson*

Painters and Painting

There is nothing more difficult for a truly creative painter than to paint a rose, because before he can do so he has first to forget all the roses that were ever painted.   *Henri Matisse*

If you could say it in words there would be no reason to paint.
                                                    Edward Hopper

Everyone wants to understand painting. Why don't they try to understand the singing of birds? People love the night, a flower, everything that surrounds them without trying to understand them. But painting — that they *must* understand.   *Pablo Picasso*

I cannot pretend to feel impartial about colours. I rejoice with the brilliant ones and am genuinely sorry for the poor browns.   *Winston Churchill*

I hope with all my heart there will be painting in heaven.
                                                    Jean Baptiste Corot

Painting is a blind man's profession. He paints not what he sees, but what he feels, what he tells himself about what he has seen.   *Pablo Picasso*

Painting, n: the art of protecting flat surfaces from the weather and exposing them to the critic.   *Ambrose Bierce*

As a painter I shall never signify anything of importance. I feel it absolutely.
                                                    Vincent van Gogh

A portrait is a painting with something wrong with the mouth.
                                                    John Singer Sargent

To say to the painter that Nature is to be taken as she is, is to say to the player that he may sit on the piano.   *James McNeill Whistler*

The fingers must be educated, the thumb is born knowing. *Marc Chagall*

I paint objects as I think them, not as I see them.   *Pablo Picasso*

The idea is in my head; to put it down is nothing   *Milton Avery*

There are three kinds of people in the world: those who can't stand Picasso, those who can't stand Raphael and those who've never heard of either of them.   *John White*

I dream my painting, and then I paint my dream.   *Vincent van Gogh*

A picture can become for us a highway between a particular thing and a universal feeling.   *Lawren Harris*

For me, painting is a way to forget life. It is a cry in the night, a strangled laugh.   *Georges Rouault*

Landscape painting is the obvious resource of misanthropy.   *William Hazlitt*

I paint from the top down. First the sky, then the mountains, then the hills, then the houses, then the cattle, and then the people.   *Grandma Moses*

A good painter is to paint two main things, namely men and the working of man's mind.   *Leonardo da Vinci*

I do not paint a portrait to look like the subject, rather does the person grow to look like his portrait.   *Salvador Dali*

All colours are the friends of their neighbours and the lovers of their opposites.   *Marc Chagall*

The purest and most thoughtful minds are those which love colour the most.   *John Ruskin*

Painting is just another way of keeping a diary.   *Pablo Picasso*

Sir, when their backsides look good enough to slap, there's nothing more to do.   *Peter Paul Rubens*

A painter who has the feel of breasts and buttocks is saved.   *Auguste Renoir*

Some day they will know what I mean.   *Tom Thomson*

Modern art is what happens when painters stop looking at girls and persuade themselves they have a better idea.   *John Ciardi*

When I look at a painting it isn't only the painting that I see but the thing that I am. If there is more in the painting than I am, then I won't see it.   *Ivan Eyre*

Parenthood

Parenthood remains the greatest single preserve of the amateur.
Alvin Toffler

The best brought-up children are those who have seen their parents as they are. Hypocrisy is not the parents' first duty. *George Bernard Shaw*

Everyone likes to think that he has done reasonably well in life, so that it comes as a shock to find our children believing differently. The temptation is to tune them out; it takes much more courage to listen.
John D. Rockefeller III

You don't have to deserve your mother's love. You have to deserve your father's. He's more particular. *Robert Frost*

I demand for the unmarried mother, as a sacred channel of life, the same reverence and respect as for the married mother; for Maternity is a cosmic thing and once it has come to pass, our conventions must not be permitted to blaspheme it. *Ben Lindsey*

Who takes the child by the hand takes the mother by the heart.
German proverb

Diogenes struck the father when the son swore. *Robert Burton*

When one has not had a good father, one must create one.
Friedrich Nietzsche

Perhaps host and guest is really the happiest relation for father and son.
Evelyn Waugh

Mother is the name for God in the lips and hearts of children.
William Makepeace Thackeray

To bring up a child in the way he should go, travel that way yourself once in a while. *Josh Billings*

Anything which parents have not learned from experience they can now learn from their children. *Anon.*

A father is a banker provided by nature. *French proverb*

To become a father is not hard,
To be a father is, however. *Wilhelm Busch*

Our sons, who so easily recognize our errors, and rightly denounce them, will have to confess their own, later on, and they may be as bad as ours, perhaps worse. *Bruce Hutchison*

A mother who is really a mother is never free. *Honoré de Balzac*

God could not be everywhere and therefore he made mothers. *Jewish proverb*

A mother is a person who if she is not there when you get home from school you wouldn't know how to get your dinner, and you wouldn't feel like eating it anyway. *Anon.*

The first half of our lives is ruined by our parents and the second half by our children. *Clarence S. Darrow*

Tired mothers find that spanking takes less time than reasoning and penetrates sooner to the seat of the memory. *Will Durant*

Every parent is at some time the father of the unreturned prodigal, with nothing to do but keep his house open to hope. *John Ciardi*

The fundamental defect of fathers is that they want their children to be a credit to them. *Bertrand Russell*

Don't limit a child to your own learning, for he was born in another time. *Rabbinical saying*

An ounce of mother is worth a pound of clergy. *Spanish proverb*

No matter how old a mother is, she watches her middle-aged children for signs of improvement. *Florida Scott-Maxwell*

Whatever you would have your children become, strive to exhibit in your own lives and conversation. *Lydia H. Sigourney*

Train a child in the way he should go, and when he is old he will not depart from it. *Proverbs 12:4*

I must study politics and war, that my sons may have the liberty to study mathematics and philosophy, geography, natural history, and naval architecture, navigation, commerce, and agriculture, in order to give their children a right to study painting, poetry, music, architecture, statuary, tapestry and porcelain. *John Adams*

The thing about having a baby is that thereafter you have it. *Jean Kerr*

The best way to bring up some children is short. *Anthony J. Pettito*

What the mother sings to the cradle goes all the way down to the coffin. *Henry Ward Beecher*

The mother-child relationship is paradoxical and, in a sense, tragic. It requires the most intense love on the mother's side, yet this very love must help the child grow away from the mother and to become fully independent. *Erich Fromm*

Who doesn't desire his father's death? *Fyodor Dostoevsky*

Insanity is hereditary — you can get it from your children. *Sam Levinson*

Parents are the bones on which children cut their teeth. *Peter Ustinov*

Your children need your presence more than your presents. *Jesse Jackson*

People should be free to find or make for themselves the kinds of educational experiences they want their children to have. *John Holt*

It is the malady of our age that the young are so busy teaching us that they have no time left to learn. *Eric Hoffer*

Passion and the Heart

What our age lacks is not reflection but passion. *Søren Kierkegaard*

It is with our passions as it is with fire and water — they are good servants, but bad masters. *Roger l'Estrange*

The happiness of a man in this life does not consist in the absence but in the mastery of his passions. *Alfred, Lord Tennyson*

The ruling passion, be it what it will,
The ruling passion conquers reason still.   *Alexander Pope*

There is no passion like that of a functionary for his function.
                                        Georges Clemenceau

An intense feeling carries with it its own universe, magnificent or wretched
as the case may be.   *Albert Camus*

He disliked emotion, not because he felt lightly, but because he felt deeply.
                                              John Buchan

People don't ask for facts in making up their minds. They would rather have
one good, soul-satisfying emotion than a dozen facts.
                                        Robert Keith Leavitt

If we resist our passions, it is more due to their weakness than to our strength.
                                           La Rochefoucauld

A sentimentalist is simply one who desires to have the luxury of an emotion
without paying for it.   *Oscar Wilde*

Is it not strange
That desire should so many years outlive performance?
                                Shakespeare, 'Henry IV' Part II

The world is a comedy to those who think; a tragedy to those who feel.
                                            Horace Walpole

Follow your heart, and you perish.   *Margaret Laurence*

The only people for me are the mad ones, the ones who are mad to live,
mad to talk, mad to be saved . . . the ones who never yawn and say a com-
monplace thing, but burn, burn, burn, like fabulous yellow roman candles
exploding like spiders across the stars.   *Jack Kerouac*

Fanaticism consists in redoubling your efforts when you have forgotten your
aim.   *George Santayana*

Disappointments should be cremated, not embalmed.   *Henry S. Haskins*

Artificial manners vanish the moment the natural passions are touched.
                                            Maria Edgeworth

Hands have not tears to flow.   *Dylan Thomas*

A good heart is better than all the heads in the world.
Edward Bulwer-Lytton

Where the mind is past hope, the heart is past shame. *John Lyly*

Nobody has ever measured, even poets, how much a heart can hold.
Zelda Fitzgerald

The logic of the heart is absurd. *Julie de Lespinasse*

Our hearts were drunk with a beauty
Our eyes could never see. *George W. Russell*

The same heart beats in every human breast. *Matthew Arnold*

The heart has its reasons which reason knows nothing of. *Blaise Pascal*

Man *becomes* man only by the intelligence, but he is man only by the heart.
Henri Frédéric Amiel

From the solitude of the wood, (Man) has passed to the more dreadful solitude
of the heart. *Loren Eiseley*

Seeing's believing, but feeling's the truth. *Thomas Fuller*

We are adhering to life now with our last muscle — the heart.
Djuna Barnes

The great art of life is sensation, to feel that we exist, even in pain.
Lord Byron

Weak people cannot be sincere. *La Rochefoucauld*

Patience

Have patience with all things, but chiefly have patience with yourself. Do
not lose courage in considering your own imperfections, but instantly set
about remedying them — every day begin the task anew.
St. Francis de Sales

Patience makes a woman beautiful in middle age. *Elliot Paul*

Life on the farm is a school of patience; you can't hurry the crops or make an ox in two days.   *Henri Fournier Alain*

There is nothing so bitter, that a patient mind cannot find some solace for it.   *Seneca*

Patience has its limits. Take it too far, and it's cowardice.
                                                                        George Jackson

With time and patience the mulberry leaf becomes a silk gown.
                                                                        Chinese proverb

Never cut what you can untie.   *Joseph Joubert*

I am as poor as Job, my lord, but not so patient.
                                                        Shakespeare, 'Henry IV' Part II

A handful of patience is worth more than a bushel of brains.
                                                                            Dutch proverb

The more haste, the less speed.   *John Heywood*

Hasten slowly.   *Augustus Caesar*

People in a hurry cannot think, cannot grow, nor can they decay. They are preserved in a state of perpetual puerility.   *Eric Hoffer*

There are no short cuts to Heaven, only the ordinary way of ordinary things.
                                                                        Vincent McNabb

Never think that God's delays are God's denials. Hold on; hold fast; hold out. Patience is genius.   *Comte de Buffon*

Patriotism and Nationalism

One of the great attractions of patriotism —it fulfills our worst wishes. In the person of our nation we are able, vicariously, to bully and cheat. Bully and cheat, what's more, with a feeling that we are profoundly virtuous.
                                                                        Aldous Huxley

Patriotism is not short, frenzied outbursts of emotion, but the tranquil and steady dedicaton of a lifetime.   *Adlai Stevenson*

True patriotism hates injustice in its own land more than anywhere else.
Clarence Darrow

A nation is a body of people who have done great things together.
Ernest Renan

Each man must for himself alone decide what is right and what is wrong,
which course is patriotic and which isn't. You cannot shirk this and be a man.
Mark Twain

The French have a passion for revolution but an abhorrence of change.
Old Saying

God made the ocean, but the Dutch made Holland.   *Dutch proverb*

The Creator made Italy with designs by Michelangelo.   *Mark Twain*

Men may be linked in friendship. Nations are linked only by interests.
Rolf Hochhuth

What makes a nation great is not primarily its great men, but the stature
of its innumerable mediocre ones.   *José Ortega y Gasset*

There is Ontario patriotism, Quebec patriotism, or Western patriotism; each
based on the hope that it may swallow up the others, but there is no Canadian patriotism, and we can have no Canadian nation when we have no Canadian patriotism.   *Henri Bourassa*

I'm troubled. I'm dissatisfied. I'm Irish.   *Marianne Moore*

The mind supplies the idea of a nation, but what gives this idea its sentimental force is a community of dreams.   *André Malraux*

My favourite example (of ex-patriotism) is James Joyce, who left Ireland
at nineteen and never came back. But he spent the rest of his life writing
about Ireland from the perspective of living in Paris.   *Karl Beveridge*

A nation is a body of people who have done great things
together in the past and hope to do great things together in the future.
Frank Underhill

The Swiss are not a people so much as a neat, clean, quite solvent business.
William Faulkner

Ireland is a fatal disease; fatal to Englishmen and doubly fatal to Irishmen.
George Moore

Peace

One sword keeps another in the sheath. *George Herbert*

Peace is a virtual, mute, sustained victory of potential powers against probable greeds. *Paul Valéry*

Peace is not an absence of war, it is a virtue, a state of mind, a disposition for benevolence, confidence, justice. *Benedict Spinoza*

There are no makers of peace because the making of peace is at least as costly as the making of war — at least as exigent. *Daniel Berrigan*

Once you hear the details of victory, it is hard to distinguish it from a defeat. *Jean-Paul Sartre*

The peace of the man who has foresworn the use of the bullet seems to me not quite peace, but a canting impotence. *Ralph Waldo Emerson*

Where they make a desert, they call it peace. *Tacitus*

That they may have a little peace, even the best dogs are compelled to snarl occasionally. *William Feather*

Peace: in international affairs, a period of cheating between two periods of fighting. *Ambrose Bierce*

They sicken of the calm who know the storm. *Dorothy Parker*

Personal Appearance

(Abraham Lincoln's) weathered face was homely as a plowed field.
Stephen Vincent Benét

Every man over forty is responsible for his face. *Abraham Lincoln*

Don't blame the mirror if your face is faulty. *Nikolai Vasilyevich Gogol*

People are like birds — from a distance, beautiful: from close up, those sharp beaks, those beady little eyes. *Richard J. Needham*

Consider the lilies of the field, how they grow; they toil not, neither do they spin. And yet I say unto you, that even Solomon in all his glory was not arrayed like one of these. *Matthew 6:28,29*

The world is a looking glass and gives back to every man the reflection of his own face. *William Makepeace Thackeray*

He that has a great nose thinks everybody is speaking of it. *Thomas Fuller*

There's one thing about baldness — it's neat. *Don Herold*

One's eyes are what one is, one's mouth what one becomes. *John Galsworthy*

Hair is another name for sex. *Vidal Sassoon*

It is easy to be beautiful; it is difficult to appear so. *Frank O'Hara*

It is only shallow people who do not judge by appearances. The true mystery of the world is the visible, not the invisible. *Oscar Wilde*

Clothes and manners do not make the man; but, when he is made, they greatly improve his appearance. *Henry Ward Beecher*

Any man may be in good spirits and good temper when he's well dressed. There ain't much credit in that. *Charles Dickens*

Why don't you get a haircut; you look like a chrysanthemum. *P. G. Wodehouse*

Her face looks as if it had worn out two bodies. *New England saying*

A man cannot dress, without his ideas get clothed at the same time. *Laurence Sterne*

Where's the man could ease the heart
Like a satin gown? *Dorothy Parker*

Let me be dressed fine as I will,
Flies, worms, and flowers, exceed me still. *Isaac Watts*

Philosophy

All philosophy lies in two words, sustain and abstain.   *Epictetus*

In philosophy an individual is becoming himself.   *Bernard Lonergan*

Romanticism is the expression of man's urge to rise above reason and common sense, just as rationalism is the expression of his urge to rise above theology and emotion.   *Charles Yost*

Science is what you know, philosophy is what you don't know.
Bertrand Russell

Here is the beginning of philosophy: a recognition of the conflicts between men, a search for their cause, a condemnation of mere opinion . . . and the discovery of a standard of judgement.   *Epictetus*

Anything that comes easy, comes wrong.   *Josephine Tessier*

To teach how to live with uncertainty, and yet without being paralyzed by hesitation, is perhaps the chief thing that philosophy in our age can still do for those who study it.   *Bertrand Russell*

All philosophies, if you ride them home, are nonsense; but some are greater nonsense than others.   *Samuel Butler*

It is easy to build a philosophy. It doesn't have to run.
Charles F. Kettering

I've developed a new philosophy — I only dread one day at a time.
Charles M. Schulz

A man of business may talk of philosophy; a man who has none may practise it.   *Alexander Pope*

Philosophy — the purple bullfinch in the lilac tree.   *T. S. Eliot*

Philosophy has a fine saying for everything — for Death it has an entire set.
Laurence Sterne

I have a simple philosophy. Fill what's empty. Empty what's full. And scratch where it itches.   *Alice Roosevelt Longworth*

All men are Philosophers, to their inches.   *Ben Jonson*

In North America there is the general belief that everything can be fixed, that life can be fixed up. In Europe, the view is that a lot can't be fixed up and that living properly is not necessarily a question of mastering the technology so much as learning to live gracefully within the constraints that the species invents.   *Jonathan Miller*

Every day look at a beautiful picture, read a beautiful poem, listen to some beautiful music, and if possible, say some reasonable thing.   *Goethe*

When you have only two pennies left in the world, buy a loaf of bread with one, and a lily with the other.   *Chinese proverb*

Three passions, simple but overwhelmingly strong, have governed my life: the longing for love, the search for knowledge and unbearable pity for the suffering of mankind.   *Bertrand Russell*

The opposite of a correct statement is a false statement. But the opposite of a profound truth may well be another profound truth.   *Niels Bohr*

The philosophy of one century is the common sense of the next.
                    Henry Ward Beecher

Philosophy is a good horse in the stable, but an errant jade on a journey.
                    Oliver Goldsmith

Philosophy will clip an Angel's wings,
Conquer all mysteries by rule and line,
Empty the haunted air, the gnomed mine —
Unweave a rainbow.   *John Keats*

Adversity's sweet milk, philosophy.   *Shakespeare, 'Romeo and Juliet'*

Philosophy is doubt.   *Montaigne*

Be a philosopher but, amid all your philosophy be still a man.
                    David Hume

I hate the philosopher who is not wise for himself.   *Euripides*

The philosopher is Nature's pilot — and there you have our difference; to be in hell is to drift: to be in heaven is to steer.   *George Bernard Shaw*

For there was never yet philosopher
That could endure the toothache patiently.
                    Shakespeare, 'Much Ado About Nothing'

One's task is not to turn the world upside down, but to do what is necessary at the given place and with a due consideration of reality.

Dietrich Bonhoeffer

Photography

Instead of just recording reality, photographs have become the norm for the way things appear to us, thereby changing the very idea of reality and of realism.

Susan Sontag

The virtue of the camera is not the power it has to transform the photographer into an artist, but the impulse it gives him to keep on looking.

Brooks Atkinson

You see someone on the street, and essentially what you notice about them is the flaw.

Diane Arbus

If you scratch a great photograph, you find two things: a painting and a photograph.

Janet Malcolm

The camera makes everyone a tourist in other people's reality, and eventually in one's own.

Susan Sontag

Photography records the gamut of feelings written on the human face; the beauty of the earth and skies that man has inherited; and the wealth and confusion man has created. It is a major force in explaining man to man.

Edward Steichen

All I wanted was to connect my moods with those of Paris. Beauty pains, and when it pained most, I shot.

Ernst Haas

Photographers deal in things which are continually vanishing and when they have vanished there is no contrivance on earth which can make them come back again.

Henri Cartier Bresson

Photographers, along with dentists, are the two professions never satisfied with what they do. Every dentist would like to be a doctor and inside every photographer is a painter trying to get out.

Pablo Picasso

Life is not about significant details, illuminated in a flash, fixed forever. Photographs are.

Susan Sontag

I really believe there are things nobody would see if I didn't photograph them.

Diane Arbus

Poets and Poetry

I don't really feel my poems are mine at all. I didn't create them out of nothing. I owe them to my relations with other people. *Robert Graves*

There's no money in poetry, but then there's no poetry in money either.
Robert Graves

The essentials of poetry are rhythm, dance and the human voice.
Earle Birney

Colour, which is the poet's wealth, is so expensive that most take to mere outline sketches and become men of science. *Henry David Thoreau*

A poet dares to be just so clear and no clearer; he approaches lucid ground warily, like a mariner who is determined not to scrape his bottom on anything solid. A poet's pleasure is to withhold a little of his meaning, to intensify by mystification. He unzips the veil from beauty, but does not remove it. A poet utterly clear is a trifle glaring. *E. B. White*

Most joyful let the Poet be,
It is through him that all men see. *William Ellery Channing*

Most people do not believe in anything very much and our greatest poetry is given to us by those that do. *Cyril Connolly*

The poet is the priest of the invisible. *Wallace Stevens*

A good poet is someone who manages, in a lifetime of standing out in thunderstorms, to be struck by lightning five or six times.
Randall Jarrell

Poetry should be common in experience but uncommon in books.
Robert Frost

For what is a poem but a hazardous attempt at self-understanding: it is the deepest part of autobiography. *Robert Penn Warren*

When a great poet has lived certain things have been done once for all, and cannot be achieved again. *T. S. Eliot*

Before verse can be human again it must learn to be brutal. *J. M. Synge*

Poetry is all nouns and verbs. *Marianne Moore*

No honest poet can ever feel quite sure of the permanent value of what he
has written: he may have wasted his time and messed up his life for nothing.
T. S. Eliot

When you write in prose you say what you mean. When you write in rhyme
you say what you must. *Oliver Wendell Holmes*

The courage of the poet is to keep ajar the door that leads into madness.
Christopher Morley

Science is for those who learn; poetry for those who know.
Joseph Roux

Popular poets are the parish priests of the Muse, retailing her ancient divina-
tions to a long since converted public. *George Santayana*

I wish our clever young poets would remember my homely definitions of
prose and poetry; that is, prose — words in their best order; poetry — the
best words in their best order. *Samuel Taylor Coleridge*

Reason respects the differences, and imagination the similitudes of things.
Percy Bysshe Shelley

The poet's mind is . . . a receptacle for seizing and storing up numberless
feelings, phrases, images, which remain there until all the particles which
can unite to form a new compound are present together. *T. S. Eliot*

Of our conflicts with others we make rhetoric; of our conflicts with ourselves
we make poetry. *William Butler Yeats*

Poetry is a mug's game. *T. S. Eliot*

A poem begins with a lump in the throat; a homesickness or a lovesickness.
It is a reaching-out toward expression; an effort to find fulfillment. A complete poem is one where an emotion has found its thought and the thought
has found words. *Robert Frost*

An art in which the artist by means of rhythm and great sincerity can convey
to others the sentiment which he feels about life. *John Masefield*

Not reading poetry amounts to a national pastime here. *Phillis McGinley*

It is Homer who has chiefly taught other poets the art of telling lies skilfully.
Aristotle

Writing free verse is like playing tennis with the net down. *Robert Frost*

To have great poets there must be great audiences too. *Walt Whitman*

Poets aren't very useful,
Because they aren't consumeful or very produceful. *Ogden Nash*

Poetry is a way of taking life by the throat. *Robert Frost*

Poetry is the opening and closing of a door, leaving those who look through to guess what is seen during a moment. *Carl Sandburg*

Poetry is the journal of a sea animal living on land, wanting to fly in the air. *Carl Sandburg*

There are nine and sixty ways of constructing tribal lays,
And every single one of them is right. *Rudyard Kipling*

Poetry is the impish attempt to paint the colour of the wind.
Maxwell Bodenheim

For me, poetry is an evasion of the real job of writing prose.
Sylvia Plath

Politeness and Manners

(Politeness is) a tacit agreement that people's miserable defects, whether moral or intellectual, shall on either side be ignored and not be made the subject of reproach. *Arthur Schopenhauer*

Good manners are made up of petty sacrifices. *Ralph Waldo Emerson*

Politeness is good nature regulated by good sense. *Sydney Smith*

If a man didn't make sense, the Scotch felt it was misplaced politeness to try to keep him from knowing it. Better that he be aware of his reputation for this would encourage reticence which goes well with stupidity.
J. K. Galbraith

A man must have very eminent qualities to hold his own without being polite.
Jean de la Bruyère

Ah, men do not know how much strength is in poise,
That he goes the farthest who goes far enough.   *James Russell Lowell*

Questioning is not the mode of conversation among gentlemen.
Samuel Johnson

It doesn't matter what you do in the bedroom as long as you don't do it
in the streets and frighten the horses.   *Mrs. Patrick Campbell*

There is always a best way of doing everything, if it be only to boil an egg.
Manners are the happy ways of doing things.   *Ralph Waldo Emerson*

There is not a single outward mark of courtesy that does not have a deep
moral basis.   *Goethe*

Manners are the hypocrisy of a nation.   *Honoré de Balzac*

Good breeding consists in concealing how much we think of ourselves and
how little we think of the other person.   *Mark Twain*

Charming people live up to the very edge of their charm, and behave as
outrageously as the world will let them.   *Logan Pearsall Smith*

Etiquette means behaving yourself a little better than is absolutely essential.
Will Cuppy

I can't stand a naked light bulb, any more than I can stand a rude remark
or a vulgar action.   *Tennessee Williams*

Rudeness is the weak man's imitation of strength.   *Eric Hoffer*

Chivalry is the most delicate form of contempt.   *Albert Guérard*

Chivalry is a poor substitute for justice, if one cannot have both. Chivalry
is something like the icing on cake, sweet, but not nourishing.
Nellie McClung

(A gentleman) is any man who wouldn't hit a woman with his hat on.
Fred Allen

A true gentlemen is one who is never unintentionally rude.   *Oscar Wilde*

This is the final test of a gentleman: his respect for those who can be of no possible service to him.
William Lyon Phelps

A gentleman is mindful no less of the freedom of others than of his own dignity.
Livy

What is the test of good manners? Being able to bear patiently with bad ones.
Solomon ibn Gabirol

The attributes of a great lady may still be found in the rule of the four S's: Sincerity, Simplicity, Sympathy, and Serenity.
Emily Post

Politicians

I have said what I meant and meant what I said. I have not done as well as I should like to have done, but I have done my best, frankly and forthrightly; no man can do more, and you are entitled to no less.
Adlai Stevenson

I'm not a member of any organized party, I'm a Democrat. *Will Rogers*

A Conservative is a fellow who is standing athwart history yelling 'Stop!'
William F. Buckley, Jr.

Greater love hath no man than this, that he lay down his friends for his political life.
Jeremy Thorpe

I love this job. I love it to death. I love every waking minute of it.
Joey Smallwood

Now that all the members of the press are so delighted I lost, I'd like to make a statement. As I leave you I want you to know — just think how much you'll be missing. You won't have Nixon to kick around anymore because, gentlemen, this is my last press conference.
Richard Nixon (after losing California gubernatorial race in 1962. He was elected President in 1968)

A politician . . . one that would circumvent God. *Shakespeare, Hamlet*

I gave 'em a sword. And they stuck it in, and they twisted it with relish. And I guess if I had been in their position, I'd have done the same.
Richard Nixon (1977)

I have been driven many times to my knees by the overwhelming conviction that I had nowhere else to go. My own wisdom, and that of all about me seemed insufficient for the day. *Abraham Lincoln*

If we are strong, our strength will speak for itself. If we are weak, words will be no help. *John F. Kennedy*

I shall never ask, never refuse, nor ever resign an office. *George Washington*

Our Congressman are the finest body of men money can buy. *Maury Amsterdam*

A disposition to preserve, and an ability to improve, taken together, would be my standard of a statesman. *Edmund Burke*

Whenever a man has cast a longing eye on office, a rottenness begins in his conduct. *Thomas Jefferson*

Whin a man gets to be my age, he ducks political meetin's, an' reads th' papers an' weighs th' ividence an' th' argymints — pro-argymints an' con-argymints, an' makes up his mind ca'mly, an' votes th' Dimmycratic Ticket. *Finley Peter Dunne*

He knows nothing; he thinks he knows everything — that clearly points to a political career. *George Bernard Shaw*

A councillor ought not to sleep the whole night through — a man to whom the populace is entrusted, and who has many responsibilities. *Homer*

One of the luxuries of a politican's life is that you see yourself as others see you. *Joe Clark*

If I believe in something, I will fight for it with all I have. But I do not demand all or nothing. I would rather get something than nothing. Professional liberals want the fiery debate. They glory in defeat. The hardest job for a politician today is to have the courage to be a moderate. It's easy to take an extreme position. *Hubert Humphrey*

A Liberal is a man too broadminded to take his own side in a quarrel. *Robert Frost*

An honest politician is one who when he is bought will stay bought. *Simon Cameron*

You do not know, you cannot know, the difficulty of life of a politician. It means every minute of the day or night, every ounce of your energy. There is no rest, no relaxation. Enjoyment? A politician does not know the meaning of the word.
Nikita S. Khrushchev

A politician divides mankind into two classes: tools and enemies.
Friedrich Nietzsche

The art of statesmanship is to foresee the inevitable and to expedite its occurrence.
Talleyrand

Since a politician never believes what he says, he is surprised when others believe him.
Charles de Gaulle

Power is a drug on which the politicians are hooked. They buy it from the voters, using the voters' own money.
Richard J. Needham

a politician is an arse upon which everyone has sat except a man.
e. e. cummings

A ginooine statesman should be on his guard, if he must hev beliefs, not to b'lieve 'em too hard.
James Russell Lowell

A new Member requires the experience of his first session in the House to teach him how to hang up his overcoat and take his seat in a manner befitting a gentlemen.
John A. Macdonald

More men have been elected between Sundown and Sunup than ever were elected between Sunup and Sundown.
Will Rogers

Macdonald's Law: Never write a letter if you can help it, and never destroy one.
John A. Macdonald

He is a pragmatist. He is not right wing, nor left wing nor any wing.
Robert Stanfield

Politicians make good company for a while just as children do — their self-enjoyment is contagious. But they soon exhaust their favourite subjects — themselves.
Garry Wills

Your representative owes you, not his industry only, but his judgement; and he betrays instead of serving you if he sacrifices it to your opinion.
Edmund Burke

The most important office is that of private citizen.   *Louis D. Brandeis*

I'm not an old, experienced hand at politics. But I am now seasoned enough to have learned that the hardest thing about any political campaign is how to win without proving that you are unworthy of winning.
Adlai Stevenson

Never retract, never explain, never apologize — get the thing done and let them howl.   *Nellie McClung*

A Conservative is a man who will not look at the new moon, out of respect for that ancient institution, the old one.   *Douglas Jerrold*

Politics

The essential ingredient of politics is timing.   *Pierre Elliott Trudeau*

It was a storm in a tea cup, but in politics we sail in paper boats.
Harold Macmillan

Practical politics consists in ignoring facts.   *Henry Adams*

Party-spirit . . . which at best is but the madness of many for the gain of a few.   *Alexander Pope*

Ultimately politics in a democracy reflects values much more than it shapes them.   *Arnold A. Rogow*

Politics is not a good location or a vocation for anyone lazy, thin-skinned or lacking a sense of humour.   *John Bailey*

A question which can be answered without prejudice to the government is not a fit question to ask.   *John G. Diefenbaker*

I have never found, in a long experience of politics, that criticism is ever inhibited by ignorance.   *Harold Macmillan*

Politics, as a practice, whatever its professions, has always been the systematic organization of hatreds.   *Henry Adams*

Politics, and the fate of mankind, are shaped by men without ideals and without greatness.   *Albert Camus*

If you ever injected truth into politics you would have no politics.
Will Rogers

The sad duty of politics is to establish justice in a sinful world.
Reinhold Niebuhr

There is no worse heresy than that the office sanctifies the holder of it.
Lord Acton

Poetry was the maiden I loved, but politics was the harridan I married.
Joseph Howe

Damn your principles! Stick to your party!   *Benjamin Disraeli*

Politics is a field where action is one long second best and where the choice constantly lies between two blunders.   *John Morley*

Politics is the science of how who gets what, when and why.
Sidney Hillman

Politics is but the common pulse beat.   *Wendell Phillips*

Politics is the gizzard of society, full of gut and gravel.
Henry David Thoreau

The more you read about politics, the more you got to admit that each party is worse than the other.   *Will Rogers*

In academic life you seek to state absolute truths; in politics you seek to accommodate truth to the facts around you.   *Pierre Elliott Trudeau*

Politics. The diplomatic name for the law of the jungle.   *Ely Culbertson*

There is a certain satisfaction in coming down to the lowest ground of politics, for then we get rid of cant and hypocrisy.
Ralph Waldo Emerson

In politics a community of hatred is almost always the foundation of friendships.   *Alexis de Tocqueville*

Politics has got so expensive that it takes lots of money to even get beat with.
Will Rogers

In politics a week is a very long time.   *Harold Wilson*

Honest statesmanship is the wise employment of individual meannesses for the public good.
Abraham Lincoln

Politics is war without bloodshed, and war is politics with blood.
Mao Tse-Tung

This proves what a purifying effect women would have on politics.
Nellie McClung (to a heckler who had said that the Prime Minister would quit politics if a woman were ever elected)

Congress is so strange. A man gets up to speak and says nothing. Nobody listens, then everybody disagrees.
Boris Marshalov

This organization (United Nations) is created to prevent you from going to hell. It isn't created to take you to heaven.
Henry Cabot Lodge, Jr.

Nothing was ever done so systematically as nothing is being done now.
Woodrow Wilson

It will not be any European statesman who will unite Europe: Europe will be united by the Chinese.
Charles de Gaulle

There is no excitement anywhere in the world, short of war, to match the excitement of the American presidential campaign.
Theodore White

A dictatorship is a country where they have taken the politics out of politics.
Sam Himmel

Vote for the man who promises least; he'll be the least disappointing.
Bernard Baruch

What counts is not necessarily the size of the dog in the fight — it's the size of the fight in the dog.
Dwight D. Eisenhower

Someone asked me... how I felt and I was reminded of a story that a fellow townsman of ours used to tell — Abraham Lincoln. They asked him how he felt once after an unsuccessful election. He said he felt like a little boy who has stubbed his toe in the dark. He said that he was too old to cry, but it hurt too much to laugh.
Adlai Stevenson

Democracy is good. I say this because other systems are worse.
Jawaharlal Nehru

There are two problems in my life. The political ones are insoluble and the economic ones are incomprehensible.
Alexander Douglas-Home

The lady's not for turning.   *Margaret Thatcher*

I have never regarded politics as the arena of morals. It is the arena of interests.   *Aneurin Bevan*

In politics, a straight line is the shortest distance to disaster.
                                               John P. Roche

In order to become the master, the politician poses as the servant.
                                               Charles de Gaulle

Politicians are the same all over. They promise to build a bridge even when there is no river.   *Nikita S. Khrushchev*

You know very well that whether you are on page one or page thirty depends on whether they fear you. It is just as simple as that.   *Richard Nixon*

The job of a citizen is to keep his mouth open.   *Gunter Grass*

If people have to choose between freedom and sandwiches they will take sandwiches.   *Lord Boyd-Orr*

Once upon a time my political opponents honored me as possessing the fabulous intellectual and economic power by which I created a worldwide depression all by mself.   *Herbert Hoover*

In our age there is no such thing as 'keeping out of politics.' All issues are political issues.   *George Orwell*

As I learnt very early in my life in Whitehall, the acid test of any political question is: What is the alternative?   *Lord Trent*

Dirksen's Three Laws of Politics:
1. Get elected.
2. Get re-elected.
3. Don't get mad, get even.

Forgiving is all; forgetting is another thing.   *Bob Rae*

He's like a football coach who's smart enough to win the game, and dumb enough to think it's important.   *Eugene McCarthy*

Deep down he is shallow.   *Political saying*

The Senate is the last primitive society in the world. We still worship the elders of the tribe and honour the territorial imperative.

Eugene McCarthy

To the victor belong the spoils of the enemy. *William L. Marcy*

I pledge you, I pledge myself, to a new deal for the American people. Let us all here assembled constitute ourselves prophets of a new order of competence and courage. This is a call to arms.

Franklin D. Roosevelt accepting Presidential nomination, 1932

A statesman is an easy man,
He tells his lies by rote;
A journalist makes up his lies
And takes you by the throat;
So stay at home and drink your beer
And let the neighbours vote. *William Butler Yeats*

This is the first convention of the space age — where a candidate can promise the moon and mean it. *David Brinkley*

Politics is more dangerous than war, for in war you are only killed once.

Winston Churchill

Money is the mother's milk of politics. *Jesse Unruh*

One fifth of the people are against everything all the time.

Robert F. Kennedy

Those who make peaceful revolution impossible will make violent revolution inevitable. *John F. Kennedy*

Poverty

Poverty makes you sad as well as wise. *Bertolt Brecht*

The child was diseased at birth — stricken with an hereditary ill that only the most vital men are able to shake off. I mean poverty — the most deadly and prevalent of all diseases. *Eugene O'Neill*

There is no scandal like rags, nor any crime so shameful as poverty.

George Farquhar

The poor on the borderline of starvation live purposeful lives. To be engaged in a desperate struggle for food and shelter is to be wholly free from a sense of futility. *Eric Hoffer*

It is easy enough to say that poverty is no crime. No, if it were men wouldn't be ashamed of it. It's a blunder, though, and is punished as such.
Jerome K. Jerome

If a free society cannot help the many who are poor, it cannot save the few who are rich. *John F. Kennedy*

The poor don't know that their function in life is to exercise our generosity.
Jean-Paul Sartre

Poverty is an anomaly to rich people: it is very difficult to make out why people who want dinner do not ring the bell. *Walter Bagehot*

Short of genius, a rich man cannot imagine poverty. *Charles Péguy*

The conspicuously wealthy turn up urging the character-building value of privation for the poor. *J. K. Galbraith*

Modern poverty is not the poverty that was blest in the Sermon on the Mount.
George Bernard Shaw

The poor will always be with you. *John 12:8*

This is one of the bitter curses of poverty: it leaves no right to be generous.
George Gissing

Poverty is less a matter of income than of prospects. While the incomes of the poor have steadily risen through Great Society largesse, their prospects have plummeted as families have broken into dependent fragments.
George Gilder

Power

Power never takes a back step — only in the face of more power.
Malcolm X

Power is always right, weakness always wrong. Power is always insolent and despotic. *Noah Webster*

Power only tires those who don't exercise it.   *Pierre Elliott Trudeau*

The only justification in the use of force is to reduce the amount of force necessary to be used.   *Alfred North Whitehead*

Not believing in force is the same as not believing in gravitation.
Leon Trotsky

The first principle of a civilized state is that the power is legitimate only when it is under contract.   *Walter Lippmann*

He was one of those men who possess almost every gift, except the gift of the power to use them.   *Charles Kingsley*

Force is never more operative than when it is known to exist but is not brandished.   *Alfred Thayer Mahan*

The main task of a free society is to civilize the struggle for power. Slavery of the acquiescent majority to the ruthless few is the hereditary state of mankind; freedom, a rarely-acquired characteristic.   *R. H. S. Crossman*

Power corrupts the few, while weakness corrupts the many.   *Eric Hoffer*

His countenance was like lightning, and his raiment white as snow.
Matthew 28:3

Power is the recognition of necessity.   *Abraham Rotstein*

If absolute power corrupts absolutely, where does that leave God?
George Daacon

Power is the ultimate aphrodisiac.   *Henry Kissinger*

Liberal — a power worshipper without power.   *George Orwell*

Power is like a woman you want to stay in bed with forever.
Patrick Anderson

The illegal we do immediately, the unconstitutional takes a little longer.
Henry Kissinger

Power tends to connect; absolute power connects absolutely.
Peter Newman

Macho does not prove mucho.   *Zsa Zsa Gabor*

Praise and Flattery

Among the smaller duties in life, I hardly know any one more important than that of not praising when praise is not due. *Sydney Smith*

Praise to the undeserving is severe satire. *Benjamin Franklin*

It's pleasant to hear these nice words while I'm still alive. I'd rather have the taffy than the epitaphy. *Chauncey Depew*

Commendation, n: the tribute that we pay to achievements that resemble, but do not equal, our own. *Ambrose Bierce*

Applause is the spur of noble minds, the end and aim of weak ones. *Charles Caleb Colton*

The meanest, most contemptible kind of praise is that which first speaks well of a man, and then qualifies it with a 'but.' *Henry Ward Beecher*

He who gladly does without the praise of the crowd will not miss the opportunity of becoming his own fan. *Karl Kraus*

Flattery is all right — if you don't inhale. *Adlai Stevenson*

The advantage of doing one's praising to oneself is that one can lay it on so thick and exactly in the right places. *Samuel Butler*

Some praise at morning what they blame at night. *Alexander Pope*

What really flatters a man is that you think him worth flattery. *George Bernard Shaw*

Our credulity is greatest concerning the things we know least about. And since we know least about ourselves, we are ready to believe all that is said about us. Hence the mysterious power of both flattery and calumny. *Eric Hoffer*

Some fellows pay a compliment like they expected a receipt. *Kin Hubbard*

I can live for two months on a good compliment. *Mark Twain*

A compliment is a gift, not to be thrown away carelessly unless you want to hurt the giver. *Eleanor Hamilton*

'Tis an old maxim in the schools,
That flattery's the food of fools;
Yet now and then your men of wit
Will condescend to take a bit.

Jonathan Swift

The true test of independent judgement is being able to dislike someone who admires us.

Sydney J. Harris

Once in a century a man may be ruined or made insufferable by praise. But surely once a minute something generous dies for want of it.

John Masefield

Few human beings are proof against the implied flattery of rapt attention.

Jack Woodford

Some natures are too good to be spoiled by praise.

Ralph Waldo Emerson

An ingenuous mind feels in unmerited praise the bitterest reproof.

Walter Savage Landor

It is simpler and easier to flatter men than to praise them.

Jean Paul Richter

Prayer

God be kind to all good Samaritans and also bad ones. For such is the kingdom of heaven.

John Gardner

It is not well for a man to pray cream and live skim milk.

Henry Ward Beecher

Pray, v: to ask that the laws of the universe be annulled in behalf of a single petitioner confessedly unworthy.

Ambrose Bierce

'Mr. President, I am praying for you.'
'Which way, Senator?'

Woodrow Wilson and Albert B. Fall

We offer up prayers to God only because we have made Him after our own image. We treat Him like a Pasha, or a Sultan, who is capable of being exasperated and appeased.

Voltaire

The fewer the words, the better the prayer.

Martin Luther

In prayer we call ourselves 'worms of the dust,' but it is only on a sort of tacit understanding that the remark shall not be taken at par.

Mark Twain

Give us grace and strength to preserve. Give us courage and gaiety and the quiet mind. Spare to us our friends and soften to us our enemies. Give us the strength to encounter that which is to come, that we may be brave in peril, constant in tribulation, temperate in wrath and in all changes of fortune, and down to the gates of death, loyal and loving to one another.

Robert Louis Stevenson

I have lived to thank God that all my prayers have not been answered.

Jean Ingelow

God punishes us mildly by ignoring our prayers and severely by answering them.

Richard J. Needham

Only man, among living things, says prayers. Or needs to.

Peter Bowman

What men usually ask of God when they pray is that two and two not make four.

Anon.

In certain trying circumstances, urgent circumstances, desperate circumstances, profanity furnishes a relief denied even to prayer.

Mark Twain

Prejudice and Bigotry

Prejudice is the child of ignorance. *William Hazlitt*

Passion and prejudice govern the world; only under the name of reason.

John Wesley

How it infuriates a bigot, when he is forced to drag out his dark convictions! *Logan Pearsall Smith*

Everyone is a prisoner of his own experiences. No one can eliminate prejudices — just recognize them. *Edward R. Murrow*

We are chameleons, and our partialities and prejudices change places with an easy and blessed facility. *Mark Twain*

Fortunately for serious minds, a bias recognized is a bias sterilized.
A. Eustace Haydon

Without the aid of prejudice and custom, I should not be able to find my way across the room. *William Hazlitt*

One may no more live in the world without picking up the moral prejudices of the world than one will be able to go to hell without perspiring.
H. L. Mencken

We hate some persons because we do not know them; and will not know them because we hate them. *Charles Caleb Colton*

The mind of a bigot is like the pupil of the eye; the more light you pour upon it, the more it will contract. *Oliver Wendell Holmes, Jr.*

It is not healthy when a nation lives within a nation, as coloured Americans are living inside America. A nation cannot live confident of its tomorrow if its refugees are among its own citizens. *Pearl Buck*

The Presidency

The president is the representative of the whole nation and he's the only lobbyist that all the one hundred and sixty million people in this country have.
Harry S. Truman

Trying to make the presidency work these days is like trying to sew buttons on a custard pie. *James David Barber*

Th' prisidincy is th' highest office in th' gift iv th people. Th' vice-prisidincy is th' next highest an' the lowest. It isn't a crime exactly. Ye can't be sint to jail f'r it, but it's a kind iv a disgrace. *Finley Peter Dunne*

Seriously, I do not think I am fit for the presidency. *Abraham Lincoln*

An eminent American is reported to have said to friends who wished to put him forward, 'Gentlemen, let there be no mistake. I should make a good president, but a very bad candidate.' *James Bryce*

Well, I wouldn't say that I was in the 'great' class, but I had a great time while I was trying to be great. *Harry S. Truman*

The presidency does not yield to definition. Like the glory of a morning sunrise, it can be experienced — it can not be told.   *Calvin Coolidge*

When the president does it, that means it is not illegal.   *Richard Nixon*

A president's hardest task is not to do what's right, but to know what's right.
Lyndon B. Johnson

Had I been chosen president again, I am certain I could not have lived another year.   *John Adams*

The four most miserable years of my life . . .   *John Adams*

If you are as happy, my dear sir, on entering this house as I am in leaving it and returning home, you are the happiest man in the country.
James Buchanan (to Abraham Lincoln)

I feel like the man who was tarred and feathered and ridden out of town on a rail. To the man who asked how he liked it he said: 'If it wasn't for the honour of the thing, I'd rather walk.'   *Abraham Lincoln*

The office of president requires the constitution of an athlete, the patience of a mother, the endurance of an early Christian.
Harold Wilson

Within the first few months I discovered that being a president is like riding a tiger. A man has to keep riding or be swallowed.   *Harry S. Truman*

Harricum! Harricum! Give 'em hell, Harricum!
Oxford University cheer for former president, Harry Truman

In America, any boy may become president, and I suppose it's just one of the risks he takes.   *Adlai Stevenson*

I have no expectation of making a hit every time I come to bat.
Franklin D. Roosevelt

I think the American public wants a solemn ass as a president, and I think I'll go along with them.   *Calvin Coolidge*

I desire to so conduct the affairs of this administration that if, at the end . . . I have lost every friend on earth, I shall have one friend left, and that friend shall be down inside me.   *Abraham Lincoln*

The final greatness of the presidency lies in the truth that it is not just an office of incredible power but a breeding ground of indestructible myth.
Clinton Rossiter

I beg leave to assure the Congress that no pecuniary consideration could have tempted me to accept this arduous employment at the expense of my domestic ease and happiness. I do not wish to make any profit from it.
George Washington

Nothing in life is so exhilarating as to be shot at without result.
Ronald Reagan (referring to Winston Churchill's words) after the assassination attempt in March, 1981

Don't let it be forgot,
That once there was a spot —
For one brief shining moment
That was known as Camelot.
John F. Kennedy's favourite lines from the Alan Lerner script of the musical, 'Camelot'

The buck stops here.   *Sign on the desk of President Harry S. Truman*

Pride

Pride has a greater share than goodness of heart in the remonstrances we make to those who are guilty of faults; we reprove not so much with a view to correct them as to persuade them that we are exempt from those faults ourselves.   *La Rochefoucauld*

Pride is seldom delicate: it will please itself with very mean advantages.
Samuel Johnson

The truly proud man is satisfied with his own good opinion, and does not seek to make converts to it.   *William Hazlitt*

Pride is the mask of one's own faults.   *Jewish proverb*

Pride is the direct appreciation of oneself.   *Arthur Schopenhauer*

There is a certain noble pride, through which merits shine brighter than through modesty.   *Jean Paul Richter*

The sun will set without thy assistance.   *The Talmud*

When a proud man hears another praised, he feels himself injured.

English proverb

A confessional passage has probably never been written that didn't stink a little bit of the writer's pride in having given up his pride.

J. D. Salinger

I do not believe that any peacock envies another peacock his tail, because every peacock is persuaded that his own tail is the finest in the world. The consequence of this is that peacocks are peaceable birds.

Bertrand Russell

Pride, perceiving humility honourable, often borrows her cloak.

Thomas Fuller

There is a paradox in pride: it makes some men ridiculous, but prevents others from becoming so.   *Charles Caleb Colton*

Pride had rather go out of the way than go behind.   *Thomas Fuller*

Progress

This world of ours is a new world, in which the unit of knowledge, the nature of human communities, the order of society, the order of ideas, the very notions of society and culture have changed, and will not return to what they have been in the past. What is new is new, not because it has never been there before, but because it has changed in quality.

J. Robert Oppenheimer

All progress is based upon the universal innate desire on the part of every organism to live beyond its income.   *Samuel Butler*

And from the discontent of man
The world's best progress springs.   *Ella Wheeler Wilcox*

Every gain made by individuals or society is almost instantly taken for granted.   *Aldous Huxley*

Do not seek to follow in the footsteps of the men of old; seek what they sought.   *Matsuo Basho*

Once you sink that first stake, they'll never make you pull it up.

Robert Moses

Flight is the only true sensation that men have achieved in modern history.
James Dickey

The fundamental magic of flying is a miracle that has nothing to do with any of its practical purposes — purposes of speed, accessibility and convenience — and will not change as they change. *Anne Morrow Lindbergh*

The really great visual experience today is to fly over a huge city and look down into the night. It's like a tremendous jubilant Christmas tree. You just feel life is worth living — when you come down you may have some doubts.
Gyorgy Kepes

A great devotee of the gospel of getting on. *George Bernard Shaw*

The century on which we are entering can be and must be the century of the common man. *Henry A. Wallace*

To spur a willing horse. *Latin proverb*

Removing the faults in a stage-coach may produce a perfect stage-coach, but it is unlikely to produce the first motor car. *Edward de Bono*

Progress might have been all right once, but it's gone on too long.
Ogden Nash

A thousand things advance; nine hundred and ninety-nine retreat; that is progress. *Henri Frédéric Amiel*

The simple faith in progress is not a conviction belonging to strength, but one belonging to acquiescence and hence to weakness. *Norbert Wiener*

The major advances in civilization are processes which all but wreck the societies in which they occur. *Alfred North Whitehead*

Behold the turtle. He makes progress only when he sticks his neck out.
James Bryant Conant

Always remember that the soundest way to progress in any organization is to help the man ahead of you to get promoted. *L. S. Hamaker*

What saves a man is to take a step. Then another step. It is always the same step, but you have to take it. *Antoine de Saint-Exupéry*

Is it progress if a cannibal uses knife and fork? *Stanislaw Lec*

Daring ideas are like chessmen moved forward. They may be beaten, but they may start a winning game.   *Goethe*

The rule is jam tomorrow and jam yesterday — but never jam today.
                                                            Lewis Carroll

The art of progress is to preserve order amid change, and to preserve change amid order.   *Alfred North Whitehead*

Now here, you see, it takes all the running you can do to keep in the same place. If you want to get somewhere else, you must run at least twice as fast as that!   *Lewis Carroll*

There is nothing new except what has become antiquated.   *Mlle. Bertin*

It so happens that the world is undergoing a transformation to which no change that has yet occurred can be compared, either in scope or in rapidity.   *Charles de Gaulle*

Modern kitchen — where the pot calls the kettle chartreuse.   *Anon.*

If Jesus Christ were to come today, people would not even crucify him. They would ask him to dinner, and hear what he had to say, and make fun of him.   *Thomas Carlyle*

Man is flying too fast for a world that is round. Soon he will catch up with himself in a great rear-end collision and Man will never know that what hit him from behind was Man.   *James Thurber*

Every step of progress the world has made has been from scaffold to scaffold, and from stake to stake.   *Wendell Phillips*

Today every invention is received with a cry of triumph which soon turns into a cry of fear.   *Bertolt Brecht*

Once a man would spend a week patiently waiting if he missed a stage coach, but now he rages if he misses the first section of a revolving door.
                                                          Simeon Strunsky

The reasonable man adapts himself to the world; the unreasonable one persists in trying to adapt the world to himself. Therefore all progress depends upon the unreasonable man.   *George Bernard Shaw*

There is no royal road to anything. One thing at a time, and all things in succession. That which grows slowly endures.   *J. G. Holland*

Growth for the sake of growth is the ideology of the cancer cell.
Edward Abbey

The world owes all its onward impulses to men ill at ease. The happy man inevitably confines himself within ancient limits.   *Nathaniel Hawthorne*

That which comes into the world to disturb nothing deserves neither respect nor patience.   *René Char*

Occasionally we sigh for an earlier day when we could just look at the stars without worrying whether they were theirs or ours.   *Bill Vaughan*

Every year it takes less time to fly across the Atlantic, and more time to drive to the office.   *Anon.*

Is it progress if a cannibal uses knife and fork.   *Stanislaw Lec*

Change is certain, progress is not.   *E.H. Carr*

Proof and Certainty

There are no facts, only interpretations.   *Friedrich Nietzsche*

Statistics are no substitute for judgement.   *Henry Clay*

Get your facts first, and then you can distort 'em as much as you please.   *Mark Twain*

'For example' is not proof.   *Jewish proverb*

A half truth, like half a brick, is always more forcible as an argument than a whole one. It carries better.   *Stephen Leacock*

He that will not apply new remedies must expect new evils, for time is the greatest innovator.   *Francis Bacon*

You are all you will ever have for certain,.   *June Havoc*

Doubt is not a pleasant condition, but certainty is.   *Voltaire*

To believe with certainty we must begin with doubting.
Stanislaus, King of Poland

Modest doubt is call'd
The beacon of the wise.   *Shakespeare, 'Troilus and Cressida'*

What men want is not knowledge, but certainty.   *Bertrand Russell*

Psychiatry

If you talk to God, you are praying; if God talks to you, you have schizophrenia.   *Thomas Szasz*

The psychiatrist must become a fellow traveller with his patient.
R. D. Laing

Those modern analysts, they charge so much! In my day, for five marks Freud himself would treat you. For ten marks he would treat you and press your pants. For fifteen marks Freud would let *you* treat *him* — that included a choice of any two vegetables.   *Woody Allen*

Psychiatry enables us to correct our faults by confessing our parents' short-comings.   *Laurence J. Peter*

Psychoanalysis is confession without absolution.   *G. K. Chesterton*

Psychiatry is the care of the id by the odd.   *Anon.*

The point of therapy is get unhooked, not to thrash around on how you got hooked.   *Maryanne Walters*

The four-letter word for psychotherapy is 'talk.'   *Anon.*

I can feel guilty about the past, apprehensive about the future, but only in the present can I act. The ability to be in the present moment is a major component of mental wellness.   *Abraham Maslow*

Mental health problems do not affect three or four out of every five persons, but one out of one.   *William Menninger*

The trouble with being a hypochondriac these days is that antibiotics have cured all the good diseases.   *Caskie Stinnet*

The best cure for hypochondria is to forget about your own body and get interested in someone else's.   *Goodman Ace*

Depression is the inability to construct a future. *Rollo May*

Depression is rage spread thin. *Paul Tillich*

Fortunately, analysis is not the only way to resolve inner conflicts. Life itself remains a very effective therapist. *Karen Horney*

Anyone who goes to a psychiatrist ought to have his head examined.
Sam Goldwyn

Quips and Comments

I hate quotations. *Ralph Waldo Emerson*

It is a sobering thought, that when Mozart was my age, he had been dead for two years. *Tom Lehrer*

He wouldn't give a duck a drink if he owned Lake Michigan. *Anon.*

Show me a man with both feet on the ground and I'll show you a man who can't put his pants on. *Arthur K. Watson*

My idea of an agreeable person is a person who agrees with me.
Benjamin Disraeli

Alimony: the cash surrender value of a husband. *Anon.*

Kiss principle: Keep it simple, stupid. *Anon.*

Nothing is impossible for the person who doesn't have to do it.
Weller's Law

His shortcoming is his long staying. *Anon.*

He has all of the virtues I dislike and none of the vices I admire.
Winston Churchill

Sherard Blaw, the dramatist who had discovered himself, and who had given so unstintingly of his discovery to the world. *Saki*

The Right Honourable gentleman is indebted to his memory for his jests and to his imagination for his facts. *Richard Brinsley Sheridan*

Her face was her chaperone.   *Rupert Hughes*

Angels fly because they take themselves lightly.   *G. K. Chesterton*

Any man who hates dogs and babies can't be all bad.   *W.C. Fields*

When people don't want to come, nothing will stop them.   *Sol Hurok*

Venice is like eating an entire box of chocolate liqueurs in one go.
                                                    Truman Capote

More and more these days I find myself pondering on how to reconcile my
net income with my gross habits.   *John Kirk Nelson*

A verbal contract isn't worth the paper it's written on.   *Sam Goldwyn*

Epigram: a wisecrack that has played Carnegie Hall.   *Oscar Levant*

Include me out.   *Sam Goldwyn*

A hole is nothing at all, but you can break your neck in it.
                                                   Austin O'Malley

Mother: It's broccoli, dear.
Child: I say it's spinach, and I say the hell with it.
          Carl Rose, E.B. White — New Yorker cartoon, 1928

Flint must be an extremely wealthy town; I see that each of you bought two
or three seats.
          Victor Borge, playing to a half-filled house in Flint, Michigan.

In uplifting, get underneath.   *George Ade*

If there were any justice in the world, people would be able to fly over pigeons
for a change.   *Anon.*

When the mouse laughs at the cat there's a hole nearby.
                                                 Nigerian proverb

Fatigue is the best pillow.   *Hindu proverb*

The ugliest of trades have their moments of pleasure. Now, if I was a grave
digger, or even a hangman, there are some people I could work for with a
great deal of enjoyment.   *Douglas Jerrold*

What happens to the hole when the cheese is gone?   *Bertolt Brecht*

God made me on a morning when he had nothing else to do.

C. F. Lloyd

When Babe Ruth was asked in 1930 how he felt about making more money
that the President of the United States, he replied 'I had a better year than
he did.'

When Tom Snyder was asked in 1977 how he felt about making more money
per year than President Carter, he replied, 'I have to go out and buy my
own 707.'   *Cleveland Amory*

Nothing succeeds like one's own successor.   *Clarence H. Hincks*

Whom the gods wish to destroy, they first call promising.

Cyril Connolly

We also serve who only punctuate.   *Brian Moore*

In California everyone goes to a therapist, is a therapist, or is a therapist
going to a therapist.   *Truman Capote*

Every director bites the hand that lays the golden egg.   *Sam Goldwyn*

If Roosevelt were alive he'd turn in his grave.   *Sam Goldwyn*

There's a wonderful family called Stein,
There's Gert, and there's Epp and there's Ein:
Gert's poems are bunk,
Epp's statues are junk,
And no one can understand Ein.   *Anon.*

Automatic simply means that you can't repair it yourself.

Frank Capra

A thick skin is a gift from God.   *Konrad Adenauer*

While you're saving your face you're losing your ass. Never trust a man whose
eyes are too close to his nose. I never trust a man unless I've got his pecker
in my pocket. Better inside the tent pissing out than outside the tent pissing in.

Lyndon B. Johnson

Parsely
is gharsley.   *Ogden Nash*

Oats, n.s. A grain which in England is generally given to horses, but in Scotland supports the people.   *Samuel Johnson*

Coffee in England is just toasted milk.   *Anon.*

Epitaph to a waiter: By and by
                    God caught his eye.   *David McCord*

A dimple in the chin; a devil within.   *Irish proverb*

Some people approach every problem with an open mouth.
                                                     Adlai Stevenson

The butler entered the room, a solemn procession of one.
                                                    P. G. Wodehouse

And what's a butterfly? At best,
He's but a caterpillar, drest.   *John Grey*

If I look like this, I need the trip.
                          Gloria Swanson (of her passport photo)

Early to bed, early to rise, work like hell, and advertise.
                                                   Laurence J. Peter

'Tis better than riches
To scratch when it itches.   *Anon.*

When you have got an elephant by the hind leg, and he is trying to run away, it is best to let him run.   *Abraham Lincoln*

Too much of a good thing can be wonderful.   *Mae West*

As old as the itch.   *English proverb*

All would live long, but none would be old.   *Proverb*

Bland as a Jesuit, sober as a hymn.   *William Ernest Henley*

I never forget a face, but in your case I'll make an exception.
                                                       Groucho Marx

'Are you lost daddy?' I asked tenderly.
'Shut up,' he explained.   *Ring Lardner*

Geography is about maps,
But biography is about chaps. *E. C. Bentley*

In the world of mules there are no rules. *Ogden Nash*

There are some people so addicted to exaggeration that they can't tell the truth without lying. *Josh Billings*

Since the house is on fire let us warm ourselves. *Italian saying*

I used to be snow-white . . . but I drifted. *Mae West*

Equal opportunity is good, but special privilege even better.
Anna Chennault

It's better to be quotable than to be honest. *Tom Stoppard*

A man of words and not of deeds,
Is like a garden full of weeds. *English proverb*

Shake a bridle over a Yorkshireman's grave, and he'll rise and steal a horse.
Lancashire proverb

An indecent mind is a perpetual feast. *Old saying*

If you can't bite, don't show your teeth. *Yiddish proverb*

Only the shallow know themselves. *Oscar Wilde*

Don't quote me; that's what you heard, not what I said.
Lawrence K. Frank

Thin people are beautiful but fat people are adorable. *Jackie Gleason*

I don't see what's wrong with giving Bobby a little experience before he starts to practise law.
John F. Kennedy (after appointing his brother Attorney General)

I had always assumed that cliché was a suburb of Paris, until I discovered it to be a street in Oxford. *Philip Guedalla*

He'd give the devil ulcers. *Anon.*

When I'm good, I'm very good, but when I'm bad, I'm better. *Mae West*

Reality

Human kind cannot bear very much reality.   *T. S. Eliot*

If anything is poisoning our lives and weakening our society, it is reality —
and not the fabrication of television writers and producers.
Martin Maloney

There is no reality except the one contained within us. That is why so many
people live such an unreal life. They take the images outside them for reality
and never allow the world within to assert itself.   *Hermann Hesse*

Nothing which is at all times and in every way agreeable to us can have objective reality. It is of the very nature of the real that it should have sharp
corners and rough edges, that it should be resistant, should be itself. Dream-
furniture is the only kind on which you never stub your toes or bang your
knee.   *C. S. Lewis*

We take our shape, it is true, within and against that cage of reality bequeath-
ed us at our birth, and yet it is precisely through our dependence on this
reality that we are most endlessly betrayed.   *James Baldwin*

Facts as facts do not always create a spirit of reality, because reality is a spirit.
G. K. Chesterton

You too must not count overmuch on your reality as you feel it today, since,
like that of yesterday, it may prove an illusion for you tomorrow.
Luigi Pirandello

All our interior world is reality — and that perhaps more so than our apparent world.   *Marc Chagall*

The field of consciousness is tiny. It accepts only one problem at a time.
Get into a fist fight, put your mind on the strategy of the fight, and you
will not feel the other fellow's punches.   *Antoine de Saint-Exupéry*

Reason

When the human mind exists in the light of reason and no more than reason,
we may say with absolute certainty that Man and all that made him will be
in that instant gone.   *Loren Eiseley*

I have hardly ever known a mathematician who was capable of reasoning.
Plato

Reason is God's gift, but so are the passions. Reason is as guilty as passion.
Cardinal Newman

The man who is master of his passions is Reason's slave.
Cyril Connolly

Human reason needs only to will more strongly than fate, and she *is* fate.
Thomas Mann

Reason deserves to be called a prophet; for in showing up the consequence and effect of our actions in the present, does it not tell us what the future will be?
Arthur Schopenhauer

The difference between the reason of man and the instinct of the beast is this, that the beast does but know, but the man knows that he knows.
John Donne

Reason is also choice.
John Milton

Reason is an emotion for the sexless.
Heathcote Williams

Never try to reason the prejudice out of a man. It was not reasoned into him, and cannot be reasoned out.
Sydney Smith

The last advance of reason is to recognize that it is surpassed by innumerable things; it is feeble if it cannot realize that.
Blaise Pascal

All our reasoning ends in surrender to feeling.
Blaise Pascal

Rebellion, Revolution and Reform

Inferiors revolt in order that they may be equal, and equals that they may be superior.
Aristotle

Resistance to tyrants is obedience to God.
Benjamin Franklin

In almost any society, I think, the quality of the non-conformists is like to be just as good as, and no better than that of the conformists.

Margaret Mead

Whatever little we have gained, we have gained by agitation, while we have uniformly lost by moderation. *Daniel O'Connell*

Every generation revolts against its fathers and makes friends with its grandfathers. *Lewis Mumford*

One revolution is like one cocktail, it just gets you organized for the next.

Will Rogers

A reformer is a guy who rides through a sewer in a glass-bottomed boat.

James J. Walker

A reformer is one who sets forth cheerfully toward sure defeat.

Richard S. Childs

The overwhelming pressure of mediocrity, sluggish and indomitable as a glacier, will mitigate the most violent, and depress the most exalted revolution.

T.S. Eliot

It is essential to the triumph of reform that it shall never succeed.

William Hazlitt

It is a dangerous thing to reform anyone. *Oscar Wilde*

Reformers have the idea that change can be achieved by brute sanity.

George Bernard Shaw

It is not the prisoners who need reformation, it is the prisons.

Oscar Wilde

It is possible for a single individual to defy the whole might of an unjust empire to save his honour, his religion, his soul, and lay the foundation for that empire's fall or its regeneration. *Gandhi*

By gnawing through a dyke, even a rat may drown a nation.

Edmund Burke

The times spat at me. I spit back at the times. *Andrei Voznesensky*

All reform except a moral one will prove unavailing. *Thomas Carlyle*

I hold it, that a little rebellion now and then is a good thing, and as necessary in the political world as storms in the physical. *Thomas Jefferson*

Riots are the voices of the unheard. *Martin Luther King, Jr.*

If we should promise people nothing better than only revolution, they would scratch their heads and say, 'Isn't it better to have good goulash?'
Nikita S. Khrushchev

I survived. (J'ai vécu.) *Emmanuel Joseph Sieyès*
(when asked what he did during the French Revolution)

Big Brother is watching you. *George Orwell*

Religion

Each religion, by the help of more or less myth which it takes more or less seriously, proposes some method of fortifying the human soul and enabling it to make its peace with its destiny. *George Santayana*

The good news is that Jesus is coming back. The bad news is that he's really pissed off. *Bob Hope*

The merit claimed for the Anglican Church is that, if you let it alone, it will let you alone. *Ralph Waldo Emerson*

Most people believe that the Christian commandments are intentionally a little too severe — like setting a clock half an hour ahead to make sure of not being late in the morning. *Søren Kirkegaard*

Three things are good in little measure and evil in large: yeast, salt and hesitation. *The Talmud*

Mystic: a person who is puzzled before the obvious, but who understands the non-existent. *Elbert Hubbard*

Faith means intense, usually confident, belief that is not based on evidence sufficient to command assent from every reasonable person.
Walter Kaufmann

Men will wrangle for religion, write for it, fight for it, die for it, anything but live for it. *Charles Caleb Colton*

I have never yet met a healthy person who worries very much about his health, or a really good person who worries much about his own soul.

J. B. S. Haldane

We Jews have a secret weapon in our struggle with the Arabs — we have no place to go.

Golda Meir

Men are idolaters, and want something to look at and kiss and hug, or throw themselves down before; they always did, they always will, and if you don't make it of wood, you must make it of words.

Oliver Wendell Holmes

The various modes of worship which prevailed in the Roman world were all considered by the people as equally true; by the philosopher as equally false; and by the magistrate as equally useful.

Edward Gibbon

Nothing in human life, least of all in religion, is ever right until it is beautiful.

Harry Emerson Fosdick

I think if you ask people what their concept of heaven is, they would say, if they are honest, that it is a big department store, with new things every week — all the money to buy them, and maybe a little more than the neighbours.

Erich Fromm

We have grasped the mystery of the atom, and rejected the Sermon on the Mount.

Omar Bradley

Religion is a great force — the only real motive force in the world; but you must get at a man through his own religion, not through yours.

George Bernard Shaw

It must require an inordinate share of vanity and presumption after enjoying so much that is good and beautiful on earth, to ask the Lord for immortality in addition to it all.

Heinrich Heine

Oysters are more beautiful than any religion . . . there's nothing in Christianity or Buddhism that quite matches the sympathetic unselfishness of an oyster.

Saki

A gentle Quaker, hearing a strange noise in his house one night, got up and discovered a burglar busily at work. He went and got his gun, came back and stood quietly in the doorway. 'Friend,' he said, 'I would do thee no harm for the world, but thou standest where I am about to shoot.'

James Hines

Religion is a way of walking, not a way of talking.   *William R. Inge*

Puritanism — the haunting fear that someone, somewhere may be happy.
H. L. Mencken

The worst moment for the atheist is when he is really thankful, and has nobody to thank.   *Dante Gabriel Rossetti*

The mystery of the beginning of all things is insoluble by us; and I for one must be content to remain agnostic.   *Charles Darwin*

Don't be agnostic — be something.   *Robert Frost*

Religion converts despair, which destroys, into resignation, which submits.
Lady Blessington

For the wonderful thing about saints is that they were human. They lost their tempers, got angry, scolded God, were egotistical or testy or impatient in their turns, made mistakes and regretted them. Still they went on doggedly blundering toward heaven.   *Phyllis McGinley*

Audible at five miles, painful at three, and lethal at one.
Said of the Winchester Cathedral organ

With soap baptism is a good thing.   *Robert G. Ingersoll*

When a man is freed of religion, he has a better chance to live a normal and wholesome life.   *Sigmund Freud*

The Church of England is the Tory party at prayer.   *Anon.*

A Unitarian very earnestly disbelieves what everyone else believes.
W. Somerset Maugham

There's no reason to bring religion into it. I think we ought to have as great a regard for religion as we can, so as to keep it out of as many things as possible.   *Sean O'Casey*

If the thunder is not loud, the peasant forgets to cross himself.
Russian proverb

While I cannot be regarded as a pillar, I must be regarded as a buttress of the church, because I support it from outside.   *Lord Melbourne*

Religion is the opium of the people.   *Karl Marx*

Infidel, n: in New York, one who does not believe in the Christian religion;
in Constantinople, one who does.   *Ambrose Bierce*

An atheist is a man who has no invisible means of support.
Fulton Sheen

Atheism is rather in the lip than in the heart of Man.   *Francis Bacon*

Yes, I am a Jew, and when the ancestors of the right honourable gentlemen
were brutal savages in an unknown land, mine were priests in the Temple
of Solomon.   *Benjamin Disraeli*

As for a future life, every man must judge for himself between conflicting
vague possibilities.   *Charles Darwin*

My theology, briefly,
Is that the universe
Was dictated
But not signed.   *Christopher Morley*

My atheism, like that of Spinoza, is true piety towards the universe and denies
only gods fashioned by men in their own image, to be servants of their human
interests.   *George Santayana*

There is a crack in everything God has made.   *Ralph Waldo Emerson*

Christianity might be a good thing if anyone ever tried it.
George Bernard Shaw

The voice of the people is the voice of God. (Vox populi, vox dei.)
Latin proverb

Men prefer to believe that they are degenerated angels, rather than elevated
apes.   *W. Winwood Roade*

Let's all give God a great big hand. I've seen the last page of the bible and
it's all going to turn out all right.   *Anon.*

I'm not ok — you're not ok, and that's ok.
Rev. William Sloane Coffin

You have not converted a man because you have silenced him.
John Morley

I consider myself a Hindu, Christian, Moslem, Jew, Buddhist, and Confucian. *Gandhi*

Repentance and Apology

He's half absolv'd
Who has confess'd. *Matthew Prior*

It is a very delicate job to forgive a man, without lowering him in his estimation, and yours too. *Josh Billings*

The sinning is the best part of repentance. *Arabic proverb*

Apology is only egotism wrong side out. *Oliver Wendell Holmes*

Apologize, v: to lay the foundation for a future offence. *Ambrose Bierce*

Apology — a desperate habit, and one that is rarely cured. *Oliver Wendell Holmes*

No sensible person ever made an apology. *Ralph Waldo Emerson*

Repentance is for little children. *Adolf Eichmann*

Repentance is but want of power to sin. *John Dryden*

Make it a rule of life never to regret and never look back. Regret is an appalling waste of energy; you can't build on it; it's good only for wallowing in. *Katharine Mansfield*

If I die, I forgive you: if I recover, we shall see. *Spanish proverb*

It is a good rule in life never to apologize. The right sort of people do not want apologies, and the wrong sort take a mean advantage of them. *P.G. Wodehouse*

God will pardon me. It's his business. *Heinrich Heine (as he died)*

I suppose you've heard all those wicked stories about me. Well, I've lived my life as it came and I've done bloody marvels with a bad hand. *Libby Holman*

Retirement

The role of a retired person is no longer to possess one.
Simone de Beauvoir

When men reach their sixties and retire, they go to pieces. Women just go right on cooking. *Gail Sheehy*

Retirement: statutory senility. *Emmett O'Donnell*

Two weeks is about the ideal length of time to retire. *Alex Comfort*

Absence of occupation is not rest,
A mind quite vacant is a mind distress'd. *William Cowper*

Don't think of retiring from the world until the world will be sorry that you retire. *Samuel Johnson*

Far from the madding crowd's ignoble strife. *Thomas Gray*

Retirement, rural quiet, friendship, books. *James Thomson*

Few men of action have been able to make a graceful exit at the appropriate time. *Malcolm Muggeridge*

Dismiss the old horse in good time, lest he fail in the lists and the spectators laugh. *Horace*

Ruin

Nations have passed away and left no traces,
And history gives the naked cause of it —
One single simple reason in all cases;
They fell because their peoples were not fit. *Rudyard Kipling*

So in the Libyan fable it is told
That once an eagle, stricken with a dart,
Said, when he saw the fashion of the shaft,
'With our own feathers, not by others' hands,
Are we now smitten.' *Aeschylus*

No man is demolished but by himself. *Thomas Bentley*

What does not destroy me, makes me strong.   *Friedrich Nietzsche*

I never was ruined but twice — once when I lost a lawsuit, and once when I gained one.   *Voltaire*

All men that are ruined are ruined on the side of their natural propensities.   *Edmund Burke*

My downfall raises me to infinite heights.   *Napoleon Bonaparte*

Candour and generosity, unless tempered by due moderation, lead to ruin.   *Tacitus*

Italians come to ruin most generally in three ways — women, gambling and farming. My family chose the slowest one.   *Pope John XXIII*

Sanity and Insanity

One is healthy when one can laugh at the earnestness and zeal with which one has been hypnotized by any single detail of one's life.   *Friedrich Nietzsche*

When we remember that we are all mad, the mysteries disappear and life stands explained.   *Mark Twain*

Madness is part of all of us, all the time, and it comes and goes, waxes and wanes.   *Otto Friedrich*

A man should not strive to eliminate his complexes, but to get into accord with them: they are legitimately what directs his conduct in the world.   *Sigmund Freud*

Work and love — these are the basics; waking life is a dream controlled.   *George Santayana*

Outside, among your fellows, among strangers, you must preserve appearances, a hundred things you cannot do; but inside, the terrible freedom!   *Ralph Waldo Emerson*

Sanity is very rare; every man almost, and every woman, has a dash of madness.   *Ralph Waldo Emerson*

Mad, bad and dangerous to know.   *Lady Caroline Lamb of Lord Byron*

We are all born mad. Some remain so.   *Samuel Beckett*

There is a pleasure sure,
In being mad, which none but madmen know!   *John Dryden*

Scholars and Scholarship

He not only overflowed with learning, but stood in the slop.
Sydney Smith of Macaulay

If we wish to know the force of human genius, we should read Shakespeare.
If we wish to see the insignificance of human learning, we may study his
commentators.   *William Hazlitt*

The clever men at Oxford
Know all there is to be knowed —
But they none of them know as half as much
As intelligent Mr. Toad.   *Kenneth Graham*

Research, as the college student will come to know it, is relatively thorough
investigation, primarily in libraries, of a properly limited topic, and presen-
tation of the results of this investigation in a carefully organized and
documented paper of some length.
Cecil B. Williams and Alan H. Stevenson

A man should keep his little brain attic stocked with all the furniture that
he is likely to use, and the rest he can put away in the lumber-room of his
library, where he can get it if he wants it.   *Arthur Conan Doyle*

What is research, but a blind date with knowledge?   *Will Henry*

If I had read as much as other men, I should have known no more than they.
Thomas Hobbes

Deep-versed in books
And shallow in himself.   *John Milton*

Learning is the knowledge of that which none but the learned know.
William Hazlitt

I would live to study, not study to live.   *Francis Bacon*

Almost all important questions are important precisely because they are not susceptible to quantitative answer.   *Arthur Schlesinger, Jr.*

Science and Technology

Technology — the knack of so arranging the world that we don't have to experience it.   *Max Frisch*

The great tragedy of Science: the slaying of a beautiful hypothesis by an ugly fact.   *Thomas Huxley*

Technology means the systematic application of scientific or other organized knowledge to practical tasks.   *J. K. Galbraith*

Whenever science makes a discovery, the devil grabs it while the angels are debating the best way to use it.   *Alan Valentine*

Science cannot stop while ethics catches up — and nobody should expect scientists to do all the thinking for the country.   *Elvin Stackman*

Science must constantly be reminded that her purposes are not the only purposes and that the order of uniform causation which she has use for, and is therefore right in postulating, may be enveloped in a wider order, on which she has no claim at all.   *William James*

Science is the attempt to make the chaotic diversity of our sense-experience correspond to a logically uniform system of thought.   *Albert Einstein*

Though many have tried, no one has ever yet explained away the decisive fact that science, which can do so much, cannot decide what it ought to do.
                                    Joseph Wood Krutch

Results? Why man, I have gotten a lot of results. I know 50,000 things that won't work.   *Thomas A. Edison*

It may be bizarre, but in my opinion, science offers a sure path to God and religion.   *Paul Davies*

As both the Mercury and Apollo programs have shown, our science and technology are so powerful that, if an intense effort is made, we can do almost anything we want in say, ten years — provided we are not in conflict with the laws of nature.   *Hannes Alfvén*

The new electronic interdependence recreates the world in the image of a global village.
Marshall McLuhan

Research is the process of going up alleys to see if they are blind.
Marston Bates

Research is to see what everybody has seen, and to think what nobody else has thought.
Albert Szent-Györgyi

No scientific theory achieves public acceptance until it has been thoroughly discredited.
Douglas Yates

The first rule of intelligent tinkering is to save all the parts.
Paul R. Ehrlich

Computers can figure out all kinds of problems, except the things in the world that just don't add up.
James Magary

The World would be a safer place,
If someone had a plan,
Before exploring Outer Space,
To find the Inner Man.
E. Y. Harburg

No amount of experimentation can ever prove me right; a single experiment can prove me wrong.
Albert Einstein

I think and think for months and years. Ninety-nine times, the conclusion is false. The hundredth time I am right.
Albert Einstein

In science the credit goes to the man who convinces the world, not to the man to whom the idea first occurs.
William Osler

There is more than a mere suspicion that the scientist who comes to ask metaphysical questions and turns away from metaphysical answers may be afraid of those answers.
Gregory Zilboorg

The perfect computer has been developed. You just feed in your problems, and they never come out again.
Al Goodman

Electric clocks reveal to you
Precisely when your fuses blew.
Leonard Schiff

The telephone is the most important single technological resource of later life.
Alex Comfort

$E = MC^2$ Energy equals mass times the speed of light squared.

Albert Einstein

Space isn't remote at all. It's only an hour's drive away if your car could go straight upwards. *Fred Hoyle*

It is very seldom that the same man knows much of science, and about the things that were known before science came. *Lord Dunsany*

A science which hesitates to forget its founders is lost.

Alfred North Whitehead

Pollution is nothing but resources we're not harvesting.

Buckminster Fuller

The best defence against the atom bomb is not to be there when it goes off.

The British Army Journal

A few observations and much reasoning lead to error; many observations and a little reasoning to truth. *Alexis Carrel*

The most important of my discoveries have been suggested to me by my failures. *Sir Humphrey Davy*

Basic research is when I'm doing what I don't know what I'm doing.

Werner von Braun

Sit down before fact as a little child, be prepared to give up every preconceived notion, follow humbly wherever and to whatever abyss nature leads, or you shall learn nothing. *Thomas Huxley*

If I have seen farther it is by standing on the shoulders of giants.

Isaac Newton

The Sea

The sea possesses a power over one's moods that has the effect of a will. The sea can hypnotize. Nature in general can do so. *Henrik Ibsen*

Roll on, thou deep and dark blue ocean — roll!
Ten thousand fleets sweep over thee in vain;
Man marks the earth with ruin — his control
Stops with the shore. *Lord Byron*

The sea — the truth must be confessed — has no generosity. No display of manly qualities — courage, hardihood, endurance, faithfulness — has ever been known to touch its irresponsible consciousness of power.

Joseph Conrad

Being in a ship is being in a jail, with the chance of being drowned.

Samuel Johnson

The sea hath no king but God alone.   *Anon.*

Love the sea? I dote upon it — from the beach.   *Douglas Jerrold*

I liked to sail alone. The sea was the same as a girl to me — I did not want anyone else along.   *E. B. White*

I do not love the sea. The look of it is disquieting. There is something in the very sound of it that stirs the premonition felt while we listen to noble music; we become inexplicably troubled.   *H. M. Tomlinson*

I have observed, on board a steamer, how men and women easily give way to their instinct for flirtation, because water has the power of washing away our sense of responsibility, and those who on land resemble the oak in their firmness behave like floating seaweed when on the sea.

Rabindranath Tagore

A poor woman from Manchester, on being taken to the seaside, is said to have expressed her delight on seeing for the first time something of which there was enough for everybody.   *John Lubbock*

The only cure for seasickness is to sit on the shady side of an old church in the country.   *Anon.*

There's never an end for the sea.   *Samuel Beckett*

The Seasons

To every thing there is a season, and a time to every purpose under the heaven; A time to be born, and a time to die; a time to plant, and a time to pluck up that which is planted.   *Ecclesiastes 3:1,2*

The nicest thing about the promise of spring is that sooner or later she'll have to keep it.   *Mark Beltaire*

Now is the winter of our discontent
Made glorious summer by this sun of York.

Shakespeare, 'King Richard III'

Every April, God rewrites the Book of Genesis. *Anon.*

The changing year's progressive plan
Proclaims mortality to man.

Horace

The English winter — ending in July, to recommence in August.

Lord Byron

Summer is the mother of the poor. *Italian proverb*

Take a winter as you find him and he turns out to be a thoroughly honest
fellow with no nonsense in him: and tolerating none in you, which is a great
comfort in the long run. *James Russell Lowell*

'Heat, ma'am!' I said, 'It was so dreadful here, that I found there was nothing
left for it but to take off my flesh and sit in my bones.' *Sydney Smith*

Summer ends, and Autumn comes, and he who would have it otherwise would
have high tide always and a full moon every night. *Hal Borland*

June's too soon, July's too late — for summer. *Siberian saying*

April,
Comes like an idiot, babbling, and strewing flowers.

Edna St. Vincent Millay

Autumn arrives in the early morning, but spring at the close of a winter's
day. *Elizabeth Bowen*

Autumn is the bite of a harvest apple. *Christina Petrowsky*

May is a pious fraud of the almanac
A ghastly parody of real Spring
Shaped out of snow and breathed with eastern wind.

James Russell Lowell

The first day of spring was once the time for taking the young virgins into
the fields, there in dalliance to set an example in fertility for Nature to follow.
Now we just set the clock an hour ahead and change the oil in the crankcase.

E. B. White

Secrets and Secrecy

Nothing is so burdensome as a secret.   *French proverb*

Shy and unready men are great betrayers of secrets; for there are few wants more urgent for the moment than the want of something to say.
                                                         Henry Taylor

In the mind and nature of a man a secret is an ugly thing, like a hidden physical defect.   *Isak Dinesen*

Be secret and exult,
Because of all things known
That is most difficult.   *William Butler Yeats*

If you wish to preserve your secret, wrap it up in frankness.
                                                       Alexander Smith

Where secrecy reigns, carelessness and ignorance delight to hide — skill loves the light.   *Daniel C. Gelman*

Whatsoever ye have spoken in darkness shall be heard in the light; and that which ye have spoken in the ear in closets shall be proclaimed upon the housetops.   *Luke 12:13*

Even in your thought, do not curse the king, nor in your bedchamber curse the rich; for a bird of the air will carry your voice, or some winged creature tell the matter.   *Ecclesiastes 10:20*

Self and Self-Knowledge

I have never seen a greater monster or miracle in the world than myself.
                                                          Montaigne

We are all serving a life sentence in the dungeon of self. *Cyril Connolly*

If a man really knew himself he would utterly despise the ignorant notions others might form on a subject in which he had such matchless opportunities for observation.   *George Santayana*

One may understand the cosmos, but never the ego; the self is more distant than any star.   *G. K. Chesterton*

We judge ourselves by our motives and others by their actions.

Dwight Morrow

There is nothing noble about being superior to some other man. The true nobility is in being superior to your previous self.   *Hindu proverb*

Self-confidence is the first requisite to great undertakings.

Samuel Johnson

Never to talk of oneself is a form of hypocrisy.   *Friedrich Nietzsche*

Goethe said there would be little left of him if you were to discard what he owed to others.   *Charlotte Cushman*

Be yourself. Who else is better qualified?   *Frank J. Giblin, II*

I don't think anyone is free — one creates one's own prison.

Graham Sutherland

I am I plus my circumstances.   *José Ortega y Gasset*

I think somehow we learn who we really are and then live with that decision.   *Eleanor Roosevelt*

There is nothing will kill a man so soon as having nobody to find fault with but himself.   *George Eliot*

I am as bad as the worst, but, thank God, I am as good as the best.

Walt Whitman

If you really do put a small value upon yourself, rest assured that the world will not raise your price.   *Anon.*

If I am not for myself, who will be?   *Pirke Avot*

The greatest success is successful self-acceptance.   *Ben Sweet*

Compassion for myself is the most powerful healer of them all.

Theodore Isaac Rubin

Self-respect is the root of discipline: the sense of dignity grows with the ability to say no to oneself.   *Abraham J. Heschel*

If you know nothing, be pleased to know nothing.   *John Newlove*

I am more afraid of my own heart than of the Pope and all his cardinals.
I have within me the great Pope, Self.   *Martin Luther*

The happy man is he who knows his limitations, yet bows to no false gods.
                                                          Robert Service

From without, no wonderful effect is wrought within ourselves, unless some
interior, responding wonder meets it.   *Herman Melville*

Nobody knows what's in him until he tries to pull it out. If there's nothing,
or very little, the shock can kill a man.   *Ernest Hemingway*

Blessed are they who heal us of self-despisings. Of all services which can be
done to man, I know of none more precious.   *William Hale White*

When three people call you an ass, put on a bridle.   *Spanish proverb*

A complete life may be one ending in so full an identification with the not-
self that there is no self left to die.   *Bernard Berenson*

A man can stand a lot as long as he can stand himself. He can live without
hope, without friends, without books, even without music, as long as he can
listen to his own thoughts.   *Axel Munthe*

A show of envy is an insult to oneself.   *Yevgeny Yevtushenko*

Maturity consists of no longer being taken in by oneself.
                                                 Kajetan von Schlaggenberg

Our own interests are still an exquisite means for dazzling our eyes agreeably.
                                                            Blaise Pascal

To penetrate one's being, one must go armed to the teeth.   *Paul Valéry*

Men at some time are masters of their fates:
The fault, dear Brutus, is not in our stars,
But in ourselves, that we are underlings.   *Shakespeare, 'Julius Caesar'*

Self-reverence, self-knowledge, self-control — these three alone lead to
sovereign power.   *Alfred, Lord Tennyson*

There are limits to self-indulgence, none to self-restraint.   *Gandhi*

Integrity simply means a willingness not to violate one's identity.
                                                            Erich Fromm

The important thing is not what they think of me, it is what I think of them.
Victoria, Queen of England

I think Dostoevsky was right, that every human being must have a point at which he stands against the culture, where he says, this is me and the damned world can go to hell.   *Rollo May*

O wad some Pow'r the giftie gie us
To see oursels as others see us.
It wad frae money a blunder free us,
And foolish notion.   *Robert Burns*

Self-respecting people do not care to peep at their reflections in unexpected mirrors, or to see themselves as others see them.   *Logan Pearsall Smith*

Self-command is the main elegance.   *Ralph Waldo Emerson*

No one can make you feel inferior without your consent.
Eleanor Roosevelt

I am better than my reputation.   *Friedrich von Schiller*

Do I contradict myself?
Very well, then I contradict myself,
I am large, I contain multitudes.   *Walt Whitman*

Be thine own palace, or the world's thy jail.   *John Donne*

Do not make yourself so big. You are not so small.   *Jewish proverb*

Individualism is rather like innocence; there must be something unconscious about it.   *Louis Kronenberger*

I am as my Creator made me, and since He is satisfied, so am I.
Minnie Smith

I live in the crowds of jollity, not so much to enjoy company as to shun myself.   *Samuel Johnson*

I refuse to try to explain everything, because if you know too much about yourself, you become impotent. Better not to know what it is that makes you tick.   *Paul Wunderlich*

Every man shall bear his own burden.   *Galations 6:5*

I seem to have an awful lot of people inside me.   *Edith Evans*

There is no crime of which I do not deem myself capable.

Johann von Goethe

I shall stay the way I am
Because I do not give a damn.   *Dorothy Parker*

I have been a selfish being all my life, in practice, though not in principle.

Jane Austen

God knows, I'm no the thing I should be,
Nor am I even the thing I could be.   *Robert Burns*

I'm a vague, conjunctured personality, more made up of opinions and
academic prepossessions than of human traits and red corpuscles.

Woodrow Wilson

In the main it is not by introspection but by reflecting on our living in common with others that we come to know ourselves. What is revealed? It is
an original creation. Freely the subject makes himself what he is, never in
this life is the making finished, always it is in process, always it is a precarious
achievement that can slip and fall and shatter.   *Bernard Lonergan*

to be nobody but yourself — in a world which is doing its best, night and
day, to make you everybody else — means to fight the hardest battle which
any human being can fight, and never stop fighting.   *e. e. cummings*

Learn what you are, and be such.   *Pindar*

My great mistake, the fault for which I can't forgive myself, is that one day
I ceased my obstinate pursuit of my own individuality.   *Oscar Wilde*

A man must learn to forgive himself.   *Arthur Davison Ficke*

I have come back again to where I belong; not an enchanted place, but the
walls are strong.   *Dorothy H. Rath*

There's only one corner of the universe you can be certain of improving and
that's your own self.   *Aldous Huxley*

It is not only the most difficult thing to know oneself, but the most inconvenient one, too.   *Josh Billings*

To know oneself, one should assert oneself.   *Albert Camus*

Every new adjustment is a crisis in self-esteem.   *Eric Hoffer*

There is no greater delight than to be conscious of sincerity on self-examination.

Mencius

Whatever you may be sure of, be sure of this — that you are dreadfully like other people.

James Russell Lowell

All life is the struggle, the effort to be itself. The difficulties which I meet with in order to realize my existence are precisely what awaken and mobilize my activities, my capacities.

José Ortega y Gasset

My closest relation is myself.

Terence

Sex

Sex is the great amateur art.

David Cort

Of all sexual aberrations, perhaps the most peculiar is chastity.

Rémy de Gourmont

I've looked on a lot of women with lust. I've committed adultery in my heart many times. This is something God recognizes I will do — and I have done it — and God forgives me for it.

Jimmy Carter

The big difference between sex for money and sex for free is that sex for money usually costs a lot less.

Brendan Francis

Whatever else can be said about sex, it cannot be called a dignified performance.

Helen Lawrenson

Sex — the poor man's polo.

Clifford Odets

Lord, make me chaste — but not yet.

St. Augustine

The natural man has only two primal passions — to get and beget.

William Osler

Amoebas at the start were not complex;
They tore themselves apart and started sex.

Arthur Guiterman

As a matter of biology, if something bites you it is probably female.

Scott M. Kruse

Every animal is sad after intercourse.

Latin proverb

Sex ought to be a wholly satisfying link between two affectionate people from which they emerge unanxious, rewarded, and ready for more.

Alex Comfort

When a man tells me he's run out of steam in the sex department, I'll tell him, 'Count your blessings; you've escaped from the clutches of a cruel tyrant. Enjoy!' *Richard J. Needham*

The dead bird does not leave the nest.
The aging Winston Churchill when told in the House of Commons that his fly was open.

The only unnatural sexual behaviour is none at all. *Freud*

While a person does not give up on sex, sex does not give up on the person.
Gabriel García Márquez

Silence

Silence is the unbearable repartee. *G. K. Chesterton*

That man's silence is wonderful to listen to. *Thomas Hardy*

I believe in the discipline of silence and could talk for hours about it.
George Bernard Shaw

He has the gift of quiet. *John Le Carré*

I'm exhausted from not talking. *Sam Goldwyn*

The cruellest lies are often told in silence. *Robert Louis Stevenson*

Nature has given to men one tongue, but two ears, that we may hear from others twice as much as we speak. *Epictetus*

Silence is the most perfect expression of scorn. *George Bernard Shaw*

Speech may be barren; but it is ridiculous to suppose that silence is always brooding on a nestful of eggs. *George Eliot*

Silence propagates itself, and the longer talk has been suspended, the more difficult it is to find anything to say. *Samuel Johnson*

The most silent people are generally those who think most highly of themselves. *William Hazlitt*

The greatest triumphs of propaganda have been accomplished, not by doing something, but by refraining from doing. Great is truth, but still greater, from a practical point of view, is silence about truth. *Aldous Huxley*

Men fear silence as they fear solitude, because both give them a glimpse of the terror of life's nothingness. *André Maurois*

Silence is deep as Eternity; speech, shallow as Time. *Thomas Carlyle*

Of every noble work the silent part is best,
Of all expression that cannot be expressed. *William Wetmore Story*

Better silent than stupid. *German proverb*

It is a great misfortune neither to have enough wit to talk well nor enough judgement to be silent. *Jean de la Bruyère*

I have noticed that nothing I never said ever did me any harm. *Calvin Coolidge*

One of the best ways to persuade others is with your ears. *Dean Rusk*

It is easier to talk than to hold one's tongue. *Greek proverb*

The pause — that impressive silence, that eloquent silence, that geometrically progressive silence which often achieves a desired effect where no combination of words, howsoever felicitous, could accomplish it. *Mark Twain*

Sleep

The sleep of a labouring man is sweet, whether he eat little or much; but the abundance of the rich will not suffer him to sleep. *Ecclesiastes 5:12*

Sleep that knits up the ravelled sleave of care,
The death of each day's life, sore labour's bath,
Balm of hurt minds, great nature's second course,
Chief nourisher in life's feast. *William Shakespeare, 'Macbeth'*

Weariness
Can snore upon the flint, when resty sloth
Finds the down pillow hard.   *Shakespeare, 'Cymbeline'*

One of the most adventurous things left is to go to bed, for no one can lay a hand on our dreams.   *E. V. Lucas*

Did anyone ever have a boring dream?   *Ralph Hodgson*

Sleeping is no mean art. For its sake one must stay awake all day.
                                        Friedrich Nietzsche

Sleep faster, we need the pillows.   *Jewish proverb*

That we are not much sicker and much madder than we are is due exclusively to that most blessed and blessing of all natural graces, sleep.
                                        Aldous Huxley

I never sleep in comfort save when I am hearing a sermon or praying to God.
                                        Rabelais

Sleep — kinsman thou to death and trance and madness.
                                        Alfred, Lord Tennyson

Thou hast been called, O sleep! the friend of woe;
But 'tis the happy who have called thee so.   *Robert Southey*

Yet a little sleep, a little slumber, a little folding of the hands to sleep.
                                        Proverbs 6:10

Sleep takes off the costume of circumstance, arms us with terrible freedom, so that every will rushes to deed. A skillful man reads his dreams for his self-knowledge; yet not the details, but the quality. What part does he play in them — a cheerful, manly part, or a poor, drivelling part? However monstrous and grotesque their apparitions, they have a substantial truth.
                                        Ralph Waldo Emerson

For some must watch, while some must sleep; thus runs the world away.
                                        Shakespeare, 'Hamlet'

Snobs and Snobbishness

Laughter would be bereaved if snobbery died.   *Peter Ustinov*

The true definition of a snob is one who craves for what separates men rather than for what unites them.   *John Buchan*

A highbrow is the kind of person who looks at a sausage and thinks of Picasso.   *A. P. Herbert*

No place in England where everyone can go is considered respectable.   *George Moore*

Snobs talk as if they had begotten their ancestors.   *Herbert Agar*

A highbrow is a person educated beyond his intelligence.   *Brander Matthews*

All the people like us are We,
And everyone else is They.   *Rudyard Kipling*

The true snob never rests; there is always a higher goal to attain, and there are, by the same token, always more and more people to look down upon.   *Russell Lynes*

Society and Social Structure

Society is composed of two great classes: those who have more dinners than appetite, and those who have more appetite than dinners.   *Sebastien Chamfort*

The complacent, the self-indulgent, the soft societies are about to be swept away with the debris of history.   *John F. Kennedy*

Society is now one polished horde,
Formed of two mighty tribes,
The Bores and the Bored.   *Lord Byron*

Society, dead or alive, can have no charm without intimacy and no intimacy without an interest in trifles.   *Arthur Balfour*

To be social is to be forgiving.   *Robert Frost*

If a free society cannot help the many who are poor, it cannot save the few who are rich.   *John F. Kennedy*

The difference between our decadence and the Russians' is that while theirs is brutal, ours is apathetic.   *James Thurber*

The rich would have to eat money, but luckily the poor provide food.
                                                            Russian proverb

The cocktail party — a device for paying off obligations to people you don't want to invite to dinner.   *Charles Merrill Smith*

Vigorous societies harbour a certain extravagance of objectives.
                                                    Alfred North Whitehead

In any assembly the simplest way to stop the transacting of business and split the ranks is to appeal to a principle.   *Jacques Barzun*

Tolerably early in life I discovered that one of the unpardonable sins, in the eyes of most people, is for a man to go about unlabeled. The world regards such a person as the police do an unmuzzled dog.   *Thomas Huxley*

Twenty per cent of the people in volunteer groups do ninety per cent of the work.   *The Diamond of Psi Upsilon*

Nothing is so dangerous as being too modern; one is apt to grow old-fashioned quite suddenly.   *Oscar Wilde*

Gentleman: one who never hurts anyone's feelings unintentionally.
                                                                    Anon.

Etiquette means behaving yourself a little better than is absolutely essential.
                                                                Will Cuppy

The best things and best people rise out of their separateness; I'm against a homogenized society because I want the cream to rise.   *Robert Frost*

There are four varieties in society; the lovers, the ambitious, observers, and fools. The fools are the happiest.   *Hippolyte Taine*

Whatever people may say, the fastidious formal manner of the upper classes is preferable to the slovenly easygoing behaviour of the common middle class. In moments of crisis, the former know how to act, the latter become uncouth brutes.   *Cesare Pavese*

Necessity is the constant scourge of the lower classes, ennui of the higher ones.   *Arthur Schopenhauer*

The classes that wash most are those that work least.   *G. K. Chesterton*

Society, my dear, is like salt water, good to swim in but hard to swallow.
                                                    Arthur Stringer

Only a few human beings should grow to the square mile; they are commonly planted too close.   *William T. Davis*

'Tis the final conflict! Let each stand in his place!
The international working class shall be the human race!
                                                    'The Internationale'

Every society honours its live conformists and its dead troublemakers.
                                                    Mignon McLaughlin

In order to stand well in the eyes of the community, it is necessary to come up to a certain, somewhat indefinite, conventional standard of wealth.
                                                    Thorstein Veblen

Class is an aura of confidence that is being sure without being cocky. Class has nothing to do with money. Class never runs scared. It is self-discipline and self-knowledge. It's the sure-footedness that comes with having proved you can meet life.   *Ann Landers*

I respect kindness in human beings first of all, and kindness to animals. I don't respect the law; I have a total irreverance for anything connected with society except that which makes the roads safer, the beer stronger, the food cheaper and the old men and old women warmer in the winter and happier in the summer.   *Brendan Behan*

Every man is a consumer and ought to be a producer.
                                                    Ralph Waldo Emerson

Solitude

I was never less alone than when by myself.   *Edward Gibbon*

In the world a man lives in his own age; in solitude in all ages.
                                                    W. Matthews

I never found the companion that was so companionable as solitude.
Henry David Thoreau

If from Society we learn to live,
'Tis Solitude should teach us how to die;
It hath no flatterers.   *Lord Byron*

Solitude is as needful to the imagination as society is wholesome for the
character.   *James Russell Lowell*

One can acquire everything in solitude but character.   *Stendhal*

Solitude is the profoundest fact of the human condition. Man is the only
being who knows he is alone.   *Octavio Paz*

We're all of us sentenced to solitary confinement inside our own skins, for
life.   *Tennessee Williams*

To dare to live alone is the rarest courage; since there are many who had
rather meet their bitterest enemy in the field, than their own hearts in their
closet.   *Charles Caleb Colton*

One of the greatest necessities in America is to discover creative solitude.
Carl Sandburg

Secret, and self-contained, and solitary as an oyster.   *Charles Dickens*

Night, when words fade and things come alive, when the destructive analysis
of day is done, and all that is truly important becomes whole and sound again.
When man reassembles his fragmentary self and grows with the calm of a
tree.   *Antoine de Saint-Exupéry*

Sorrow

In extreme youth, in our most humiliating sorrow, we think we are alone.
When we are older we find that others have suffered too.
Suzanne Moarny

The deeper the sorrow the less tongue it hath.   *The Talmud*

When sorrows come, they come not as single spies,
But in battalions!   *Shakespeare, 'Hamlet'*

Men who are unhappy, like men who sleep badly, are always proud of the fact.   *Bertrand Russell*

What man is there that does not laboriously, though all unconsciously, himself fashion the sorrow that is to be the pivot of his life.
                                                                    Maurice Maeterlinck

Only one-fourth of the sorrow in each man's life is caused by outside uncontrollable elements, the rest is self-imposed by failing to analyze and act with calmness.   *George Jackson*

There is something pleasurable in calm remembrance of a past sorrow.
                                                                    Cicero

The poor and the busy have no leisure for sentimental sorrow.
                                                                    Samuel Johnson

While grief is fresh, every attempt to divert it only irritates.
                                                                    Samuel Johnson

No one can keep his griefs in their prime; they use themselves up.
                                                                    E. M. Cioran

Sorrow is a fruit; God does not allow it to grow on a branch that is too weak to bear it.   *Victor Hugo*

There are few sorrows, however poignant, in which a good income is of no avail.   *Logan Pearsall Smith*

Speakers and Speeches

It is terrible to speak well and be wrong.   *Sophocles*

All the great speakers were bad speakers at first.
                                                                    Ralph Waldo Emerson

In an easy cause any man may be eloquent.   *Ovid*

A dull speaker, like a plain woman, is credited with all the virtues, for we charitably suppose that a surface so unattractive must be compensated by interior blessings.   *A. P. Herbert*

Once you get people laughing, they're listening and you can tell them almost anything.

Herbert Gardner

When a man gets talking about himself, he seldom fails to be eloquent and often reaches the sublime.

Josh Billings

The object of oratory alone is not truth, but persuasion.

Thomas Babington Macaulay

If the announcer can produce the impression that he is a gentleman, he may pronounce as he pleases.

George Bernard Shaw

If no thought
your mind does visit
make your speech
not too explicit.

Piet Hein

Oratory: the art of making deep noises from the chest sound like important messages from the brain.

H. I. Phillips

The glittering generalities of the speaker have left an impression more delightful than permanent.

Franklin J. Dickman

Say what you have to say and the first time you come to a sentence with a grammatical ending — sit down.

Winston Churchill

First learn the meaning of what you say, and then speak.

Epictetus

When a man is asked to make a speech, the first thing he has to decide is what to say.

Gerald Ford

I've never thought my speeches were too long; I've rather enjoyed them.

Hubert Humphrey

Blessed is the man who, having nothing to say, abstains from giving us wordy evidence of the fact.

George Eliot

Look wise, say nothing, and grunt. Speech was given to conceal thought.

William Osler

I have learnt a good deal from my own talk.

Thomas Chandler Haliburton

Speech is the small change of silence.

George Meredith

Speak what you think today in words as hard as cannon balls, and tomorrow speak what tomorrow thinks in hard words again, though it contradict everything you said today.   *Ralph Waldo Emerson*

The voice is a second face.   *Gerard Bauer*

If you don't say anything, you won't be called on to repeat it.
                                                          Calvin Coolidge

In Maine we have a saying that there's no point in speaking unless you can improve on silence.   *Edmund Muskie*

If you have an important point to make, don't try to be subtle or clever. Use a pile-driver. Hit the point once. Then come back and hit it again. Then hit it a third time — a tremendous whack!   *Winston Churchill*

Mend your speech a little,
Lest it may mar your fortunes.   *Shakespeare, 'King Lear'*

He draweth out the thread of his verbosity finer than the staple of his argument.   *Shakespeare, Love's Labour's Lost*

Sport

I hate all sports as rabidly as a person who likes sports hates common sense.
                                                           H. L. Mencken

You can't think and hit at the same time.   *Yogi Berra*

Pro football is like nuclear warfare. There are no winners, only survivors.
                                                          Frank Gifford

Horses and jockeys mature earlier than people — which is why horses are admitted to race tracks at the age of two, and jockeys before they are old enough to shave.   *Dick Beddoes*

Jogging is very beneficial. It's good for your legs and your feet. It's also very good for the ground. It makes it feel needed.   *Charles M. Schulz*

It you watch a game, it's fun. If you play it, it's recreation. If you work at it, it's golf.   *Bob Hope*

Winning can be defined as the science of being totally prepared.

George Allen

When you win, nothing hurts.   *Joe Namath*

Running for money doesn't make you run fast. It makes you run first.

Ben Jipcho

Let's win this one for the Gipper.

Knute Rockne, 1921, in memory of George Gipp

Sports allow men to build up situations of emergency. What he then demands of himself is unnecessary achievement — and unnecessary sacrifice. He artificially creates the tension that he has been spared by affluent society.

Viktor Frankl

It may be the games are silly. But, then, so are human beings.

Robert Lynd

It is in games that many men discover their paradise.   *Robert Lynd*

International sport is war without shooting.   *George Orwell*

Fatigue makes cowards of us all.   *Vince Lombardi*

Sports do not build character. They reveal it.   *Heywood Broun*

Every time you win, you're reborn; when you lose you die a little.

George Allen

Becoming number one is easier than remaining number one.

Bill Bradley

If you aren't fired with enthusiasm, you'll be fired with enthusiasm.

Vince Lombardi

Sport is one area where no participant is worried about another's race, religion or wealth: and where the only concern is 'Have you come to play?'

Henry Roxborough

Behind every tennis player there is another tennis player.   *John McPhee*

Catching a fly ball is a pleasure, but knowing what to do with it is a business.

Tommy Henrich

Trying to get a fast ball past Hank Aaron is like trying to get the sun past a rooster.   *Curt Simmons*

Golf is a good walk spoiled.   *Mark Twain*

Walking is the best possible exercise. Habituate yourself to walk very far.
                                                                       Thomas Jefferson

Hockey captures the essence of the Canadian experience in the New World. In a land so inescapably and inhospitably cold, hockey is the dance of life, and an affirmation that despite the deathly chill of winter we are alive.
                                                                          Bruce Kidd

The game isn't over until it's over.   *Yogi Berra*

The race is not always to the swift nor the battle to the strong — but that's the way to bet.   *Damon Runyan*

A sportsman is a man who, every now and then, simply has to get out and kill something. Not that he's cruel. He wouldn't hurt a fly. It's not big enough.   *Stephen Leacock*

Sport begets tumultuous strife and wrath, and wrath begets fierce quarrels and war to the death.   *Horace*

Citius, altius, fortius. (Swifter, higher, stronger).
                                                           Motto of the Olympic Games

Well, God is certainly getting an earful tonight.
                        Jim Murray, sports columnist, on the death of Casey Stengel

Going to bed with a woman never hurt a ball player. It's staying up all night looking for them that does you in.   *Casey Stengel*

Knute Rockne liked 'bad losers.' He said 'good losers' lose too often.
                                                                          George Allen

Ninety per cent of this game is half-mental.   *Yogi Berra*

Success

If one advances confidently in the direction of his dreams, and endeavours to live the life which he has imagined, he will meet with a success unexpected in common hours.
Henry David Thoreau

The world belongs to the enthusiast who keeps cool.   *William McFee*

Out of every fruition of success, no matter what, comes forth something to make a new effort necessary.
Walt Whitman

Though a tree grow ever so high, the falling leaves return to the root.
Malay proverb

Success is that old A B C — ability, breaks and courage.
Charles Luckman

How can they say my life isn't a success? Have I not for more than sixty years got enough to eat and escaped being eaten?
Logan Pearsall Smith

You always pass failure on the way to success.   *Mickey Rooney*

Of course there is no formula for success except perhaps, an unconditional acceptance of life and what it brings.   *Artur Rubinstein*

High station in life is earned by the gallantry with which appalling experiences are survived with grace.   *Tennessee Williams*

Everything bows to success, even grammar.   *Victor Hugo*

Never having been able to succeed in the world, he took his revenge by speaking ill of it.   *Voltaire*

The successful people are the ones who think up things for the rest of the world to keep busy at.   *Don Marquis*

It is no use saying 'we are doing our best.' You have got to succeed in doing what is necessary.   *Winston Churchill*

Survival is triumph enough.   *Harry Crews*

It takes time to be a success, but time is all it takes.   *Anon.*

There is a passion for perfection which you will rarely see fully developed; but you may note this fact, that in successful lives it is never wholly lacking.   *Bliss Carman*

Nothing fails like success; nothing is so defeated as yesterday's triumphant cause.   *Phyllis McGinley*

The toughest thing about success is that you've got to keep on being a success.   *Irving Berlin*

Nothing fails like success because we don't learn from it. We learn only from failure.   *Kenneth Boulding*

Get place and wealth, if possible with grace;
If not, by any means get wealth and place.   *Alexander Pope*

Success is not so much what you are, but rather what you appear to be.   *Anon.*

I cannot give you the formula for success, but I can give you the formula for failure, which is — try to please everybody.   *Herbert Bayard Swope*

Before everything else, getting ready is the secret of success.
                                                                        Henry Ford

A successful man is he who receives a great deal from his fellow men, usually incomparably more than corresponds to his service to them. The value of a man, however, should be seen in what he gives and not in what he is able to receive.   *Albert Einstein*

Success is not the result of spontaneous combustion. You must set yourself on fire.   *Reggie Leach*

Success is the progressive realization of a worthy ideal.
                                                                   Earl Nightingale

Success has made failures of many men.   *Cindy Adams*

A great secret of success is to go through life as a man who never gets used up.   *Albert Schweitzer*

Success is a science. If you have the conditions, you get the result.
                                                                      Oscar Wilde

Failure changes for the better, success for the worse.   *Seneca*

Behind every successful man there's a lot of unsuccessful years.

Bob Brown

If people knew what they had to do to be successful, most people wouldn't.

Lord Thomson of Fleet

The secret of all victory lies in the organization of the non-obvious.

Oswald Spengler

Snowflakes are one of nature's most fragile things, but just look what they can do when they stick together. *Vesta M. Kelly*

Damon Runyon. A day-coach boy in a parlor car seat. *Damon Runyon*

There is only one success — to be able to spend your life in your own way.

Christopher Morley

Tact and Diplomacy

If a person has no delicacy, he has you in his power. *William Hazlitt*

Tact is the intelligence of the heart. *Anon.*

Silence is not always tact, and it is tact that is golden, not silence.

Samuel Butler

Diplomats are useful only in fair weather. As soon as it rains, they drown in every drop. *Charles de Gaulle*

A distinguished diplomat could hold his tongue in ten languages. *Anon.*

Negotiation in the classic diplomatic sense assumes parties more anxious to agree than to disagree. *Dean Acheson*

Diplomacy; the art of saying 'nice doggie' till you can find a rock.

Wynn Catlin

If any pilgrim monk come from distant parts, with wish as a guest to dwell in the monastery, and will be content with the customs which he finds in the place, and does not perchance by his lavishness disturb the monastery, but is simply content with what he finds, he shall be received for as long as he desires. If, indeed, he find fault with anything, or expose it, reasonably, and with the humility of charity, the Abbott shall discuss it prudently lest perchance God had sent him for this very thing. But, if he have been found gossipy and contumacious in the time of his sojourn as guest, not only ought he not be joined to the body of the monastery, but also, it shall be said to him, honestly, that he must depart. If he does not go, let two stout monks, in the name of God, explain the matter to him.   *Saint Benedict*

An ambassador is an honest man sent to lie abroad for the good of his country.   *Henry Wotton*

Talent

Genius does what is must, and talent does what it can.
Edward Bulwer-Lytton

In this world people have to pay an extortionate price for any exceptional gift whatever.   *Willa Cather*

There is no substitute for talent. Industry and all the virtures are of no avail.
Aldous Huxley

Talent is always conscious of its own abundance, and does not object to sharing.   *Aleksandr Solzhenitsyn*

The luck of having talent is not enough; one must also have a talent for luck.
Hector Berlioz

A talent somewhat above mediocrity, shrewd and not too sensitive, is more likely to rise in the world than genius, which is apt to be perturbable and to wear itself out before fruition.   *Charles Horton Cooley*

Great talents are the most lovely and often the most dangerous fruits on the tree of humanity. They hang upon the most slender twigs that are easily snapped off.   *Carl Jung*

Everyone has a talent. What is rare is the courage to follow the talent to the dark places where it leads.   *Erica Jong*

The crowning blessing of life — to be born with a bias to some pursuit.
S. G. Tallentyre

Taste

Good taste is the first refuge of the non-creative. It is the last ditch stand of the artist.   *Marshall McLuhan*

Taste is the feminine of genius.   *Edward Fitzgerald*

It is good taste, and good taste alone, that possesses the power to sterilize and is always the first handicap to any creative functioning.
Salvador Dali

Taste is the enemy of creativeness.   *Pablo Picasso*

Have nothing in your houses that you do not know to be useful, or believe to be beautiful.   *William Morris*

Style is a simple way of saying complicated things.   *Jean Cocteau*

Fashion exists for women with no taste, etiquette for people with no breeding.
Queen Marie of Rumania

People care more about being thought to have good taste than about being thought either good, clever or amiable.   *Samuel Butler*

We all have some taste or other, of too ancient a date to admit of our remembering that it was an acquired one.   *Charles Lamb*

Good taste and humour are a contradiction in terms, like a chaste whore.
Malcolm Muggeridge

Taste cannot be controlled by law.   *Thomas Jefferson*

One of the surest signs of the Philistine is his reverence for the superior tastes of those who put him down.   *Pauline Kael*

One man's poison ivy is another man's spinach.   *George Ade*

Taxation

The Eiffel Tower is the Empire State Building after taxes.   *Anon.*

The power to tax involves the power to destroy.   *John Marshall*

The art of taxation consists in so plucking the goose as to get the most feathers with the least hissing. *Jean Baptiste Colbert*

The point to remember is that what the government gives it must first take away. *John S. Coleman*

Next to being shot at and missed, nothing is quite as satisfying as an income tax refund. *F. J. Raymond*

The income tax has made more liars out of the American people than golf has. Even when you make a tax form out on the level, you don't know when it's through, if you are a crook or a martyr. *Will Rogers*

Governments last as long as the under-taxed can defend themselves against the over-taxed. *Bernard Berenson*

There went out a decree from Caesar Augustus that all the world should be taxed . . . And all went to be taxed, everyone into his own city.
Luke 2:1,3

The promises of yesterday are the taxes of today.
William Lyon Mackenzie King

Teachers and Teaching

A teacher affects eternity; he can never tell where his influence stops.
Henry Adams

It would be a great advantage to some schoolmasters if they would steal two hours a day from their pupils, and give their own minds the benefit of the robbery. *J. F. Boyse*

Thoroughly to teach another is the best way to learn for yourself.
Tryon Edwards

If the student fails to learn the teacher fails to teach. *Anon.*

The authority of those who profess to teach is often a positive hindrance to those who desire to learn. *Cicero*

Teaching is not a lost art, but the regard for it is a lost tradition.
Jacques Barzun

To teach is to learn twice.   *Joseph Joubert*

A high-school teacher, after all, is a person deputized by the rest of us to explain to the young what sort of world they are living in, and to defend, if possible, the part their elders are playing in it.   *Emile Capouya*

He who can does. He who can't, teaches.   *George Bernard Shaw*

Nothing that is worth knowing can be taught.   *Oscar Wilde*

I hear and I forget. I see and I remember. I do and I understand.
                                                      Chinese proverb

The secret of teaching is to appear to have known all your life what you learned this afternoon.   *Anon.*

No man can reveal to you aught but that which already lies half asleep in the dawning of your knowledge.   *Kahlil Gibran*

The first duty of a lecturer — to hand you after an hour's discourse a nugget of pure truth to wrap up between the pages of your notebooks and keep on the mantelpiece for ever.   *Virginia Woolf*

Television

Television? The word is half Latin and half Greek. No good can come of it.   *C. P. Scott*

Television is the literature of the illiterate, the culture of the low-brow, the wealth of the poor, the privilege of the underprivileged, the exclusive club of the excluded masses.   *Lee Loevinger*

I can get a better grasp of what is going on in the world from one good Washington dinner party than from all the background information NBC piles on my desk.   *Barbara Walters*

Television has proved that people will look at anything rather than each other.   *Ann Landers*

Television is a gold goose that lays scrambled eggs; and it is futile and probably fatal to beat it for not laying caviar.   *Lee Loevinger*

Television is chewing gum for the eyes.   *Frank Lloyd Wright*

In the age of television, image becomes more important than substance.
S. I. Hayakawa

Television is the first truly democratic culture — the first culture available
to everybody and entirely governed by what the people want. The most terrifying thing is what people do want.   *Clive Barnes*

Television has a real problem. They have no page two.   *Art Buchwald*

Good heavens, television is something you appear on, you don't watch.
Noel Coward

Television is an invention that permits you to be entertained in your living
room by people you wouldn't have in your home.   *David Frost*

Why should people pay good money to go out and see bad films when they
can stay at home and see bad television for nothing?   *Sam Goldwyn*

The television commercial is the most efficient power-packed capsule of
education that appears anywhere on TV.   *G. L. Gray*

Television is not the truth. Television is a god-damned amusement park.
Television is a circus, a carnival, a travelling troupe of acrobats, storytellers,
dancers, singers, jugglers, sideshow freaks, lion tamers and football players.
We're in the boredom-killing business.   *Paddy Chayefsky*

Dictum on television scripts: We don't want it good — we want it Tuesday.
Dennis Norden

I've had several years in Hollywood and I still think the movie heroes are
in the audience.   *Wilson Mizner*

Temptation

There are several good protections against temptation, but the surest is cowardice.   *Mark Twain*

Temptation rarely comes in working hours. It is in their leisure time that
men are made or marred.   *W. M. Taylor*

Things forbidden have a secret charm.   *Tacitus*

After listening to thousands of pleas for pardon to offenders, I can hardly recall a case where I did not feel that I might have fallen as my fellow man had done, if I had been subjected to the same demoralizing influences and pressed by the same temptations.   *Horatio Seymour*

I have a simple principle for the conduct of life — never to resist an adequate temptation.   *Max Lerner*

The only way to get rid of a temptation is to yield to it. Resist it, and your soul grows sick with longing for the things it has forbidden to itself.
Oscar Wilde

If the world were merely seductive, that would be easy. If it were merely challenging, that would be no problem. But I rise in the morning torn between a desire to improve (or save) the world and a desire to enjoy (or savour) the world. This makes it hard to plan the day.   *E. B. White*

Never give in, never give in, never, never, never, never — in nothing great or small, large or petty — never give in except to convictions of honour and good sense.   *Winston Churchill*

I generally avoid temptation unless I can't resist it.   *Mae West*

Thinking and Thought

All thought is a feat of association; having what's in front of you bring up something in your mind that you almost didn't know you knew.
Robert Frost

We only think when we are confronted with a problem.   *John Dewey*

The extra calories needed for one hour of intense mental effort would be completely met by eating one oyster cracker or one half of a salted peanut.
Francis G. Benedict

Every man who says frankly and fully what he thinks is doing a public service.   *Leslie Stephen*

Thought is the strongest thing we have. Work done by true and profound thought — that is a real force.   *Albert Schweitzer*

When a man knows he is to be hanged in a fortnight, it concentrates his mind wonderfully.   *Samuel Johnson*

We find it hard to believe that other people's thoughts are as silly as our own, but they probably are.   *James Harvey Robinson*

Thinking is like loving and dying — each of us must do it for himself.
Josiah Royce

A man of action forced into a state of thought is unhappy until he can get out of it.   *John Galsworthy*

It is human nature to think wisely and to act in an absurd fashion.
Anatole France

Men use thought only to justify their wrongdoings, and speech only to conceal their thoughts.   *Voltaire*

And which of you with taking thought can add to his stature one cubit?
Luke 12:25

The real offence, as she ultimately perceived, was her having a mind of her own at all. Her mind was to be his — attached to his own like a small garden plot to a deer park.   *Henry James*

To be uncertain is to be uncomfortable, but to be certain is to be ridiculous.
Chinese proverb

Think wrongly, if you please, but in all cases think for yourself.
Doris Lessing

The thoughts that come often unsought, and, as it were, drop into the mind, are commonly the most valuable of any we have.   *John Locke*

We shall succeed only so far as we continue that most distasteful of all activity, the intolerable labour of thought.   *Learned Hand*

Profundity of thought belongs to youth, clarity of thought to old age.
Friedrich Nietzsche

Every real thought on every real subject knocks the wind out of somebody or other.   *Oliver Wendell Holmes*

What was once thought can never be unthought.   *Friedrich Dürrenmatt*

Many a time I have wanted to stop talking and find out what I really believed.
Walter Lippmann

Man is a slow, sloppy and brilliant thinker; the machine is fast, accurate and stupid.   *William M. Kelly*

Folks that blurt out just what they think wouldn't be so bad if they thought.   *Kin Hubbard*

Facts in books, statistics in encyclopedias, the ability to use them in men's heads.   *Fogg Brackell*

Knowledge is a process of piling up facts; wisdom lies in their simplification.   *Martin H. Fisher*

The fundamental fact about the Greek was that he had to use his mind. The ancient priests had said 'Thus far and no farther. We set the limits of thought.' The Greek said, 'All things are to be examined and called into question. There are no limits set on thought.'   *Edith Hamilton*

Thought is born of failure.   *Lancelot Law Whyte*

'What you think is an illusion created by your glands, your emotions and, in the last analysis, by the content of your stomach. That gray matter you're so proud of is like a mirror in an amusement park which transmits to you nothing but distorted signals from reality forever beyond your grasp.'
                                                        Ayn Rand

Speaking without thinking is shooting without taking aim.
                                                        Spanish proverb

Many highly intelligent people are poor thinkers. Many people of average intelligence are skilled thinkers. The power of a car is separate from the way the car is driven.   *Edward de Bono*

Belief is harder to shake than knowledge.   *Adolf Hitler*

Time

Time is a great legalizer, even in the fields of morals.   *H.L. Mencken*

Time goes, you say? Ah no! Alas, Time stays, we go.
                                                Henry Austin Dobson

Let time that makes you homely, make you sage.   *Thomas Parnell*

I don't ask for your pity, but just your understanding — no, not even that — no. Just for your recognition of me in you, and the enemy, time, in us all.   *Tennessee Williams*

All things flow, nothing abides.   *Heraclitus*

When you sit with a nice girl for two hours, you think it's only a minute. But when you sit on a hot stove for a minute, you think it's two hours. That's relativity.   *Albert Einstein*

There was a young lady named Bright
Who could travel much faster than light
She started one day
In the relative way
And came back on the previous night.   *Anon.*

Longevity conquers scandal every time.   *Shelby Foote*

What may be done at any time will be done at no time. *Scottish proverb*

One of these days is none of these days.   *English proverb*

Punctuality is the thief of time.   *Oscar Wilde*

Enjoy the present hour,
Be thankful for the past,
And neither fear nor wish
Th' approaches of the last.   *Abraham Cowley*

The only true time which a man can properly call his own, is that which he has all to himself; the rest, though in some sense he may be said to live it, is other people's time, not his.   *Charles Lamb*

I want to go ahead of Father Time with a scythe of my own.
H.G. Wells

Time is a great teacher, but unfortunately it kills all its pupils.
Hector Berlioz

One third of the people of the world are asleep at any given moment. The other two thirds are awake and probably stirring up trouble somewhere.
Dean Rusk

Time and I against any two.   *Baltasar Gracián*

Time discovered truth.   *Seneca*

Horus non numero nisi serenas (I count only the sunny hours).
                          Motto on sundial quoted by William Hazlitt

Time gives good advice.   *Maltese proverb*

What a day may bring, a day may take away.   *Thomas Fuller*

Time is a kindly god.   *Sophocles*

Time goes by: reputation increases, ability declines. *Dag Hammarskjöld*

Time cools, time clarifies; no mood can be maintained quite unaltered through
the course of hours.   *Thomas Mann*

Every minute starts an hour.   *Paul Gondola*

Time wounds all heels.   *Jane Ace*

The apparent serenity of the past is an oil spread by time.
                                            Lloyd Frankenberg

Time is a sort of river of passing events, and strong is its current; no sooner
is a thing brought to sight than it is swept by and another takes its place,
and this too will be swept away.   *Marcus Aurelius*

It takes time to save time.   *Joe Taylor*

The mind of man works with strangeness upon the body of time. An hour,
once it lodges in the queer element of the human spirit, may be stretched
to fifty or a hundred times its clock length; on the other hand, an hour may
be accurately represented by the timepiece of the mind by one second.
                                             Virginia Woolf

Travel and Travellers

I like terra firma — the more firma, the less terra.   *George S. Kaufman*

When I was at home, I was in a better place; but travellers must be content.
                                 Shakespeare, 'As You Like It'

I have travelled a good deal in Concord.   *Henry David Thoreau*

A bred-in-the-bone Boston lady, when asked why she never travelled, said 'Why should I? I'm already there.'

Anon.

It is better to travel hopefully than to arrive.   *Robert Louis Stevenson*

The early North American Indian made a great mistake by not having an immigration bureau.

Anon.

Travel is fatal to prejudice, bigotry and narrow-mindedness.

Mark Twain

Every perfect traveller always creates the country where he travels.

Nikos Kazantzakis

If an ass goes travelling, he'll not come back a horse.   *Thomas Fuller*

No man should travel until he has learned the language of the country he visits, otherwise he voluntarily makes himself a great baby — so helpless and ridiculous.   *Ralph Waldo Emerson*

As the Spanish proverb says, 'He who would bring home the wealth of the Indies, must carry the wealth of the Indies with him.' So it with traveling. A man must carry knowledge with him if he would bring home knowledge.

Samuel Johnson

How much a dunce that has been sent to roam
Excels a dunce that has been kept at home!   *William Cowper*

The traveller's-eye view of men and women is not satisfying. A man might spend his life in trains and restaurants and know nothing of humanity at the end. To know, one must be an actor as well as a spectator.

Aldous Huxley

Usually speaking, the worst-bred person in company is a young traveller just returned from abroad.   *Jonathan Swift*

For my part, I travel not to go anywhere, but to go. I travel for travel's sake. The great affair is to move.   *Robert Louis Stevenson*

I met a lot of people in Europe. I even encountered myself.

James Baldwin

Travel is ninety per cent anticipation and ten per cent recollection.

Edward Streeter

If one had but a single glance to give the world, one should gaze on Istanbul.   *Alphonse de Lamartine*

There is no unhappiness like the misery of sighting land again after a cheerful, careless voyage.   *Mark Twain*

Before he sets out, the traveller must possess fixed interests and facilities, to be served by travel. If he drifted aimlessly from country to country he would not travel but only wander, ramble as a tramp. The traveller must be somebody and come from somewhere so his definite character and moral traditions may supply an organ and a point of comparison for his observations.   *George Santayana*

Following the sun we left the old world.
                              Inscription on one of Columbus' caravels

When you travel, remember that a foreign country is not designed to make you comfortable. It is designed to make its own people comfortable.
                                                         Clifton Fadiman

Wherever I travel, I'm too late. The orgy has moved elsewhere.
                                                        Mordecai Richler

My favourite thing is to go where I've never been.   *Diane Arbus*

(Airplanes) may kill you, but they ain't likely to hurt you. *Satchel Paige*

If you are lucky enough to have lived in Paris as a young man, then wherever you go for the rest of your life, it stays with you, for Paris is a movable feast.   *Ernest Hemingway*

Russia is the only country of the world you can be homesick for while you're still in it.   *John Updike*

Old men and far travellers may lie with authority.   *Anon.*

Trust

It is better to suffer wrong than to do it, and happier to be sometimes cheated than not to trust.   *Samuel Johnson*

I think that we may safely trust a good deal more than we do.
                                                  Henry David Thoreau

To put one's trust in God is only a longer way of saying that one will chance it.   *Samuel Butler*

To be trusted is a greater compliment than to be loved.
                                                          George Macdonald

Trust me, but look to thyself.   *Irish proverb*

Trust thyself only, and another shall not betray thee.   *Thomas Fuller*

Make yourself necessary to somebody.   *Ralph Waldo Emerson*

Trust one who has tried.   *Virgil*

Truth

The man who speaks the truth is always at ease.   *Persian proverb*

Every man has a right to utter what he thinks is truth, and every other man has a right to knock him down for it.   *Samuel Johnson*

Don't be consistent, but be simply true.   *Oliver Wendell Holmes*

It makes all the difference in the world whether we put truth in the first place, or in the second place.   *John Morley*

Rough work, iconoclasm, but the only way to get at the truth.
                                                    Oliver Wendell Holmes

When one has no design but to speak plain truth, he may say a great deal in a very narrow compass.   *Richard Steele*

One can live in this world on soothsaying but not on truth saying.
                                                       G.C. Lichtenberg

For my part, whatever anguish of spirit it may cost, I am willing to know the whole truth — to know the worst and provide for it. *Patrick Henry*

Truth has a handsome countenance but torn garments. *German proverb*

God offers to every mind its choice between truth and repose. Take which you please; you can never have both.   *Ralph Waldo Emerson*

Some people handle the truth carelessly;
Others never touch it at all.   *Anon.*

Truth for him was a moving target; he never aimed for the bull and rarely pierced the outer ring.   *Hugh Cudlipp on William Randolph Hearst*

I tore myself away from the safe comfort of certainties through my love for truth; and truth rewarded me.   *Sylvia Ashton-Warner*

There is only one truth, steadfast, healing, salutary, and that is the absurd.
Andrew Salmon

Every emancipation has in it the seeds of a new slavery, and every truth easily becomes a lie.   *I. F. Stone*

Seeing's believing — but feeling is God's own truth.   *Irish proverb*

In every generation there has to be some fool who will speak the truth as he sees it.   *Boris Pasternak*

Every truth passes through three stages before it is recognized. In the first it is ridiculed, in the second it is opposed, in the third it is regarded as self-evident.   *Arthur Schopenhauer*

No one can bar the road to truth, and to advance its cause I'm ready to accept even death.   *Aleksandr Solzhenitsyn*

The passion for truth is silenced by answers which have the weight of undisputed authority.   *Paul Tillich*

A truth that's told with bad intent
Beats all the lies you can invent.   *William Blake*

He who, when called upon to speak a disagreeable truth, tells it boldly and has done, is both bolder and milder than he who nibbles in a low voice and never ceases nibbling.   *Johann Kaspar Lavater*

We call first truths those we discover after all the others.   *Albert Camus*

As scarce as truth is, the supply has always been in excess of the demand.
Josh Billings

I speak the truth, not so much as I would, but as much as I dare; and I dare a little more, as I grow older.   *Montaigne*

The truth is cruel, but it can be loved, and it makes free those who have loved it. *George Santayana*

Between whom there is hearty truth, there is love. *Henry David Thoreau*

Everything has to be taken on trust; truth is only that which is taken to be true. It's the currency of living. There may be nothing behind it, but it doesn't make any difference so long as it is honoured. *Tom Stoppard*

One truth discovered, one pang of regret at not being able to express it, is better than all the fluency and flippancy in the world. *William Hazlitt*

If you speak the truth have a foot in the stirrup. *Turkish proverb*

The man who fears no truths has nothing to fear from lies.
Thomas Jefferson

Truth is the daughter of time. *Anon.*

Pretty much all the honest truthtelling there is in the world is done by children.
Anon.

There are truths that are not for all men, nor for all times. *Voltaire*

A thing is not necessarily true because a man dies for it. *Oscar Wilde*

What I tell you three times is true. *Lewis Carroll*

Peace if possible, but truth at any rate. *Martin Luther*

It takes two to speak the truth — one to speak, and another to hear.
Henry David Thoreau

If you tell the truth you don't have to remember anything. *Mark Twain*

There's such a thing as moderation, even in telling the truth.
Vera Johnson

Truth is something you stumble into when you think you're going some place else. *Jerry Garciá*

We shall return to proven ways — not because they are old, but because they are true. *Barry Goldwater*

Truth emerges more readily from error than from confusion.

Francis Bacon

If you are out to describe the truth, leave elegance to the tailor.

Albert Einstein

I don't give them hell. I just tell the truth and they think it is hell.

Harry S. Truman

Vice

Vice goes a long way tow'rd makin' life bearable. A little vice now an' thin is relished by th' best iv men.   *Finley Peter Dunne*

When I religiously confess myself to myself, I find that the best virtue I have has in it some tincture of vice.   *Montaigne*

One big vice in a man is apt to keep out a great many smaller ones.

Bret Harte

Vice is as much a part of human nature as folly, and pornography may be as necessary to vent vice as satire is to vent folly.   *Mavor Moore*

He who hates vice hates men.   *John Morley*

Nurse one vice in your bosom. Give it the attention it deserves and let your virtues spring up modestly around it. Then you'll have the miser who's no liar; and the drunkard who's the benefactor of a whole city.

Thornton Wilder

The vices we scoff at in others, laugh at us within ourselves.

Thomas Browne

It is the function of vice to keep virtue within reasonable grounds.

Samuel Butler

When our vices leave us, we flatter ourselves with the credit of having left them.   *La Rochefoucauld*

Many without punishment, none without sin.   *John Ray*

If individuals have no virtues, their vices may be of use to us.   *Junius*

If you don't want anyone to know it, don't do it. *Chinese proverb*

Ill habits gather by unseen degrees,
As brooks make rivers, rivers run to seas. *John Dryden*

Vice can be learnt, even without a teacher. *Seneca*

There's a small choice in rotten apples.
Shakespeare, 'The Taming of the Shrew'

Everyone has his faults which he continually repeats; neither fear nor shame
can cure them. *Jean de la Fontaine*

Violence

Violence is the quest for identity. When identity disappears with technological
innovation, violence is the natural recourse. *Marshall McLuhan*

Violence is essentially wordless, and it can begin only where thought and
rational communication have broken down. *Thomas Merton*

You know what I think about violence. For me it is profoundly moral —
more moral than compromises and transactions. *Benito Mussolini*

Violence is just, where kindness is vain. *Corneille*

It is unfair to blame man too fiercely for being pugnacious; he learned the
habit from Nature. *Christopher Morley*

Is some cases non-violence requires more militancy than violence.
Cesar Chavez

We are all shot through with enough motives to make a massacre, any day
of the week that we want to give them their head. *Jacob Bronowski*

In a war of ideas it is people who get killed. *Stanislaw J. Lee*

The private terror of the liberal spirit is invariably suicide, not murder.
Norman Mailer

Violence is, essentially, a confession of ultimate inarticulateness.
Time Magazine

Non-violence is a powerful and just weapon. It is a weapon unique in history, which cuts without wounding and enobles the man who wields it. It is a sword that heals.   *Martin Luther King, Jr.*

Today violence is the rhetoric of the period.   *José Ortega y Gasset*

Virtue

Few men have virtue to withstand the highest bidder.
George Washington

Purity is obscurity.   *Ogden Nash*

I know myself too well to believe in pure virtue.   *Albert Camus*

There are few chaste women who are not tired of their trade.
La Rochefoucauld

Ascetic: one who makes a necessity of virtue.   *Friedrich Nietzsche*

A virtue to be serviceable must, like gold, be alloyed with some commoner but more durable metal.   *Samuel Butler*

The Saints are the Sinners who keep on trying. *Robert Louis Stevenson*

No doubt alcohol, tobacco, and so forth, are things that a saint must avoid, but sainthood is also a thing that human beings must avoid.
George Orwell

If a man has no vices, he's in great danger of making vices about his virtues, and there's a spectacle.   *Thornton Wilder*

When men grow virtuous in their old age, they only make a sacrifice to God of the devil's leavings.   *Jonathan Swift*

If virtue were its own reward, it would no longer be a human quality, but supernatural.   *Vauvenargues*

Let him who believes in immortality enjoy his happiness in silence without giving himself airs about it.   *Goethe*

War

War is much too important a matter to be left to the generals.

Georges Clemenceau

War is mainly a catalogue of blunders.

Winston Churchill

War is a series of catastrophes which result in victory.

Georges Clemenceau

It would indeed be a tragedy if the history of the human race proved to be nothing more than the story of an ape playing with a box of matches on a petrol dump.

David Ormsby Gore

Either war is obsolete, or men are.

Buckminster Fuller

War appeals to young men because it is fundamentally auto-eroticism.

Northrop Frye

Wars are not fought for territory, but for words. Man's deadliest weapon is language. He is susceptible to being hypnotized by slogans as he is to infectious diseases. And where there is an epidemic, the group-mind takes over.

Arthur Koestler

A war regarded as inevitable or even probable, and therefore much prepared for, has a very good chance of eventually being fought.

Anaïs Nin

If you know the enemy and know yourself you need not fear the results of a hundred battles.

Sun Tzu

Today the real test of power is not capacity to make war but capacity to prevent it.

Anne O'Hare McCormick

War is the unfolding of miscalculations.

Barbara Tuchman

As long as war is regarded as wicked, it will always have its fascination. When it is looked upon as vulgar, it will cease to be popular.

Oscar Wilde

What the hell difference does it make, left or right? There were good men lost on both sides.

Brendan Behan

The supreme excellence is not to win a hundred victories in a hundred battles. The supreme excellence is to subdue the armies of your enemies without even having to fight them.

Sun Tzu

Frankly I'd like to see the government get out of war altogether and leave the whole field to private industry.   *Joseph Heller*

War is the national industry of Prussia.   *Mirabeau*

It is a fearful thing to lead this great peaceful people into war, into the most terrible and disastrous of all wars, civilization itself seeming to be in the balance. But the right is more precious than peace, and we shall fight for the things which we have always carried nearest our hearts — for democracy.
Woodrow Wilson

Sweet is war to those who have never experienced it.   *Latin proverb*

Among the calamities of wars may be justly numbered the diminution of the love of truth by the falsehoods which interest dictates and credulity encourages.   *Samuel Johnson*

The possibility of war increases in direct proportion to the effectiveness of the instruments of war.   *Norman Cousins*

I don't know what effect these men will have on the enemy, but by God, they frighten *me*.
Attributed to the Duke of Wellington reviewing his troops

Boys are the cash of war. Whoever said: we're not free spenders — doesn't know our like.   *John Ciardi*

In time of war the first casualty is truth.   *Boake Carter*

World War II was the last government program that really worked.
George Will

It's one of the most serious things that can possibly happen to one in a battle — to get one's head cut off.   *Lewis Carroll*

No one can guarantee success in war, but only deserve it.   *Winston Churchill*

There is no such thing as inevitable war. If war comes it will be from failure of human wisdom.   *Bonar Law*

The world will never have lasting peace so long as men reserve for war the finest human qualities.   *John Foster Dulles*

War would end if the dead could return.   *Stanley Baldwin*

If they want peace, nations should avoid the pinpricks that precede cannon
shots.   *Napoleon Bonaparte*

Sometime they'll give a war and nobody will come.   *Carl Sandburg*

A man who experiences no genuine satisfaction in life does not want peace.
People court war to escape meaninglessness and boredom, to be relieved of
fear and frustration.   *Nels F. S. Ferre*

The object of war is to survive it.   *John Irving*

So far war has been the only force that can discipline a whole community,
and until an equivalent discipline is organized, I believe that war must have
its way.   *William James*

Men love war because it allows them to look serious; because it is the only
thing that stops women laughing at them.   *John Fowles*

War hath no fury like a non-combatant.   *E. C. Montague*

Most sorts of diversion in men, children and other animals, are in imitation
of fighting.   *Jonathan Swift*

Nothing except a battle lost can be half so melancholy as a battle won.
                                                          Duke of Wellington

Human war has been the most successful of all our cultural traditions.
                                                            Robert Ardrey

War is the trade of kings.   *John Dryden*

The whole art of war consists of guessing at what is on the other side of
the hill.   *Duke of Wellington*

It is well that war is so terrible — we would grow too fond of it.
                                                            Robert E. Lee

Men grow tired of sleep, love, singing and dancing sooner than of war.
                                                                  Homer

Most people coming out of war feel lost and resentful. What had been a
minute-to-minute confrontation with yourself, your struggle with what
courage you have against discomfort, at the least, and death at the other
end, ties you to the people you have known in the war and makes for a time
others seem alien and frivolous.   *Lillian Hellman*

Vice stirs up war; virtue fights. *Vauvenargues*

In peace, sons bury their fathers; in war, fathers bury their sons.
Herodotus

War will exist until that distant day when the conscientious objector enjoys the same reputation and prestige that the warrior does today.
John F. Kennedy

The weak against the strong,
Is always in the wrong. *Ivan Krylov*

But, in case signals can neither be seen or perfectly understood, no captain can do very wrong if he places his ship alongside the enemy.
Horatio Nelson

Something must be left to chance; nothing is sure in a sea fight beyond all others. *Horatio Nelson*

War is like love, it always finds a way. *Bertolt Brecht*

The guerilla must live amongst the people as the fish lives in the water.
Mao Tse-Tung

It simply is not true that war never settles anything. *Felix Frankfurter*

War does not determine who is right — only who is left. *Anon.*

There are no atheists in the foxholes. *William Thomas Cummings*

There is many a boy here today who looks on war as all glory, but boys, it is all hell. *William T. Sherman*

There will be no veterans of World War III. *Walter Mondale*

Wealth

The human race has had long experience and a fine tradition in surviving adversity. But we now face a task for which we have little experience, the task of surviving prosperity. *Alan Gregg*

Riches enlarge, rather than satisfy appetites. *Thomas Fuller*

It is better to live rich than to die rich. *Samuel Johnson*

Australia is so kind that, just tickle her with a hoe, and she laughs with a harvest. *Douglas Jerrold*

We can have democracy in this country or we can have great wealth concentrated in the hands of a few, but we can't have both. *Louis D. Brandeis*

I am opposed to millionaires, but it would be dangerous to offer me the position. *Mark Twain*

Sleep, riches and health to be truly enjoyed must be interrupted. *Jean Paul Richter*

The wealth of a nation consists not in its mass of material things, but in its system. The natural resources of South America are not inferior to those of the United States, but the wealth of the two regions is vastly different. The land of India is far richer than that of Japan, but the comparative wealth of the two nations is reversed. *George Brockway*

I have enough money to get by. I'm not independently wealthy, just independently lazy, I suppose. *Montgomery Clift*

I have no complex about wealth. I have worked hard for my money, producing things people need. I believe that the able industrial leader who creates wealth and employment is more worthy of historical notice than politicians or soldiers. *Paul Getty*

I was born into it and there was nothing I could do about it. It was there, like air or food, or any other element. The only question with wealth is what you do with it. *John D. Rockefeller, Jr.*

Riches do not consist in the possession of treasures, but in the use made of them. *Napoleon Bonaparte*

I wish to become rich, so that I can instruct the people and glorify honest poverty a little, like those kind-hearted, fat, benevolent people do. *Mark Twain*

In big houses in which things are done properly, there is always the religious element. The diurnal cycle is observed with more feeling when there are servants to do the work. *Elizabeth Bowen*

Wickedness and Cruelty

Men are always wicked at bottom unless they are made good by some compulsion.
Niccolo Machiavelli

God bears with the wicked, but not forever.
Cervantes

Weak men are apt to be cruel because they stick at nothing that may repair the ill effect of their mistakes.
George, Lord Halifax

All cruelty springs from weakness.
Seneca

I must be cruel
Only to be kind.
Shakespeare, 'Hamlet'

We are oftener treacherous through weakness than through calculation.
La Rochefoucauld

When we do evil,
We and our victims
Are equally bewildered.
W. H. Auden

Half of the harm that is done in this world
Is due to people who want to feel important.
They don't mean to do harm — but the harm does not interest them.
T. S. Eliot

We all have flaws, and mine is being wicked.
James Thurber

Why inflict pain on oneself, when so many others are ready to save us the trouble?
George W. Pacaud

Will and Determination

The difference between perseverance and obstinacy is that one often comes from a strong will, and the other from a strong won't.
Henry Ward Beecher

This free-will business is a bit terrifying anyway. It's almost pleasanter to obey, and make the most of it.
Ugo Betti

Fall seven times, stand up eight.
Japanese proverb

Don't fall before you're pushed.   *English proverb*

Where the willingness is great, the difficulties cannot be great.
                                                    Niccolo Machiavelli

The will is the strong blind man who carries on his shoulders the lame man who can see.   *Arthur Schopenhauer*

Obstinacy is the result of the will forcing itself into the place of the intellect.   *Arthur Schopenhauer*

Make voyages. Attempt them. There's nothing else. *Tennessee Williams*

Do what you can, with what you have, where you are.
                                                    Theodore Roosevelt

Our strength is often composed of the weakness that we're damned if we are going to show.   *Mignon McLaughlin*

Nothing in the world can take the place of persistence. Talent will not; nothing is more common than unsuccessful men of talent. Genius will not; unrewarded genius is almost a proverb. Education will not; the world is full of educated derelicts. Persistence and determination alone are omnipotent.
                                                    Calvin Coolidge

All happiness depends on courage and work. I have had many periods of wretchedness, but with energy and above all with illusions, I pulled through them all.   *Honoré de Balzac*

Man is both determined and self-determining.   *Stein and Vidichon*

Don't let your will roar when your power only whispers. *Thomas Fuller*

Those who live are those who fight.   *Victor Hugo*

If you start to take Vienna — take Vienna.   *Napoleon Bonaparte*

If you would convince others, seem open to conviction yourself.
                                                    Lord Chesterfield

You have to pay the price — but if you do you can only win.
                                                    Frank Leahy

Victory — a matter of staying power.   *Elbert Hubbard*

In war, as in life, it is often necessary, when some cherished scheme has failed, to take up the best alternative open, and if so, it is folly not to work for it with all your might. *Winston Churchill*

It isn't the mountain ahead that wears you out — it's the grain of sand in your shoe. *Robert Service*

Wisdom and the Wise

The road to wisdom? Well, it's plain
And simple to express:
Err
And err
And err again
But less
And less
And less. *Piet Hein*

A wise man hears one word and understands two. *Jewish proverb*

The art of being wise is the art of knowing what to overlook.
William James

Through wisdom a house is built and through understanding it is established.
Proverbs 24:3

Great men are not always wise. *Job 32:9*

A wise man gets more use from his enemies than a fool from his friends.
Baltasar Gracián

Who is wise? He that learns from everyone.
Who is powerful? He that governs his passions.
Who is rich? He that is content.
Who is that? Nobody. *Benjamin Franklin*

Not to know certain things is a great part of wisdom. *Hugo Grotius*

It is characteristic of wisdom not to do desperate things.
Henry David Thoreau

A word to the wise is infuriating. *Anon.*

The wise only possess ideas; the greater part of mankind are possessed by them. *Samuel Taylor Coleridge*

Learning passes for wisdom among those who want both.
William Temple

A man that is young in years may be old in hours, if he has lost no time.
Francis Bacon

Every man is a damn fool for at least five minutes every day; wisdom consists in not exceeding the limit. *Elbert Hubbard*

It is not wise to be wiser than is necessary. *Philippe Quinault*

A wise man sees as much as he ought, not as much as he can.
Montaigne

A proverb is one man's wit and all men's wisdom. *John Russell*

Almost every wise saying has an opposite one, no less wise, to balance it.
George Santayana

We should be careful to get out of an experience only the wisdom that is in it — and stop there, lest we be like the cat that sits down on a hot stovelid. She will never sit down on a hot stove-lid again — and that is well; but also she will never sit down on a cold one anymore. *Mark Twain*

All human wisdom is summed up in two words — wait and hope.
Alexandre Dumas the Elder

It's taken me all my life to understand that it is not necessary to understand everything. *René Coty*

What a man knows at fifty that he did not know at twenty is for the most part incommunicable. *Adlai Stevenson*

Nine-tenths of wisdom consists in being wise in time.
Theodore Roosevelt

Deliberate often — decide once. *Latin proverb*

Nothing contributes so much to tranquilize the mind as a steady purpose — a point on which the soul may fix its intellectual eye.
Mary Wollstonecraft Shelley

Knowledge comes, but wisdom lingers.   *Alfred, Lord Tennyson*

In much wisdom is much grief: and he that increaseth knowledge increaseth sorrow.   *Ecclesiastes 1:18*

I prefer the errors of enthusiasm to the indifference of wisdom.
        Anatole France

The wise have a solid sense of silence and the ability to keep a storehouse of secrets. Their capacity and character are respected.   *Baltasar Gracián*

God Almighty never created a man half as wise as he looks.
        Thomas Carlyle

Where ignorance is bliss
'Tis folly to be wise.   *Thomas Gray*

Everyone whose deeds are more than his wisdom, his wisdom endures. And everyone whose wisdom is more than his deeds, his wisdom does not endure.
        The Talmud

Wit

Wit consists in knowing the resemblance of things which differ and the difference of things which are alike.   *Madame de Staël*

If you want to be witty, work on your character and say what you think on every occasion.   *Stendhal*

Melancholy men are of all others the most witty.   *Aristotle*

The well of true wit is truth itself.   *George Meredith*

An epigram is a half-truth so stated as to irritate the person who believes the other half.   *Shailer Mathews*

A brilliant epigram is a solemn platitude gone to a masquerade ball.
        Lionel Strachey

What is perfectly true is perfectly witty.   *La Rochefoucauld*

Wit is the sudden marriage of ideas which, before their union, were not perceived to have any relation.   *Mark Twain*

True wit is Nature to advantage dress'd
What oft was thought, but ne'er so well express'd.   *Alexander Pope*

A man often runs the risk of throwing away a witticism if he admits that
it is his own.   *Jean de la Bruyère*

Wit is the epitaph of an emotion.   *Friedrich Nietzsche*

Wit has truth in it; wisecracking is simply calisthenics with words.
Dorothy Parker

Wit is far more often a shield than a lance.   *Anon.*

What is an epigram? A dwarfish whole,
Its body brevity, and wit its soul.   *Samuel Taylor Coleridge*

Brevity is the soul of wit.   *Shakespeare, 'Hamlet'*

Belief in form, but disbelief in content — that's what makes an aphorism
charming.   *Friedrich Nietzsche*

Women

Have you any notion how many books are written about women in the course
of one year? Have you any notion how many are written by men? Are you
aware that you are, perhaps, the most discussed animal in the universe?
Virginia Woolf

A woman is the only thing I am afraid of that I know will not hurt me.
Abraham Lincoln

Music and women I cannot but give way to, whatever my business is.
Samuel Pepys

A woman never sees what we do for her, she only sees what we don't do.
Georges Courteline

What does a woman want?   *Sigmund Freud*

You have to go back to the Children's Crusade in 1212 AD to find as unfortunate and fatuous an attempt at manipulated hysteria as the Women's
Liberation Movement.   *Helen Lawrenson*

A woman is always buying something.   *Ovid*

Educating a beautiful woman is like pouring honey into a fine Swiss watch: everything stops.   *Kurt Vonnegut*

By nice women . . . you probably mean selfish women who have no more thought for the underprivileged, overworked women than a pussycat in a sunny window for the starving kitten in the street. Now in that sense I am not a nice woman, for I do care.   *Nellie McClung*

A kiss can be a comma, a question mark or an exclamation point. That's a basic spelling that every woman should know.   *Mistin Guett*

A beautiful woman who is pleasing to men is good only for frightening fish when she falls into the water.   *Zen proverb*

Whether women are better than men I cannot say — but I can say they are certainly no worse.   *Golda Meir*

Of my two 'handicaps,' being female put many more obstacles in my path than being black.   *Shirley Chisholm*

The toughest thing about being a housewife is you have no place to stay home from.   *Patricia C. Beudoin*

The economic dependence of women is perhaps the greatest injustice that has been done to us, and has worked the greatest injury to the race.
                                                      Nellie McClung

Whatever women do they must do twice as well as men to be thought half as good. Luckily, this is not difficult.   *Charlotte Whitton*

All women's dresses are merely variations on the eternal struggle between the admitted desire to dress and the unadmitted desire to undress.
                                                        Lin Yutang

If you can make a woman laugh you can do anything with her.
                                                   Nicol Williamson

Woman is at once apple and serpent.   *Heinrich Heine*

The more underdeveloped the country, the more overdeveloped the women.
                                                     J. K. Galbraith

One is not born a woman — one becomes one.   *Simone de Beauvoir*

Nature says to a woman: 'Be beautiful if you can, wise if you want to, but be respected, that is essential.'   *Beaumarchais*

A modest woman, dressed out in all her finery, is the most tremendous object of the whole creation.   *Oliver Goldsmith*

Why should human females become sterile in their forties, while female crocodiles continue to lay eggs into their third century?   *Aldous Huxley*

You don't know a woman until you have had a letter from her.
                                                    Ada Levenson

Housework is what woman does that nobody notices unless she hasn't done it.   *Evan Esar*

The worst thing about work in the house or home is that whatever you do is destroyed, laid waste or eaten within twenty-four hours. *Lady Kasluck*

The woman who thinks she is intelligent demands equal rights with men. A woman who is intelligent does not.   *Colette*

Most women still need a room of their own and the only way to find it may be outside their own home.   *Germaine Greer*

Women are the true maintenance class. Society is built upon their acquiescence and upon their small and necessary labours.   *Sally Kempton*

It is hard to fight an enemy who has outposts in your head.
                                                    Sally Kempton

A woman past forty should make up her mind to be young — not her face.
                                                    Billie Burke

There is nothing enduring in life for a woman except what she builds in a man's heart.   *Judith Anderson*

I know the nature of women;
When you want to, they don't want to;
And when you don't want to, they desire exceedingly.   *Terence*

Honest women are inconsolable for the mistakes they haven't made.
                                                    Sacha Guitry

Even the most respectable woman has a complete set of clothes in her wardrobe ready for a possible abduction.   *Sacha Guitry*

My vigour, vitality and cheek repel me. I am the kind of woman I would run from.   *Lady Astor*

I have met with women who I really think would like to be married to a poem, and to be given away by a novel.   *John Keats*

A beautiful woman should break her mirror early.   *Baltasar Gracián*

I don't know of anything better than a woman if you want to spend money where it will show.   *Kin Hubbard*

In our civilization men are afraid they will not be men enough, and women are afraid they might be considered only women.   *Theodore Reik*

It takes all the fun out of a bracelet if you have to buy it yourself.
Peggy Joyce

Age cannot wither, her nor custom stale her infinite variety; other women cloy the appetites they feed, but she makes hungry where most she satisfies.
Shakespeare, 'Antony and Cleopatra'

The cave-dweller's wife complained that he hadn't dragged her anywhere in months.   *Laurence J. Peter*

There is but an hour a day between a good housewife and a bad one.
English proverb

If a woman likes another woman, she's cordial. If she doesn't like her, she's very cordial.   *Irvin S. Cobb*

Next to the wound, what women makes best is the bandage.
Barbey d'Aurevilly

Social science affirms that a woman's place in society marks the level of civilization.   *Elizabeth Cady Stanton*

Nobody objects to a woman being a good writer or sculptor or geneticist if at the same time she manages to be a good wife, good mother, good looking, good tempered, well groomed and unaggressive. *Leslie M. McIntyre*

When thou goest to woman, take thy whip.   *Friedrich Nietzsche*

It was a woman who drove me to drink — and, you know, I never even thanked her.   *W. C. Fields*

Has a woman who knew that she was well dressed ever caught a cold?
Friedrich Nietzsche

Each suburban housewife spends her time presiding over a power plant sufficient to have staffed the palace of a Roman emperor with a hundred slaves.
Margaret Mead

Boys don't make passes at female smart-asses.   *Letty Cottin Pogrebin*

As a woman, to be competitive is to be passive.   *Marianne Partridge*

Women are like elephants. They are interesting to look at, but I wouldn't like to own one.   *W. C. Fields*

No woman can call herself free who does not own and control her body. No woman can call herself free until she can choose consciously whether she will or will not be a mother.   *Margaret Sanger*

Women are most adorable when they are afraid; that's why they frighten so easily.   *Ludwig Börne*

Can we today measure devotion to husband and children by our indifference to everything else?   *Golda Meir*

Women are perfectly well aware that the more they seem to obey the more they rule.   *Jules Michelet*

Some women blush when they are kissed; some call for the police; some swear; some bite. But the worst are those who laugh.   *Anon.*

What will not woman, gentle woman dare
When strong affection stirs her spirit up?   *Robert Southey*

Women keep a special corner of their hearts for sins they have never committed.   *Cornelia Otis Skinner*

Nature is in earnest when she makes a woman.   *Oliver Wendell Holmes*

The only question left to be settled now is, are women persons?
Susan B. Anthony

Women do not find it difficult nowadays to behave like men, but they often find it extremely difficult to behave like gentlemen. *Compton Mackenzie*

In various stages of her life, a woman resembles the continents of the world. From 13 to 18, she's like Africa — virgin territory, unexplored; from 18 to 30, she's like Asia — hot and exotic; from 30 to 45, she's like America — fully explored and free with her resources; from 45 to 55, she's like Europe — exhausted, but not without places of interest; after 55, she's like Australia — everybody knows it's down there but nobody much cares. *Al Boliska*

Woman's place is in the wrong.   *James Thurber*

There are no ugly women, only lazy ones.   *Helena Rubenstein*

A woman without a man is like a fish without a bicycle. *Gloria Steinem*

I dress for women — and I undress for men.   *Angie Dickinson*

When a woman dresses up for an occasion, the man should become the black velvet pillow for the jewel.   *John Weitz*

The average girl would rather have beauty than brains because she knows the average man can see much better than he can think.
Ladies' Home Journal

She was not a woman likely to settle for equality when sex gave her an advantage.   *Anthony Delano*

Whether they give or refuse, women are glad to have been asked.   *Ovid*

One can find women who have never had a love affair, but it is rare indeed to find any who have had only one.   *La Rochefoucauld*

The mirror is the conscience of women; they never do a thing without first consulting it.   *Moritz G. Saphir*

Simpson succeeded in proving that there was no harm in giving anaesthetics to men, because God put Adam into a deep sleep when He extracted his rib. But male ecclesiastics remained unconvinced as regards the sufferings of women, at any rate in childbirth.   *Bertrand Russell*

The cleverest woman finds a need for foolish admirers.   *Anon.*

Women who set a low value on themselves make life hard for all women.
Nellie McClung

Women have simple tastes. They get pleasure out of the conversation of children in arms and men in love.   *H. L. Mencken*

Women are the cowards they are because they have been semi-slaves for so long. The number of women prepared to stand up for what they really think, feel, experience, with a man they are in love with is still very small.

Doris Lessing

Woman's normal occupations in general run counter to creative life, or contemplative life, or saintly life.   *Anne Morrow Lindbergh*

Men know that women are an overmatch for them, and therefore they choose the weakest or the most ignorant. If they did not think so, they never could be afraid of women knowing as much as themselves.   *Samuel Johnson*

If woman had no existence save in the fiction written by men, one would imagine her a person of the utmost importance; very various; heroic and mean; splendid and sordid; infinitely beautiful and hideous in the extreme; as great as a man, some think even better.   *Virginia Woolf*

No man is as anti-feminist as a really feminine woman.

Frank O'Connor

The ideal woman which is in every man's mind is evoked by a word or phrase or the shape of her wrist, her hand. The most beautiful description of a woman is by understatement. Remember, all Tolstoy ever said to describe Anna Karenina was that she was beautiful and could see in the dark like a cat. Every man has a different idea of what's beautiful, and it's best to take the gesture, the shadow of the branch, and let the mind create the tree.

William Faulkner

Words and Language

Since the concepts people live by are derived only from perceptions and from language and since the perceptions are received and interpreted only in light of earlier concepts, man comes pretty close to living in a house that language built.   *Russell R. W. Smith*

If a conceptual distinction is to be made, the machinery for making it ought to show itself in language. If a distinction cannot be made in language, it cannot be made conceptually.   *N. R. Hanson*

Often I am struck in amazement about a word: I suddenly realize that the complete arbitrariness of our language is but a part of the arbitrariness of our own world in general.   *Christian Morgenstern*

Understanding is nothing else than conception caused by speech.
Thomas Hobbes

Who does not know another language, does not know his own. *Goethe*

To me, the term 'middle-class' connotes a safe, comfortable, middle-of-the-road policy. Above all, our language is 'middle-class' in the middle of our road. To drive it to one side or the other or even off the road, is the noblest task of the future. *Christian Morgenstern*

Similies are like songs of love:
They much describe, they nothing prove. *Matthew Prior*

Words are the physicians of a mind diseased. *Aeschylus*

A language is a dialect with its own army and navy. *Max Weinreich*

Words are wise men's counters, they do but reckon by them; but they are the money of fools. *Thomas Hobbes*

'When I use a word,' Humpty Dumpty said in rather a scornful tone, 'it means just what I choose it to mean — neither more nor less.'
'The question is,' said Alice, 'whether you can make words mean so many different things.'
'The question is,' said Humpty Dumpty, 'which is to be master — that's all.' *Lewis Carroll*

The word is half his that speaks, and half his that hears it. *Montaigne*

A single word often betrays a great design. *Jean Baptiste Racine*

Words once spoken, can never be recalled. *Wentworth Dillon*

Some words are like the old Roman galleys; large-scaled and ponderous. They sit low in the water even when their cargo is light. *William Jovanovich*

It's as interesting and as difficult to say a thing well as to paint it. There is the art of lines and colours, but the art of words exists too, and will never be less important. *Vincent van Gogh*

The difference between the right word and the almost right word is the difference between lightning and the lightning bug. *Mark Twain*

Words, like eyeglasses, blur everything that they do not make clear.
Joseph Joubert

There is only one way to degrade mankind permanently and that is to destroy language.   *Northrop Frye*

The limits of my language mean the limits of my world.
                                                    Ludwig Wittgenstein

More than kisses, letters mingle souls.   *John Donne*

To have another language is to possess a second soul.   *Charlemagne*

A good catchword can obscure analysis for fifty years.   *Johan Huisinga*

I wonder what language truck drivers are using, now that everyone is using theirs?   *Beryl Pfizer*

The two words 'information' and 'communication' are often used interchangeably, but they signify quite different things. Information is giving out; communication is getting through.   *Sydney J. Harris*

England and America are two countries separated by the same language.
                                                    George Bernard Shaw

The Englishman loves to roll his tongue around the word, 'extraordinary.' It so pleases him that he is reluctant to finish the sound which goes on into harmonics and overtones. The American publisher is likewise inclined.
                                                    R. I. Fitzhenry

Words are feminine; deeds are masculine.   *Baltasar Gracián*

Let it not be said that I have said nothing new. The arrangement of the material is new.   *Blaise Pascal*

When an idea is wanting, a word can always be found to take its place.
                                                    Goethe

Speech is civilization itself. The word, even the most contradictory word, preserves contact — it is silence which isolates.   *Thomas Mann*

In certain trying circumstances, urgent circumstances, desperate circumstances, profanity furnishes a relief denied even to prayer.
                                                    Mark Twain

Like stones, words are laborious and unforgiving, and the fitting of them together, like the fitting of stones, demands great patience and strength of purpose and particular skill.   *Edmund Morrison*

In Paris they simply stared when I spoke to them in French; I never did succeed in making those idiots understand their own language. *Mark Twain*

Great literature is simply language charged with meaning to the utmost possible degree. *Ezra Pound*

One way of looking at speech is to say it is a constant stratagem to cover nakedness. *Harold Pinter*

The downtrodden, who are the great creators of slang, hurl pithiness and colour at poverty and oppression. *Anthony Burgess*

Slang is language which takes off its coat, spits on its hands — and goes to work. *Carl Sandburg*

Work

As a remedy against all ills — poverty, sickness, and melancholy — only one thing is absolutely necessary: a liking for work. *Charles Baudelaire*

They intoxicate themselves with work so they won't see how they really are. *Aldous Huxley*

Most people like hard work, particularly when they're paying for it. *Franklin P. Jones*

We work to become, not to acquire. *Elbert Hubbard*

If one defines the term 'dropout' to mean a person who has given up serious effort to meet his responsibilities, then every business office, government agency, golf club and university faculty would yield its quota. *John W. Gardner*

Hasten slowly, and without losing heart, put your work twenty times upon the anvil. *Nicolas Boileau*

How many years of fatigue and punishment it takes to learn the simple truth that work, that disagreeable thing, is the only way of not suffering in life, or at all events, of suffering less. *Charles Baudelaire*

Miracles sometimes occur, but one has to work terribly hard for them. *Chaim Weizmann*

Beware all enterprises that require new clothes.   *Henry David Thoreau*

Employment is nature's physician, and is essential to human happiness.
Galen

Work is the grand cure of all the maladies and miseries that ever beset mankind.   *Thomas Carlyle*

The secret of being miserable is to have leisure to bother about whether you are happy or not. The cure for it is occupation.   *George Bernard Shaw*

Chance favours only those who know how to court her.   *Charles Nicolle*

Work is man's most natural form of relaxation.   *Dagobert Runes*

Work is not man's punishment. It is his reward and his strength, his glory and his pleasure.   *George Sand*

If a man loves the labour of his trade, apart from any question of success or fame, the gods have called him.   *Robert Louis Stevenson*

When white-collar people get jobs, they sell not only their time and energy, but their personalities as well. They sell by week, or month, their smiles and their kindly gestures, and they must practise prompt repression of resentment and aggression.   *C. Wright Mills*

He that can work is a born king of something.   *Thomas Carlyle*

Love of bustle is not industry.   *Seneca*

The joy about our work is spoiled when we perform it not because of what we produce but because of the pleasure with which it can provide us, or the pain against which it can protect us.   *Paul Tillich*

Productive work is the central purpose of a rational man's life, the central value that integrates and determines the hierarchy of all his other values. Reason is the source, the precondition of his productive work — pride is the result.   *Ayn Rand*

Because it is less structured than work, leisure time leaves workaholics at a loss for what to do. Workaholics practically climb the wall when they can't work.   *Marilyn Machlowitz*

Workaholics commit slow suicide by refusing to allow the child inside them to play.   *Dr. Laurence Susser*

Man works primarily for his own self-respect and not for others or for profit . . . the person who is working for the sake of his own satisfaction, the money he gets in return serves merely as fuel, that is, as a symbol of reward and recognition, in the last analysis, of acceptance by one's fellowmen.

Otto Rank

The people people work with best are often very queer.

Charlotte Perkins Gilman

To travel hopefully is a better thing than to arrive, and the true success is to labour. *Robert Louis Stevenson*

By the work one knows the workman. *Jean de la Fontaine*

Work brings its own relief;
He who most idle is
Has most of grief. *Eugene Fitch Ware*

In a professional once engaged, the performance of the job comes first.

Garson Kanin

If a little labour, little are our gains.
Man's fortunes are according to his pains. *Robert Herrick*

Work is the curse of the drinking classes. *Oscar Wilde*

A man must love a thing very much if he not only practises it without any hope of fame and money, but even practises it without any hope of doing it well. *G. K. Chesterton*

A hobby is hard work you wouldn't do for a living. *Anon.*

A task becomes a duty from the moment you suspect it to be an essential part of that integrity which alone entitles a man to assume responsibility.

Dag Hammarskjöld

God gave man work, not to burden him, but to bless him, and useful work, willingly, cheerfully, effectively done, has always been the finest expression of the human spirit. *Walter R. Courtenay*

Work is more fun than fun. *Noel Coward*

When more and more people are thrown out of work, unemployment results.

Calvin Coolidge

We can redeem anyone who strives unceasingly.   *Goethe*

Man's usual routine is to work and to dream and work and dream.
                                                    Raymond Queneau

The Gods rank work above virtues.   *Hesiod*

Anyone can do any amount of work provided it isn't the work he is supposed to be doing at that moment.   *Robert Benchley*

It is not upon thee to finish the work; neither art thou free to abstain from it.   *The Talmud*

Work banishes those three great evils, boredom, vice, and poverty.
                                                            Voltaire

Amateurs hope. Professionals work.   *Garson Kanin*

Work is love made visible. And if you cannot work with love but only with distaste, it is better that you should leave your work and sit at the gate of the temple and take alms of those who work with joy.   *Kahlil Gibran*

There is dignity in work only when it is work freely accepted.
                                                        Albert Camus

If a man will not work, he shall not eat.   *2 Thessalonians 3:10*

Anyone who is honestly seeking a job and can't find it, deserves the attention of the United States government, and the people. *John F. Kennedy*

Work is the inevitable condition of human life, the true source of human welfare.   *Leo Tolstoy*

He who shuns the millstone, shuns the meal.   *Erasmus*

Rest is the sweet sauce of labour.   *Plutarch*

God gives every bird its food, but he does not throw it into the nest.
                                                        J. G. Holland

When your work speaks for itself, don't interrupt.   *Henry J. Kaiser*

I work as my father drank.   *George Bernard Shaw*

For it is commonly said: accomplished labours are pleasant.   *Cicero*

While I am busy with little things, I am not required to do greater things.
St. Francis de Sales

A people so primitive that they did not know how to get money except by working for it.
George Ade

Work expands so as to fill the time available for its completion.
C. Northcote Parkinson

If all the year were playing holidays
To sport would be as tedious as to work.
Shakespeare, 'Henry IV' Part I

I am only an average man, but, by George, I work harder at it than the average man.
Theodore Roosevelt

Work is accomplished by those employees who have not yet reached their level of incompetence.
Laurence J. Peter

When I was a young man I observed that nine out of ten things I did were failures. I didn't want to be a failure, so I did ten times more work.
George Bernard Shaw

The worst crime against working people is a company which fails to operate at a profit.
Samuel Gompers

How do I work? I grope.
Albert Einstein

It is the privilege of any human work which is well done to invest the doer with a certain haughtiness. He can well afford not to conciliate, whose faithful work will answer for him.
Ralph Waldo Emerson

Work and love — these are the basics. Without them there is neurosis.
Theodor Reik

The effectiveness of work increases according to geometric progression if there are no interruptions.
André Maurois

Writers and Writing

Take care of the sense and the sounds will take of themselves.
Lewis Carroll

The truth is, we've not really developed a fiction that can accommodate the full tumult, the zaniness and crazed quality of modern experience.

Saul Bellow

There is today an extraordinary interest with the data of modern experience per se. Our absorption in our contemporary historical state is very high right now. It's not altogether unlike a similar situation in seventeenth century Holland, where wealthy merchants wanted their portraits done with all their blemishes included. It is the height of egotism, in a sense, to think even one's blemishes are of significance. So today Americans seem to want their writers to reveal all their weaknesses, their meannesses, to celebrate their very confusions. And they want it in the most direct possible way — they want it served up neat, as it were, without the filtering and generalizing power of fiction.

Saul Bellow

I can write better than anyone who can write faster, and I can write faster than anyone who can write better.

A. J. Liebling

Writing: I certainly do rewrite my central myth in every book, and would never read or trust any writer who did not also do so.

Northrop Frye

Every human being has hundreds of separate people living under his skin. The talent of a writer is his ability to give them their separate names, identities, personalities and have them relate to other characters living with him.

Mel Brooks

There is one last thing to remember: writers are always selling somebody out.

Joan Didion

The writer must write what he has to say, not speak it.

Ernest Hemingway

Writers should be read — but neither seen nor heard.

Daphne du Maurier

A person who publishes a book appears willfully in public with his pants down.

Edna St. Vincent Millay

The beginning is easy; what happens next is much harder.

Anon.

There should be two main objectives in ordinary prose writing: to convey a message and to include in it nothing that will distract the reader's attention or check his habitual pace of reading — he should feel that he is seated at ease in a taxi, not riding a temperamental horse through traffic.

Robert Graves and Allan Hodge

If we try to envisage an 'average Canadian writer' we can see him living near a campus, teaching at least part-time at university level, mingling too much for his work's good with academics, doing as much writing as he can for the CBC, and always hoping for a Canada Council Fellowship.

George Woodcock

The writer is committed when he plunges to the very depths of himself with the intent to disclose, not his individuality, but his person in the complex society that conditions and supports him. *Jean-Paul Sartre*

I struggled in the beginning. I said I was going to write the truth, so help me God. And I thought I was. I found I couldn't. Nobody can write the absolute truth. *Henry Miller*

For a dyed-in-the-wool author nothing is as dead as a book once it is written . . . she is rather like a cat whose kittens have grown up. While they were a-growing she was passionately interested in them but now they seem hardly to belong to her — and probably she is involved with another batch of kittens as I am involved with other writing. *Rumer Godden*

Every author, however modest, keeps a most outrageous vanity chained like a madman in the padded cell of his breast. *Logan Pearsall Smith*

Never believe anything a writer tells you about himself. A man comes to believe in the end the lies he tells himself about himself.

George Bernard Shaw

I am always at a loss to know how much to believe of my own stories.

Washington Irving

That's not writing, that's typing. *Truman Capote (on Jack Kerouac)*

There is an accuracy that defeats itself by the overemphasis of details. I often say that one must permit oneself, and quite advisedly and deliberately, a certain margin of misstatement. *Benjamin N. Cardozo*

I suppose some editors are failed writers — but so are most writers.

T. S. Eliot

I think with my right hand. *Edmund Wilson*

Writers are the engineers of human souls. *Joseph Stalin*

A great many people now reading and writing would be better employed in keeping rabbits. *Edith Sitwell*

The process of writing a book is infinitely more important than the book that is completed as a result of the writing, let alone the success or failure that book may have after it is written . . . the book is merely a symbol of the writing. In writing the book, I am living. I am growing. I am tapping myself. I am changing. The process is the product.

Theodore Isaac Rubin

Writing is no trouble: you just jot down ideas as they occur to you. The jotting is simplicity itself — it is the occurring which is difficult.

Stephen Leacock

Writing, when properly managed (as you may be sure I think mine is) is but a different name for conversation.   *Laurence Sterne*

My method is to take the utmost trouble to find the right thing to say, and then to say it with the utmost levity.   *George Bernard Shaw*

Caesar had perished from the world of men
Had not his sword been rescued by his pen.   *Henry Vaughan*

Every great and original writer, in proportion as he is great and original, must himself create the taste by which he is to be relished.

William Wordsworth

Writers write to influence their readers, their preachers, their auditors, but always, at bottom, to be more themselves.   *Aldous Huxley*

We are as much informed of a writer's genius by what he selects as by what he originates.   *Ralph Waldo Emerson*

I quote others in order to better express my own self.   *Montaigne*

In any really good subject, one has only to probe deep enough to come to tears.   *Edith Wharton*

He is limp and damp and milder than the breath of a cow.

Virginia Woolf of E.M. Forster

The most essential gift for a good writer is a built-in, shockproof shit detector. This is the writer's radar and all great writers have had it.

Ernest Hemingway

It is a sobering thought that each of us gives his hearers and his readers a chance to look into the inner working of his mind when he speaks or writes.

J. M. Barker

Read over your compositions, and when you meet a passage which you think is particularly fine, strike it out.   *Samuel Johnson*

When you're a writer, you no longer see things with the freshness of the normal person. There are always two figures that work inside you, and if you are at all intelligent you realize that you have lost something. But I think there has always been this dichotomy in a real writer. He wants to be terribly human, and he responds emotionally, but at the same time there's this cold observer who cannot cry.   *Brian Moore*

When I am dead, I hope it may be said:
'His sins were scarlet, but his books were read.'   *Hilaire Belloc*

The best part of every author is in general to be found in his book, I assure you.   *Samuel Johnson*

The obscurity of a writer is generally in proportion to his incapacity.
                                      Quintilian

Life cannot defeat a writer who is in love with writing — for life itself is a writer's love until death.   *Edna Ferber*

Get black on white.   *Guy de Maupassant*

Just get it down on paper, and then we'll see what to do with it.
                                      Maxwell Perkins (advice to Marcia Davenport)

Advice to young writers who want to get ahead without any annoying delays: don't write about Man, write about a man.   *E. B. White*

Vigorous writing is concise. A sentence should contain no unnecessary words, a paragraph no unnecessary sentences, for the same reason that a drawing should have no unnecessary lines and a machine no unnecessary parts. This requires not that the writer make all his sentences short, or that he avoid all detail and treat his subjects only in outline, but that every word tell.
                                      William Strunk

Tennessee Williams said if he got rid of his demons, he would lose his angels.
                                      Dakin Williams

There is but one art, to omit.   *Robert Louis Stevenson*

A man really writes for an audience of about ten persons. Of course if others like it, that is clear gain. But if those ten are satisfied, he is content.
                                      Alfred North Whitehead

Self-expression is for babies and seals, where it can be charming. A writer's business is to affect the reader. *Vincent McHugh*

It is in the hard rockpile labour of seeking to win, hold, or deserve a reader's interest that the pleasant agony of writing comes in. *John Mason Brown*

Write something, even if it's just a suicide note. *Anon.*

Flaubert had infinite correction to perform. *Roland Barthes*

Nature, not content with denying him the ability to think, has endowed him with the ability to write. *A. E. Housman*

Beauty and truth may be attributes of good writing, but if the writer deliberately aims at truth, he is likely to find that what he has hit is the didactic. *Northrop Frye*

When an author is yet living, we estimate his powers by his worst performance; and when he is dead, we rate them by his best. *Samuel Johnson*

How vain it is to sit down to write when you have not stood up to live. *Henry David Thoreau*

A writer is someone who can make a riddle out of an answer. *Karl Kraus*

The man who is asked by an author what he thinks of his work is put to the torture and is not obliged to speak the truth. *Samuel Johnson*

Style is the hallmark of a temperament stamped upon the material at hand. *André Maurois*

Every writer, without exception, is a masochist, a sadist, a peeping Tom, an exhibitionist, a narcissist, an injustice collector and a depressed person constantly haunted by fears of unproductivity. *Edmund Bergler*

My novels point out that the world consists entirely of exceptions. *Joyce Carey*

We like that a sentence should read as if its author, had he held a plough instead of a pen, could have drawn a furrow deep and straight to the end. *Henry David Thoreau*

The reason a writer writes a book is to forget a book and the reason a reader reads one is to remember it. *Thomas Wolfe*

I work every day — or at least I force myself into office or room. I may get nothing done, but you don't earn bonuses without putting in time. Nothing may come for three months, but you don't earn the fourth without it.   *Mordecai Richler*

Less is more.   *Robert Browning*

John the Baptist pretending to be Karl Marx.
                                  Anonymous description of G. B. Shaw

Every word she writes is a lie, including 'and' and 'the.'
                                  Mary McCarthy (of Lillian Hellmann)

It fell dead from the Press.   *Old bookseller saying.*

When you put down the good things you ought to have done, and leave out the bad things you did do — well, that's memoirs.   *Will Rogers*

Journalism allows it's readers to witness history. Fiction gives its readers an opportunity to live it.   *John Hersey*

His (the writer's) standard of fidelity to the truth should be so high that his invention, out of his experience, should produce a truer account than anything factual can be.   *Ernest Hemingway*

The most lasting reputation I have is for an almost ferocious aggressiveness, when in fact I am amiable, indulgent, affectionate, shy and rather timid at heart.   *J. B. Priestley*

The life of a writer is tragic: the more we advance, the farther there is to go and the more there is to say, the less time there is to say it.
                                                              Gabrielle Roy

It is only through fiction and the dimension of the imaginary that we can learn something real about individual experience. Any other approach is bound to be general and abstract.   *Nicola Chiaromonte*

I have only made this letter rather long because I have not had time to make it shorter.   *Blaise Pascal*

It makes a great difference in the force of a sentence whether a man be behind it or no.   *Ralph Waldo Emerson*

Footnotes, the little dogs yapping at the heels of the text. *William James*

When the style is fully formed, if it has a sweet undersong, we call it beautiful, and the writer may do what he likes in words or syntax.

Oliver Wendell Holmes

I like prefaces. I read them. Sometimes I do not read any further.

Malcolm Lowry

As for style of writing, if one has anything to say, it drops from him simply and directly, as a stone falls to the ground.   *Henry David Thoreau*

What is written without effort is in general read without pleasure.

Samuel Johnson

Proper words in proper places, make the true definition of a style.

Jonathan Swift

They're fancy talkers about themselves, writers. If I had to give young writers advice, I would say don't listen to writers talking about writing or themselves.

Lillian Hellman

The business of writing is one of the four or five most private things in the world.   *Ethel Wilson*

I conceive that the right way to write a story for boys is to write so that it will not only interest boys but strongly interest any man who has ever been a boy. That immensely enlarges the audience.   *Mark Twain*

He claimed his modest share of the general foolishness of the human race.

Irving Howe (of Thomas Hardy)

There are two kinds of writers — the great ones who can give you truths, and the lesser ones, who can only give you themselves.   *Clifton Fadiman*

My own experience is that once a story has been written, one has to cross out the beginning and the end. It is there that we authors do most of our lying . . . one must ruthlessly suppress everything that is not concerned with the subject. If, in the first chapter, you say there is a gun hanging on the wall, you should make quite sure that it is going to be used further on in the story.   *Anton Chekhov*

(Writing) — the art of applying the seat of the pants to the seat of the chair.

Mary Heaton Vorse

All a writer has to do to get a woman is to say he's a writer. It's an aphrodisiac.   *Saul Bellow*

Publication is a self-invasion of privacy. *Marshall McLuhan*

It has been said that writing comes more easily if you have something to say.
Sholem Asch

I've put my genius into my life; I've only put my talent into my works.
Oscar Wilde

Fundamentally, all writing is about the same thing: it's about dying, about the brief flicker of time we have here, and the frustrations that it creates.
Mordecai Richler

I am what libraries and librarians have made me, with a little assistance from a professor of Greek and a few poets. *B. K. Sandwell*

Our society, like decadent Rome, has turned into an amusement society, with writers chief among the court jesters — not so much above the clatter as part of it. *Saul Bellow*

If you would be a reader, read; if a writer, write. *Epictetus*

A writer and nothing else: a man alone in a room with the English language, trying to get human feelings right. *John K. Hutchens*

How can I know what I think till I see what I say? *E. M. Forster*

Please, never despise the translator. He's the mailman of human civilization. *Alexander Pushkin*

The waste basket is a writer's best friend. *Isaac Bashevis Singer*

The llama is a woolly sort of fleecy hair goat
With an indolent expression and an undulating throat —
Like an unsuccessful literary man. *Hilaire Belloc*

If a man means his writing seriously, he must mean to write well. But how can he write well until he learns to see what he has written badly. His progress toward good writing and his recognition of bad writing are bound to unfold at something like the same rate. *John Ciardi*

Words and sentences are subjects of revision; paragraphs and whole compositions are subjects of prevision. *Barrett Wendell*

There is nothing more dangerous to the formation of a prose style than the endeavour to make it poetic. *J. Middleton Murry*

The most original thing a writer can do is write like himself. It is also his most difficult task.   *Robertson Davies*

Now as through this world I ramble,
I see lots of funny men,
Some rob you with a six gun
Some with a fountain pen.   *Woody Guthrie*

It is the function of art to renew our perception. What we are familiar with we cease to see. The writer shakes up the familiar scene, and as if by magic, we see a new meaning in it.   *Anaïs Nin*

A woman must have money and a room of her own if she is to write fiction.
                                                                    Virginia Woolf

Better to write for yourself and have no public, than to write for the public and have no self.   *Cyril Connolly*

I have cultivated my hysteria with joy and terror.   *Charles Baudelaire*

Writing has power, but its power has no vector. Writers can stir the mind, but they can't direct it. Time changes things, God changes things, the dictators change things, but writers can't change anything.
                                                              Isaac Bashevis Singer

A good writer is basically a story-teller, not a scholar or a redeemer of mankind.   *Isaac Bashevis Singer*

Anybody can find out if he is a writer. If he were a writer, when he tried to write of some particular day, he would find in the effort that he could recall exactly how the light fell and how the temperature felt, and all the quality of it. Most people cannot do it. If they can do it, they may never be successful in a pecuniary sense, but that ability is at the bottom of writing, I am sure.   *Maxwell Perkins*

I believe the writer . . . should always be the final judge. I have always held to that position and have sometimes seen books hurt thereby, but at least as often helped. The book belongs to the author.   *Maxwell Perkins*

You have to throw yourself away when you write.   *Maxwell Perkins*

A memorandum is written to protect the writer — not to inform his reader.
                                                                    Dean Acheson

I write for myself and strangers. The strangers, dear Readers, are an afterthought.   *Gertrude Stein*

The great enemy of clear language is insincerity. When there is a gap between one's real and one's declared aims, one turns as if it were instinctively to long words and exhausted idioms, like a cuttlefish squirting out ink.

George Orwell

A novel must be exceptionally good to live as long as the average cat.

Hugh MacLennan

You praise the firm restraint with which they write —
I'm with you, there, of course:
They use the snaffle and the curb all right,
But where's the bloody horse?

Roy Campbell

At least half the mystery novels published violate the law that the solution, once revealed, must seem to be inevitable.

Raymond Chandler

On the trail of another man, the biographer must put up with finding himself at every turn: any biography uneasily shelters an autobiography within it.

Paul Murray Kendall

The editorial job has become, unlike the ancient age when one judged what one read, a job of making judgements on outlines, ideas, reputations, previous books, scenarios, treatments, talk and promises.

Sam Vaughan

An editor should tell the author his writing is better than it is. Not a lot better, a little better.

T. S. Eliot

Writing is a solitary occupation. Family, friends and society are the natural enemies of a writer. He must be alone, uninterrupted and slightly savage if he is to sustain and complete an undertaking.

Laurence Clark Powell

Just as there is nothing between the admirable omelette and the intolerable, so with autobiography.

Hilaire Belloc

I think it's bad to talk about one's present work, for it spoils something at the root of the creative act. It discharges the tension.

Norman Mailer

As for my next book, I am going to hold myself from writing it till I have it impending in me: grown heavy in my mind like a ripe pear, pendant, gravid, asking to be cut or it will fall.

Virginia Woolf

No man understands a deep book until he has seen and lived at least part of its contents.

Ezra Pound

How can you write if you can't cry?

Ring Lardner

Writing is easy: all you do is sit staring at the blank sheet of paper until the drops of blood form on your forehead.   *Gene Fowler*

Your manuscript is both good and original; but the parts that are good are not original, and the parts that are original are not good.
                                                            Samuel Johnson

Youth

In early youth, as we contemplate our coming life, we are like children in a theatre before the curtain is raised, sitting there in high spirits and eagerly waiting for the play to begin.   *Arthur Schopenhauer*

Much may be made of a Scotchman if he be caught young.
                                                            Samuel Johnson

Young men think old men fools and old men know young men to be so.
                                                            Anon.

The belief that youth is the happiest time of life is founded upon a fallacy. The happiest person is the person who thinks the most interesting thoughts, and we grow happier as we grow older.   *William Lyon Phelps*

When I was a boy of fourteen, my father was so ignorant I could hardly stand to have the old man around. But when I got to be twenty-one, I was astonished at how much the old man had learned in seven years.
                                                            Mark Twain

It is essential that we enable young people to see themselves as participants in one of the most exciting eras in history, and to have a sense of purpose in relation to it.   *Nelson Rockefeller*

This is a youth-oriented society, and the joke is on them because youth is a disease from which we all recover.   *Anon.*

It takes a long time to become young.   *Pablo Picasso*

Oh, to be only half as wonderful as my child thought I was when he was small, and only half as stupid as my teenager now things I am.
                                                            Rebecca Richards

When I was younger, I could remember anything, whether it had happened or not.   *Mark Twain*

The deepest definition of youth is life as yet untouched by tragedy.
Alfred North Whitehead

Only the young die good.   *Oliver Herford*

Consider well the proportion of things. It is better to be a young June bug,
than an old bird of paradise.   *Mark Twain*

I am constantly amazed when I talk to young people to learn how much they
know about sex and how little about soap.   *Billie Burke*

The joy of the young is to disobey — but the trouble is that there are no
longer any orders.   *Jean Cocteau*

To keep clear of concealment, to keep clear of the need of concealment, to
do nothing that he might not do out on the middle of Boston Common at
noonday — I cannot say how more and more that seems to me to be the
glory of a young man's life. It is an awful hour when the first necessity of
hiding anything comes. The whole life is different thenceforth. When there
are questions to be feared and eyes to be avoided and subjects that must not
be touched, then the bloom of life is gone. Put off that day as long as possible. Put if off forever if you can.   *Phillips Brooks*

The 'teenager' seems to have replaced the Communist as the appropriate
target for public controversy and foreboding.   *Edgar Z. Friedenberg*

Everyone believes in his youth that the world really began with him, and
that all merely exists for his sake.   *Goethe*

It is not possible for civilization to flow backward while there is youth in
the world. Youth may be headstrong, but it will advance its allotted length.
Helen Keller

You never see the old austerity
That was the essence of civility;
Young people hereabouts, unbridled, now
Just want.   *Molière*

The young always have the same problem — how to rebel and conform at
the same time. They have now solved this by defying their parents and copying one another.   *Quentin Crisp*

One boy's a boy, two boys are half a boy; three boys are no boy at all.
Anon.

Trouble is, kids feel they have to shock their elders and each generation grows up into something harder to shock.   *Cal Craig*

I do beseech you to direct your efforts more to preparing youth for the path and less to preparing the path for the youth.   *Ben Lindsey*

Every generation is a secret society and has incommunicable enthusiasms, tastes, and interests which are a mystery both to its predecessors and to posterity.   *John Jay Chapman*

The interests of childhood and youth are the interests of mankind.
                    Edmund Storer James

The youth gets together this material to build a bridge to the moon, or perchance, a palace or temple on earth, and at length, the middle-aged man concludes to build a woodshed with them.   *Henry David Thoreau*

Youth has become a class.   *Roger Vadim*

Don't laugh at a youth for his affectations; he's only trying on one face after another till he finds his own.   *Logan Pearsall Smith*

If one could recover the uncompromising spirit of one's youth, one's greatest indignation would be for what one has become.   *André Gide*

It is always self-defeating to pretend to the style of a generation younger than your own; it simply erases your own experience in history.
                    Renata Adler

It's all that the young can do for the old, to shock them and keep them up to date.   *George Bernard Shaw*

What though youth gave love and roses
Age still leaves us friends and wine.   *Thomas More*

Index

By the year 2000, 2 out of 3 Americans could be illiterate.

It's true.

Today, 75 million adults...about one American in three, can't read adequately. And by the year 2000, U.S. News & World Report envisions an America with a literacy rate of only 30%.

Before that America comes to be, you can stop it...by joining the fight against illiteracy today.

Call the Coalition for Literacy at toll-free **1-800-228-8813** and volunteer.

**Volunteer
Against Illiteracy.
The only degree you need
is a degree of caring.**

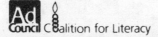 Ad Council Coalition for Literacy